CONTESTED GROUNDS

CONTESTED GROUNDS

Essays on Nature, Culture, and Power

edited by

AMITA BAVISKAR

OXFORD
UNIVERSITY PRESS

OXFORD

UNIVERSITY PRESS

YMCA Library Building, Jai Singh Road, New Delhi 110 001

Oxford University Press is a department of the University of Oxford. It furthers the
University's objective of excellence in research, scholarship, and education
by publishing worldwide in

Oxford New York

Auckland Cape Town Dar es Salaam Hong Kong Karachi Kuala Lumpur
Madrid Melbourne Mexico City Nairobi New Delhi Shanghai Taipei Toronto

With offices in
Argentina Austria Brazil Chile Czech Republic France Greece Guatemala
Hungary Italy Japan Poland Portugal Singapore South Korea Switzerland
Thailand Turkey Ukraine Vietnam

Oxford is a registered trademark of Oxford University Press
in the UK and in certain other countries

Published in India
by Oxford University Press, New Delhi

ISBN 13: 978-0-19-569585-4
ISBN 10: 0-19-569585-2

Typeset in GoudyOlSt BT 10.5/12 8
by Sai Graphic Design, New Delhi 110 055
Printed in India by Repro India Limited
Published by Oxford University Press
22 Workspace, 2nd Floor, 1/22 Asaf Ali Road, New Delhi 110002, India

Contents

Acknowledgements

The essays in this volume were originally written for a conference on 'Resources: Conceptions and Contestations' held at Kathmandu in 2003. The conference was organized by the South Asia programme of the Social Science Research Council, New York, with the support of the Ford Foundation, New Delhi. The essays were first published in 2003 as a special issue of the *Economic and Political Weekly* (*EPW*) entitled 'For a Cultural Politics of Natural Resources'. I am grateful to the late Krishna Raj for encouraging this effort and to Rammanohar Reddy, the present editor of *EPW*. The enthusiastic response to the *EPW* special issue led us to think that the essays deserved wider circulation in a more durable form. Hence this book.

I thank the authors of the essays for their sustained collaboration that made this volume possible. I am also grateful to Itty Abraham, Sanjay Chaturvedi, Ajaya Dixit, Dipak Gyawali, Marcus Moench, Ranabir Samaddar, Azra Talat Sayeed, Munmeeth Soni, and Malini Sur for their contributions to this initiative. Discussions with Donald Moore and Peter Vandergeest were crucial for formulating and clarifying the arguments presented here in the Introduction. Itty Abraham's valuable comments helped improve the final version, as did comments from the reviewers at Oxford University Press. I owe an enduring debt to Ramachandra Guha, Donald S. Moore, Mahesh Rangarajan, Dunu Roy, Vasant Saberwal, K. Sivaramakrishnan, Rohan D'Souza, Nandini Sundar, and Michael Watts, who have helped deepen and refine my understanding of the cultural politics of environment and development over the years. For their friendship and critical support through thick and thin, I thank Vasudha Dalmia, Bernadette Joseph, Brij Kothari, Saba Mahmood, Isha Ray, Raka Ray, and, most of all, Rahul N. Ram.

1

Introduction

AMITA BAVISKAR

We live in a world where conflicts over natural resources are writ large upon the landscape. Be it the struggles between farmers and corporate interests over land acquisition for Special Economic Zones (SEZs), the social movements against large dams on rivers, or the contestations around climate change: all testify to the salience of ecological conflicts in our times. The centrality of these conflicts requires that we closely examine the relations between nature, culture and power as they shape our lives and the biophysical world we inhabit. The essays in this volume collectively make a case for the study of natural resources through the lens of cultural politics. They argue that a focus on the complex material and symbolic dimensions of how 'natural resources' come to be imagined, appropriated and contested, enables one to move away from the dull rigours of economic determinism that dog political ecology. The conceptual strengths of this approach also enrich political practice. This introductory essay delineates some of the contours of cultural politics and situates the following essays within its rubric, organizing the discussion around prominent keywords used in discourses around natural resources.

RESOURCES: TECHNOLOGIES AND TRUTHS

On careful examination, almost any environmental conflict reveals the complexity and contentiousness of the political economy of natural resources. Let us take the case of the ongoing war in Iraq.[1] Many

---

[1] For a more general analysis of the relationship between wars and resource control, see McNeill (2001).

key aspects of the US invasion can be analysed in terms of empire (Anderson 2002) and capitalist control over a critical resource like oil. Yet, these explanations do not exhaust either what is at stake or the form that conflicts around natural resources take. An approach that focuses on the economy of extraction is a necessary but not sufficient condition for understanding the politics of petroleum. The politics of oil has other dimensions that are as constitutive of its meaning and power. The extraction of this resource is better understood as part of a regime of rule involving technologies, rationalities and institutions, made intelligible by regimes of truth that organize understanding and experience (Rose 1999). These hegemonic truths are challenged and struggled over through cultural politics. In this introduction, I make a case for using cultural politics as an approach that enables a more insightful analysis of the significance of natural resources in contemporary life.

The technologies of rule that develop around natural resources have most often been studied in terms of the imperial quest for stable regimes of extraction (Ludden 1992). Wars of conquest and 'pacification' are followed by occupation and the coerced re-arrangement of relations of rule, production and exchange.[2] Yet, profit—the economic calculus of private benefit—cannot be separated from passionate attachment to more lofty ideals. In the Iraqi case, as in other colonial schemes, the violence of extraction is tied to ideas of Improvement, almost echoing Mill's declaration that 'despotism is the legitimate mode of government in dealing with barbarians, provided the end be their improvement'.[3] Thus, US military occupation is presented as a way to further the welfare of ordinary Iraqis through improved management of their polity and economy. This conceit is underwritten by a key imperial ideology: stewardship (Cowen and Shenton 1996), the notion that the 'more civilized' know best

[2] The diverse forms that these processes have taken in different contexts have been described by the following environmental historians: for the African continent, see Anderson and Grove (1987), Beinart (2003), Hochschild (1998); for North America, see Cronon (1983) and Merchant (1989); and for South Asia, see Agrawal (2005), Grove et al. (1998), Guha (1989), Sivaramakrishnan (1999). Also see Bayly (2004) on imperial conquest and worldwide sedentarization in the era of European dominance.
[3] J.S. Mill (1859) On Liberty. Quoted in Drayton (2000: 94).

how to run the lives of subordinate peoples (Mehta 1999). Ideas of improvement, predicated on liberalism's constructions of cultural difference,[4] inform contemporary discourses of development; these ideas are implicit in the imperative to efficiently maximize resource use, a goal best directed by technocratic experts who lead the less educated towards an enlightened, prosperous future.

Constructing stable regimes of extraction thus requires not just brute force but also the mobilization of 'consensus' such that people be willing participants. Official narratives frame the 'problem' in ways that legitimize particular forms of action. Trying to dress up domination as consent, the US administration and media titled their project 'Operation Iraqi Freedom', where freedom was understood as an end universally desired. Terrorism was presented as the enemy of all. Saddam Hussein was demonized as a monster whose overthrow would restore democracy and capitalist business-as-usual. To the extent that Americans and others around the world acceded to these representations, the campaign worked. Much has been written on the manufacture of consent for imperialist projects.[5] I will not recapitulate those discussions except to highlight the connections they draw between imperialism and culture (Said 1993), connections that are made less often in debates about natural resources. If the war in Iraq was about oil, as it indeed was, it was also about freedom and terror, Arab nationalism and evangelical Christian fervour. One is no less real than the other; all have consequential effects. Appreciating the inseparability of the material and the symbolic dimensions of the conflict helps us understand that the political economy of a natural resource is meaningful only through the wider networks of cultural politics in which it is embedded.

While recognizing the salience of cultural politics, one must also appreciate the biophysical qualities of the resource. Oil has particular characteristics that necessitate specific forms of centralized, capital-intensive technologies of extraction that tend towards state control

[4] The most influential of these has been race, exemplified in the popular phrase that Rudyard Kipling coined: 'the white man's burden'. See Moore et al. for a wide-ranging and erudite discussion on how 'discourses of race and nature provide the resources to express truths, forge identities, and justify inequalities' (2003:1). Also see Philip (2004).

[5] See Herman and Chomsky (1988).

(Watts 2001). Hence Iraqi oil could not be appropriated by Americans without deposing the Iraqi government. Then there is the strategic importance of oil within industrialism. For all the assertions by the Bush administration that the conflict was *not* about oil, critics pithily pointed out that if Iraq's major export were olives, its political regime would not attract quite the same degree of concern. Each resource has distinctive use values that emerge in relation to particular modes of production. Petroleum in the present involves geopolitical formations like nation-states (Coronil 1997), armies, firms and research establishments that make up the military-industrial complex, those who work to process and distribute oil and the billions of consumers who use it in one form or another. It also affects the fate of those who live in the areas where it is produced, both humans and other species. 'What is called nature or the material world moves… in and out of human forms, or occurs as arrangements… that are social as well as natural, technical as well as material' (Mitchell 2002: 52; also see Williams 1980: 83).

POLITICAL ECOLOGY AND CULTURAL POLITICS

The *cultural politics* approach to natural resources attempts to displace some of the assumptions that govern *political ecology*, the conceptual rubric under which extensive research has been conducted in India and abroad.[6] Political ecology's great strength has been its unwavering focus on issues of social equality and justice at stake in conflicts over natural resources. This rich literature has examined social movements large and small that bring together diverse and distant social groups, address transnational audiences and use international and national

[6] The pioneers of political ecology (or social ecology, as they prefer to call it) are undoubtedly Ramachandra Guha and Madhav Gadgil whose published works and generous collegiality have inspired many researchers, including this one (Gadgil and Guha 1992, 1995; Guha 1989). It is always difficult to pin a label on a wide-ranging body of work, produced over at least twenty five years, but in doing so, I am following Gadgil and Guha's method, which is distinguished by a pronounced taxonomic bent. Recent political ecology collections include Peluso and Watts (2001), Saberwal and Rangarajan (2003), and Biersack and Greenberg (2006). For exemplary monographs, see Hecht and Cockburn (1989), D'Souza (2006) and Peluso (1992). For a critical commentary on political ecology, see Robbins (2004).

regulatory and judicial institutions to defend threatened livelihoods against the incursions of state-led extractive development. However, while asymmetries of power are clearly identified as crucial in political ecology's analysis, they tend to be viewed through the binaries of civil society versus state, 'virtuous peasants' versus 'vicious states'.[7] It is often assumed that the 'state' and 'communities' are separate, autonomous entities with self-evident interests that are clearly opposed. Critiques of such assumptions are now commonplace within anthropology[8] and, even in studies of resource conflicts, more complex representations are beginning to gain ground. Thus a continued fondness for singular narratives to explain natural resource struggles is inexplicable. Such an analytical frame, I would argue, takes at face value the simplified political representations that social movements must generate in order to cohere.[9] Yet this uncritical reproduction of claims, often intended as a gesture of solidarity, ignores the difficult, creative work of constructing political identities, forging alliances and transcending differences.[10] In doing so, political ecology may not only fail to offer much analytical purchase, but may also be complicit in the continued political marginalization of those excluded by dominant narratives of environmental movements.[11] Collective representations created by activists, circulated and endorsed by academics, can and do have consequential effects.

[7] See Bernstein (1990); quoted in Li (this volume). On this point, also see Sivaramakrishnan (2003: 391).

[8] On the ethnography of the state, see Fuller and Benei (2000). The ethnographic literature that complicates ideas of 'community' is too vast to be summed up since most anthropologists and sociologists (not to mention historians and political scientists) have addressed it from different theoretical perspectives and at different scales. On critical approaches to ideas of community in natural resource management, see Agrawal and Sivaramakrishnan (2000); Brara (2006); Cederlof and Sivaramakrishnan (2006); Jeffery and Sundar (1999); Sivaramakrishnan (1999).

[9] On the politics of academic practice vis-à-vis the strategy of making essentialist cultural claims within environmental movements, see Brosius (1999). On the wider issue of strategic essentialism, see Herzfeld (1997).

[10] For a discussion of the complex and contradictory politics of forging a social movement, see Baviskar (1995).

[11] Baviskar (2005) discusses the predicament of landless Dalits and urban migrant workers whose practices are tainted with greater illegitimacy, thanks to the spread of environmentalism.

6 Contested Grounds

Identities and interests are mutually formed through the contingent, lived experience of 'situated cultural practices and sedimented histories of people and place' (Moore 1999: 658). This messy process creates contradictions as subjects are formed within multiple, if unequal, fields of power. The Adivasi fighting against displacement in the Narmada valley is simultaneously a tribal, a farmer, a collector of forest produce, a woman, a mother, a consumer of manufactured goods like fertilizers and saris, a worker on state drought-relief projects, in debt to a moneylender, a migrant, an anti-dam activist, a devout member of the Gayatri Parivar sect, a panchayat leader, a voter in state and national elections, and so much more. These criss-crossing affiliations are not only intrinsic to how people live their quotidian lives, they are immensely consequential for shaping collective action. However, political ecology tends to assume that cultural identities are pre-formed, derived directly from an objective set of interests based on shared locations in terms of class, gender or ethnicity that challenge nationalism and/or capitalism.

Political ecology has also assumed that the primary significance of natural resources resides in their material use value. A forest becomes the locus of contention because its trees represent timber, fodder or fuel, material values desired by different social groups. Cultural politics suggests that natural resources have value within a larger economy of signification which crucially shapes their modes of appropriation. They are also resources for collective representations that exceed the concern with immediate material use (see Agrawal 2005). This 'social life of things'[12] is well illustrated in David Mosse's study of village water tanks in Tamil Nadu where Dalits mobilized for representation in the association that managed these bodies (Mosse 2003: 279–82). For Dalits, traditionally excluded from institutions controlling the village temple and tank, a place in the water users' association was a form of symbolic capital that mattered, perhaps more than the material gains from water. As an arena where subaltern aspirations for upward mobility and greater power within a Mudaliar-dominated village caste hierarchy could be pursued, the association's importance exceeded that of the resource it managed. Concerns about honour and respect, crystallized through a region-wide Dalit movement,

[12] See Appadurai (1986).

as much as the material practices of cultivation, became central to water management.

Cultural politics thus embeds resource struggles within a larger symbolic economy where the 'roles' that resources perform are several. Thus Iraq's invasion, while securing oil, also serves as an object lesson to impress the rest of the world with US willingness to act unilaterally—'defy us at your peril'. An 'environmental management programme' like the Madhya Pradesh Watershed Mission seeks to produce not only ecologically sustainable landscapes and livelihoods, but also legitimacy for the administration, distracting detractors from the state's other practices that are ecologically and socially rapacious (Baviskar 2007a). At stake in resource politics are concerns that relate the materiality of the resource to wider structures of meaning. Following Bourdieu (1998), one must note that expanding the notion of value beyond the material does not mean that varied elements (honour, water, patronage, votes) can be assimilated into the same metric. On the contrary, it is precisely their difference and incommensurability that is fiercely guarded (for example, honour loses its value and is compromised and corrupted if it is 'bought' or exchanged for money). Yet political ecology often tends towards unitary analyses that distil meanings down to the economic 'last instance', rendering resources as sources of only profit and subsistence, and not social life.

A cultural politics of natural resources treats identities, interests and resources, not as pre-determined givens, but as emergent products of the practices of cultural production and reproduction. By emphasizing power, process and practice, this approach treats 'culture itself as a site of political struggle' (Moore et al. 2003: 2). The analytic draws attention to the cultural work involved in reproducing and challenging inequalities and exclusions around resources. It suggests that the practices of subjects be understood not through structurally determined categories but through the specificity of their contradictory lived experience (Hale 1994). While cultural politics shares political ecology's commitment to understanding the asymmetric workings of power, it argues for a greater appreciation of the complex and contingent conditions under which people make history. Ethnography provides the tools best suited to represent that contingent process.[13]

[13] Significant monographs and collected volumes that use ethnographic

THE CULTURAL POLITICS OF NATURAL RESOURCES

The analysis of cultural politics immediately draws attention to the presumptions contained in the term 'natural resources'. 'Natural' suggests an existence outside culture, something that is not an artefact of human making: an endowment of minerals, forest wealth or the bounty of rivers. 'Resources' invoke utility, culturally produced use and exchange values, something to be efficiently managed. Linking these antinomies are notions of property and possession, stewardship and responsibility, the right to use and appropriate. In turn, these notions rest upon assumptions about space and territory, and how they relate to collectivities in the past, present and future. These cultural formations have emerged over time and across spaces that are trans-local; they are always contentious and changing.

The essays in this volume enable us to think anew the taken-for-granted aspects of natural resources. Each essay can be read as an independent and self-contained argument. At the same time, each also highlights a different facet of the natural resources debate, a distinctive theme that may be summed up in a 'keyword'. Raymond Williams used this concept to explore 'significant, indicative words' whose changing meanings trace shifts in a vocabulary of cultural practices and institutions (1976: 15). The term 'natural resource' is a contemporary keyword which, when examined along with waste, scarcity, security, territory, sovereignty, frontier, conflict, expertise and community, maps a distinctive world of meanings. Taken together, these related keywords chart out the terrain of the cultural politics of natural resources. In the following paragraphs, I outline the relations between these keywords, without attempting to summarize the papers.

The utilitarian principle of efficiency that dominates discourses around natural resources has an evil twin: *waste*. The necessity of avoiding waste entails the creation of subjects who understand that their role is to optimize the returns on a resource. As David Gilmartin argues through an account of British irrigation engineers

---

techniques to illuminate the cultural politics of the environment include: Cronon (1995); DuPuis and Vandergeest (1996); Gold and Gujar (2002); Greenough and Tsing (2003); Raffles (2002); Tsing (2005); Zerner (2003).

in the Indus basin, differing conceptions of 'waste' were connected to competing visions of indigenous community. Waste was a term central to professional engineering theory as it developed in the nineteenth century. But it was a term critical also to the structure of the colonial state's revenue system, and to its reliance on the 'village community' as a key institution linking the state to the land. Controlling waste was, in differing ways, crucial to both an agenda of increasing 'scientific' control over the environment, and to the state's political manipulation of indigenous communities. Understanding the place of waste in colonial discourse is thus a way of understanding some of the most basic contradictions underlying this resource regime.

Like waste, *scarcity* is another keyword that defines a resource and shapes its disposition. Lyla Mehta points out that scarcity is neither absolute nor 'natural'; its experience is always socially mediated.[14] Tracing the cultural constructions of drought in Kutch, Mehta shows how changing modes of appropriating water have marginalized established practices of coping with the fluctuations in rainfall. Scarcity, earlier accepted as a fact of life and part of a frugal environment that affected everyone more or less equally, is now the focus of strenuous interventions that have exacerbated social differences. Intensive private water extraction has made scarcity 'real', a social fact that has consequences. The fortunes of the poorer households decline faster than the falling level of groundwater, and impoverished residents migrate outwards. At the same time, the spectre of scarcity is presented politically as a crisis, creating anxieties that demand dramatic resolution. Mehta argues that the construction of mega-dams like Sardar Sarovar is legitimized through such tactics that conceal the inequalities that have shaped scarcity in the first place.

The scarcity of natural resources has now begun to preoccupy another set of policy makers besides conservationists and resource economists. In the post-Cold War context, conflicts over natural resources are the focus of the geopolitics of *security*. Statements such as 'the next world war will be over water' assert a simplistic causal connection between resource scarcity and violence. Glossing over

---

[14] Rosalind Shaw uses a similar approach for understanding not scarcity (drought) but excess (floods), in her Bangladesh-based study (1992).

complex, locally grounded cultural histories with which resource use is entangled, this alarmist rhetoric is usually accompanied by blueprints for action designed by the international development industry. So-called resource wars in 'weak states' like Sierra Leone are perceived as threatening international stability, necessitating authoritative interventions by the United Nations or the United States. Simon Dalby shows how environmental security debates construct the problem in ways that obscure the links between 'zones of conflict' and global circuits of resource extraction and consumption.

The security debate presumes that a *territory* is discrete, and geography and communities can be isomorphically mapped onto each other. Natural resources are believed to 'belong' to localized political entities, a system of nation-states and regions with clearly-defined proprietary powers to exclude others. Claims to territory are often based on the assertion of a 'sedentarist metaphysics' (Malkki 1992), primordial ties linking long-settled populations to landscapes. David Ludden offers a provocative challenge to this perspective by arguing that territoriality is, in fact, shaped by mobility. Delineating the long history of Sylhet, Bangladesh, he shows how the region is continually produced over time through far-flung webs of exchange. Commodity chains and circuits of labour move Sylheti resources around the world, contributing to the making of a distinctive place.

Integral to the notion of territory is that of *sovereignty*. Territory invokes a governable space within which populations and resources must be managed. And yet, as Michael Watts shows, the ordering processes suggested by Michel Foucault's concept of governmental rationality, a field of power aimed at shaping, guiding and directing conduct to achieve desired ends (Foucault 1991), collapse when multiple spatialities collide. Watts' discussion of oil politics in Nigeria examines governable spaces along three scales: chieftainship, indigeneity, and nationalism, marked by tensions and contradictions. In enclave economies where emerging ethnic identities challenge a rentier-state, violent youth gangs erupt like the gas flared from oil-rigs, illuminating Nigeria's great public secret: the fiction of the Nigerian nation.

The violence engendered around natural resources is most visible on the *frontier*, on the edge of wildness, where resources can be claimed by the resourceful and through risk-taking. Frontiers are not given but are made—as the history of the American 'Wild West' shows, frontiers are constructed and conquered through violent acts of dispossession. Anna Tsing describes the making of a 'resource frontier' in Kalimantan, Indonesia, where Meratus Dayaks have experienced the takeover of forests by armies, logging and plantation corporations, and mineral prospectors. Tsing provides a visceral account of the experience of the frontier, the instability and unevenness of its quicksilver changes. The mythos of get-rich-quick is both intoxicating and terrifying; understanding it requires not only politics but also poetics. Resource frontiers are far away from the sanitized world of World Bank deliberations on 'natural resource management' and 'decentralized governance', and yet they are created in the spaces opened up when privatization mixes with Indonesia's move from military dictatorship.

Conflict, generated as multiple groups lay claim to natural resources, is at centre-stage in cultural politics. As much as the visible, violent confrontations between groups, cultural politics is concerned with the everyday ways in which conflict is negotiated, deflected or pre-empted. The absence of conflict may indicate not harmony, but 'symbolic violence' when relations of domination are transfigured into affective relations through socially inculcated beliefs (Bourdieu 1998: 102–3). The different ways of dealing with conflict, from denial to warfare, form the substance of Michael Thompson's essay. Analysing climate change debates through the framework of Mary Douglas's cultural theory (Douglas and Wildavsky 1982), Thompson argues that disputes over the environment may not only be inevitable but may also be desirable when argumentation leads to a more constructive, democratic resolution. His paper makes a case for designing 'clumsy' institutions that accommodate the messy processes of airing and reconciling differences.

The process of decision-making around resource-related issues often accords great weight to expertise, privileging technocratic knowledge. 'Objective' scientific assessment is often legally mandated in the setting and monitoring of environmental standards. Scientific expertise shapes popular perceptions of 'problems'; its interventions organize experiences ranging from the human body (through medicine and public health) to the continental movement of rain and winds. Governments, consumers, and environmentalists, often to opposing ends, summon the authority of science. Steve Rayner points out that in contemporary industrialized countries, as decision-makers have increasingly turned to scientific experts for resolving environmental issues, electoral participation has been decreasing. The rising reliance on expertise has been accompanied by declining accountability. Rayner critically evaluates the ways in which governments have sought to incorporate public participation in the design of environmental decision-making.

Notions of participation presume a *community* of legitimate people who have rights. Cultural politics argues that the existence of such a community is not a foregone conclusion; the contentious processes of its being and becoming demand attention. Tania Li offers the tools to analyse how communities create legitimate identities in order to claim resources, and how conflicting images of community inspire different solidarities among environmentalists, human rights activists and government officials. Li presents a repertoire of terms—projects, practices, processes, positions—within a conceptualization of power in terms of sovereignty, government and politics, enabling an empirical examination of particular resource struggles. Migrant farmers in Sulawesi, Indonesia, who occupy land inside a national park, land that is also claimed by an 'indigenous' group, have to muster a virtuous environmental persona in order to be recognized. Their calls for justice invoke citizenship, mimic indigeneity, and a history of displacement. From this creative pastiche of claims is community forged.

The essays in this volume offer conceptually sophisticated and empirically rich research about the politics of the environment. By emphasizing the role of cultural politics, they attempt to take environmental debates onto grounds that may prove to be even more fertile.

2

Water and Waste*
Nature, Productivity and Colonialism in the Indus Basin

DAVID GILMARTIN

The government has embarked with all the energies it can command in the noble work of improving the condition of the people and developing the resources of the country. It has made a commencement from which it is impossible to draw back, without damage to the national character and without the sacrifice both of income and power.

James Thomason, 1851 (Quoted in Mital 1986: 44–5)

Few undertakings offered a wider field for 'developing the resources of the country' in colonial India than the application of engineering science to large-scale irrigation works. No works were more spectacular than those that transformed the Punjab in the late nineteenth and the early twentieth century. In the 1830s, British engineers began the construction of a series of interlinked irrigation canals in western Punjab that eventually opened over 14 million acres of arid land to agricultural colonization and settlement. The Punjab 'canal colonies', as these lands were called, emerged in colonial lore as one of the greatest success stories of colonial engineering, dramatizing the productive potential of an alliance between the colonial state

* I wish to thank the Social Science Research Council for inviting me to present this paper at their conference on 'Resources: Conceptions and Contestations' in Kathmandu, Nepal, in January 2003. Earlier versions of this paper were presented at the Agrarian Studies Seminar, Yale University, and the South Asia seminar of the University of Michigan. Thanks to all who made comments and suggestions.

and scientific engineering in the development of India's resources. Here, truly, to transfer Donald Worster's phrase to a more appropriate context, were 'rivers of empire', harnessed by science and the imperial state to foster agricultural production (Worster 1985).[1]

But if the linking of science and empire conjures images of aggressive efforts to control and commodify nature in order to tap its productive powers, the history of the Punjab canal colonies in fact suggests the complex character of the relationship between the state, science and nature in the colonial context. On one level, colonial water engineering in the Punjab grew out of emerging nineteenth-century European ideas about the relationship between science and political economy more broadly. These ideas defined Punjab's river waters as a 'resource', open to increasing state control for purposes of productive 'use' and 'development'. But if, as James Thomason noted, 'developing' such resources was critical to enhanced income, it was also critical to new forms of state power. Increasing state control over water—and thus over the land—defined new frameworks for the exercise of control over the local 'communities' comprising the Indus basin society.

The role of resource control in the simultaneous agendas of enhancing productivity and of increasing state control was in fact one that was marked by serious contradictions. While the application of engineering science allowed the state to commodify water in new ways, it also impinged on the structures through which the state had long sought to define its political relationship to indigenous society, and to the kin-based village 'communities' that comprised it. The contradictory character of colonial thinking about nature—and, by implication, the contradictory meanings attached by the colonial state to notions of 'development'—is the focus of this essay. The argument put forth here is that these contradictions can be highlighted by focusing on the foundational usage in the colonial context of one key term—the word 'waste'. This was a term central to professional engineering theory as it developed in the nineteenth century. But it was a term critical also to the structure of the colonial state's revenue

---

[1] For a recent study of the impact of colonial capitalism on the development of the river basin in British India (though with an emphasis primarily on flood control), see D'Souza (2006).

system, and to its reliance on the 'village community' as a central institution linking the state to the land. Controlling 'waste' was, in differing ways, central to both an agenda of increasing 'scientific' control over the environment, and to the state's political manipulation of indigenous communities. Understanding the place of 'waste' in colonial discourse is thus a key to the understanding of some of the most basic contradictions underlying the colonial resource regime.

SCIENCE AND IRRIGATION ENGINEERING

North-west India was one the great experimental centres for irrigation engineering in the late nineteenth-century world—and one in which science and professional engineering played a major role. Irrigation investment in India was hardly new in the mid-nineteenth century; the East India Company had been involved in a number of irrigation projects, largely planned and executed by military engineers, many trained at the East India Company's military college at Addiscombe. The emergence of a professional cadre of civil irrigation engineers in India can perhaps best be dated from the opening, in 1848, of the College of Civil Engineering at Roorkee (renamed the Thomason College of Civil Engineering in 1854). The founding of the college was directly linked to the growing demand for irrigation engineers created by the construction of the Ganges canal in the 1840s, but it was reorganized and expanded in the 1850s with the irrigation requirements of the newly-annexed Punjab, and its newly established Public Works Department (PWD), also in mind (Kumar 1995; Mital 1986).

Not all new PWD engineers came from Roorkee, particularly after the founding in 1871 of a new engineering college at Cooper's Hill in England funded by the Government of India. But as the histories of both Roorkee and Cooper's Hill demonstrated, colonialism in India encouraged the professionalization of British civil engineering generally, and suggested the profession's important colonial roots. As Richard Temple noted, Britain had held, as late as the 1880s, a reputation for backwardness in technical education as compared with the countries of continental Europe, since most engineering instruction tended to be conducted in 'private establishments at the industrial centres of England', and was geared largely towards private employment. But in India, the British government had come to have, as Temple wrote in 1883, 'colossal interests at stake in its public works', with a concomitant need for well-educated engineers and 'immense resources for so arranging its plans that this object shall be secured' (Temple 1986a: 304–11). From the beginning this promised to give engineers trained at Roorkee and Cooper's Hill a new sense of professional mission, and one intimately linked to colonialism.

Mathematics, the language of international science, lay at the heart of this education. Many Roorkee professors, who tended to come initially from the Royal Engineers, held, in the words of William Willcocks, an early Roorkee graduate, aspirations for 'world-wide science'. Doubtless, military irrigation engineers in India had long had an interest in what could be learned pragmatically from irrigation works in other parts of the world, but in the last decades of the nineteenth century this was linked to a growing sense of shared expertise drawn from a common body of 'theoretical' (that is mathematical) published research.[2] As Willcocks wrote of his days as a student at Roorkee in the early 1870s, 'we were taught on the sound lines of the Ecole Polytechnique in Paris, and not on the ridiculous lines generally in vogue in England at the time' (Willcocks 1935: 32).[3]

On one level, the increasing prestige and professionalism of irrigation engineers in India in the late nineteenth century was rooted particularly in the conjoining of the prestige of mathematical science to the prestige of service to the state. Central to this was a 'public' commitment to scientific control over nature, a commitment linked to service to the state, which worked powerfully on British and Indians alike. It was the ethos of disinterested service to science that empowered the self-image of many engineers as engaged in a moral enterprise, 'content', as one engineer put it, 'to let their achievements speak for themselves' even as they identified strongly with the power of the state (Punjab Public Works Department 1943: 3.50). For many

[2] As Headrick notes, both Proby Cautley and Richard Baird Smith studied Italian irrigation (Headrick 1988: 177–8). Sir Colin Scott-Moncrieff, later chairman of the Indian Irrigation Commission, was also deputed by the Government of India in the 1860s to study European irrigation (Scott-Moncrieff 1868).

[3] For a fuller discussion of Willcocks' views on irrigation and empire, see Gilmartin (2006).

Indians, like Ram Das Tandon, who graduated from Roorkee in 1898 and joined the Punjab Irrigation Department, the process of becoming an engineer at the college was like passing through a transformative 'dream', defining an entirely new 'public' identity (Tandon 1968: 28; also Srivastava 1998: 134–64). For British boys at Cooper's Hill, as Temple wrote, the aim of education was not just skill in engineering, but also the 'moral training' and 'discipline' that would prepare them for 'victorious success' (Temple 1986a: 310)—success, in this case, in 'subduing' nature, and turning its products into 'resources' that could be used for purposes of production. But it was a commitment to mathematical science that most clearly defined their distinctive professional image. As a Punjab Irrigation Department manual later suggested in tracing the development of irrigation engineering in the Punjab, the military engineers who had worked in the mid-nineteenth century had shown 'amazing courage and resources', but 'their knowledge of irrigation and hydraulics was *nil*'. They worked largely by trial and error. The Bari Doab and Sirhind canals had thus been built with 'beautifully drawn and skilfully coloured plans', but with 'shocking mistakes of design', which had been corrected only by trial and error and dogged persistence. It was only mathematical science that had moved engineering beyond this phase, so that it could be said by the 1880s that irrigation engineering as a profession was really 'on its feet' (Punjab Public Works Department 1943: 3.50–3.52).[4]

WATER'S DUTY: THE LANGUAGE OF ENGINEERING CONTROL

The vision of man's relationship to nature that underlay the professionalization of irrigation engineering in the second half of the nineteenth century was perhaps clearest in the metaphorical language that came to define the foundations of irrigation science. Perhaps no single term was more redolent of the underlying assumptions that shaped water engineering in the late nineteenth century than the term 'duty', a word that assumed foundational significance in the

---

[4] The engineering problems with the Bari Doab and Sirhind canals, and the general doubts about canal construction that they raised in the 1870s, are discussed briefly in Michel (1967: 60–1, 71–2).

nineteenth-century development of mathematical irrigation science.[5] While the term echoed the sense of moral mission increasingly important in the public profession of science, the word 'duty' was defined in technical jargon as applying directly to water; it was, in fact, the basic measure of water as a 'resource', that is, the measure of the productive 'use' to which irrigation water was put. Water 'duty' was, in the words of one leading engineer, the measure of 'the relation between the volume of water and the area of crop which it matures'. Though its precise measurement varied somewhat in different contexts, it was usually expressed in India in terms of the number of acres of cropped land that a cusec of water could be expected to bring to maturity in a particular period of time: thus, 'if 1 cubic foot a second [cusec] running continuously for four months will mature 100 acres of crop, the "duty", in that case, is said to be 100 acres to the cusec, to the base of 4 months' (Buckley 1908: 124–5). 'Duty' was thus a fundamental measure of the ultimate goal of irrigation science—the extraction of productive capacity from nature. As Herbert Wilson noted in a leading irrigation engineering textbook of the late nineteenth century,

...on the duty of water depends the financial success of every irrigation enterprise, for as water becomes scarce its value increased. In order to estimate the cost of irrigation in projecting works, it is essential to know how much water the land will require. In order to ascertain the dimensions of canals and reservoirs for the irrigation of given areas the duty of water must be known (Wilson 1893: 38).[6]

The prominent use of the term 'duty' in water engineering suggested the discipline's close connections to trends that had transformed nineteenth-century scientific conceptions of nature more generally.

---

[5] An example is the opening of the technical discussion of irrigation in Phillips (1908: 154): 'On the duty of water depends the financial success of every irrigation enterprise...' This precise phrase, probably initially that of Herbert Wilson, was echoed in many textbooks.

[6] Wilson's textbook was intended for American engineers, and yet it drew significantly on Indian experience, reflecting, in fact, the strong influence of Indian colonial irrigation practice on US engineers in the late nineteenth century. Wilson himself had visited India and published on Indian irrigation. For a discussion of his views, see Wescoat (2002).

Most critically, it suggested the vital importance of measurement as scientific engineering's defining feature.[7] But it also suggested the metaphoric vision of natural systems that increasingly influenced the world view of nineteenth-century engineers. In origin, the term 'duty' was one that was first technically applied in Britain in the late eighteenth century as a measurement for assessing the efficiency of steam engines. As used by James Watt, for example, the efficiency of a steam engine in pumping water was measured by the 'duty' (or work) it could perform: the number of pounds of water that the engine could raise one foot per bushel of coal as fuel (Dickinson 1936: 106).[8] The concept of 'duty' was thus rooted in the concern for the efficiency of energy use within a closed mechanical system.

The foundational usage of 'duty' in late nineteenth-century irrigation engineering transformed its meaning in critical ways. But its use in irrigation engineering nevertheless suggested the firm grounding of the discipline in the larger transformations in British scientific thinking about energy that marked the middle decades of the nineteenth century and that shaped the broader professionalization of engineering. As M. Norton Wise and Crosbie Smith have argued, these decades witnessed a fundamental shift in the dominant view of nature among scientists from one stressing a mechanical 'balance' of natural forces, tending towards equilibria (a vision dating back to Newton's clockwork universe), to one that stressed the importance in nature of perpetual change and of the tendency of natural systems to move relentlessly towards energy dissipation. In the realm of scientific thinking, this shift was captured perhaps most prominently in the articulation at mid-century of the second law of thermodynamics

[7] This was perhaps most clearly expressed in the words of Sir William Thomson (Lord Kelvin) in 1883 as he sought to systematize the units of measurement that came to be central to electrical engineering: 'In physical science a first essential step in the direction of learning any subject is to find principles of numerical reckoning and methods for practicably measuring some quality concerned with it. I often say that when you can measure what you are speaking about, and express it in numbers, you know something about it, but when you cannot measure it, when you cannot express it in numbers, your knowledge is of a meagre kind: it may be the beginning of knowledge, but you have scarcely in your thoughts, advanced to the stage of *science*...' Quoted in Smith and Wise (1989: 684).

[8] According to the Oxford English Dictionary, the term was 'introduced' by Watt.

which postulated, through the concept of entropy, the fundamental notion of natural energy systems tending towards ever-increasing disorder. The science of energy conservation and control thus came to be central to scientific technique in the nineteenth century; 'work' and 'waste', as Wise and Smith argue, emerged as the critical terms defining human interactions with nature, even as these came to be increasingly central too in shaping thinking about the human economies through which production was organized. As a result, the early to mid-nineteenth century tended to witness a gradual shift from the clock (which mechanically suggested nature's 'balance') to the engine (whose purpose was production) as a root metaphor for conceptualizing human relations with nature in mechanical terms. And with this, the extraction of 'work' for human use and the minimization of 'waste' from the energies of nature came to define the mission of the professional engineer (Wise and Smith 1989–90).

With its emphasis on water's 'duty' as the fundamental measure of irrigational value, irrigation engineering clearly imported this engine model into its own metaphorical language. Canal systems, like machines, drew on nature's energy, in this case the productive, life-giving power of scarce water, carried through river systems. The central technique of water engineering was thus geared towards building structures, and mathematically modelling water flow, so as to maximize the productive work that water could perform. 'We may look on [a canal system] as a great machine composed of many parts', wrote one prominent engineer in the 1870s, 'and go about calculating its efficiency much in the same way as that of a steam-engine'.[9] The moral imperative of irrigation engineering was to counter the natural tendency of water, like energy, to run to waste. As Bruno Latour has put it, any good water engineer 'should begin with the principle that if water can leak away, it will' (Latour 1987: 57–8).[10] It was this

[9] J.S. Beresford, 'Memo on the Irrigation Duty of Water and the Principles on which its Increase Depends', August 1875. Beresford was writing specifically here of the Ganges canal. See Punjab Irrigation Branch Papers, No. 10 ('Remodelling of Distributaries on Old Canals'), 1905.

[10] Latour here uses the metaphor of water control to describe, by analogy, the structure of scientific argument as well. His metaphor suggests how the model of nature as tending to dissipation metaphorically defined even the work

preoccupation—thwarting the natural tendency towards waste—
that defined both the moral mission of most irrigation engineers
and their discipline as a mathematical craft (a craft concerned with
using mathematics first to model nature to understand its processes,
and then to construct mechanical means to tap its energy—as a
resource—for productive use).

Such a vision of 'waste'—and a concern for making efficient use of
scarce resources—held implications also for how users themselves were
incorporated into such a system. Fundamental to the notion of duty
was that efficiency depended not just on the flow of water in canals
and distributaries, but also on how water was used in farmers' fields.
As a mathematical construct, the 'duty' of water depended critically
on efficiency of individual use, for it was only when water reached the
root zones of plants in individual fields that its productive energies
were unleashed. As Herbert Wilson noted in a late nineteenth-
century irrigation textbook, calculations of 'duty' thus depended not
just on the soil, the rainfall, and the condition of the ditches, but also
on 'the skill of the irrigator' (Wilson 1909: 47–50). Measurements
of duty inevitably hinged on calculations of 'waste' (water losses) in
all the parts of canal systems, including the irrigators' fields. R.G.
Kennedy, later chief engineer of the Punjab, thus estimated in 1883
that for every 100 cubic feet of water entering the Bari Doab canal at
its river intake at Madhopur, 20 cubic feet were lost in transit in the
main canal, 6 cubic feet in *rajbahas* (distributaries), 21 cubic feet in
village watercourses, and 25 cubic feet by waste in everyday usage,
thus yielding an overall efficiency rating for 'the canal as a machine'
(or duty measured at the canal intake) of 28 per cent.[11] Duty could
only be measured when all these variables (and others) were taken
into account.

---

of the scientist, or engineer himself, in building and controlling a scientific
argument.

[11] 'Considering the canal as a machine', Kennedy wrote, 'its efficiency was 28 per
cent' (that is, only 28 per cent of the water taken from the river at the canal head
reached the root zone of plants to perform its 'work'). 'Note on the Irrigation Duty of
the Bari Doab Canal', April 1883, by R.G. Kennedy, Executive Engineer, Bari Doab
Canal. See Punjab Irrigation Branch Papers, No. 10 ('Remodelling of Distributaries
on Old Canals'), 1905.

But the place of the user in such calculations—however important in theory—remained, in practice, highly problematic. Textbook engineering doctrine in the late nineteenth century hinged on a vision of the user as a maximizing producer, who was thus joined with the engineer (in theory) in a community defined by a common struggle for production against a wasteful nature. The language of opposition between engineering science and natural 'waste' paralleled the dominant language of market efficiency shaping late nineteenth-century ideas of political economy and economic man. But in practice, colonial engineers rarely incorporated users effectively into their formulas for canal design, or, in fact, into their thinking about the efficient control of water as a resource.

On one level, this was the result of the virtually insurmountable practical problems that engineers faced in delivering water in measurable quantities to individual users. Only by providing a measured volume of water to each user could canal administrators charge for water in such a way as to create incentives for individual producers to behave as profit maximizers, thus maximizing the efficiency of use and distribution within larger irrigation systems. In practice, however, colonial irrigation engineers despaired in the first half of the twentieth century of devising a practical system of water gauging that was both tamper-proof, and inexpensive enough to be used effectively for measuring the quantities of water delivered to individuals. Though they repeatedly remarked on the inefficiencies in water use encouraged by the absence of volumetric water charges in the Indus basin (and proposed numerous hypothetical expedients for gauging water so that users would be forced to pay for the actual quantities of water consumed), they never developed the mechanical or social technology to solve this problem (Ali 1988: 169–77). Water charges in the Indus basin were thus, in practice, taken throughout the colonial period and beyond, not on quantities of water used, but on the basis of matured crop areas under irrigation (Stone 1984: 159–94). This had the advantage of linking water charges to the actual 'work' that water performed (in terms of crop returns), but it undercut all efforts to encourage (or measure) individual human efficiency as a vital part of the overall irrigating 'machine'. Indeed, to the extent that engineers were able to encourage non-wasteful water use in individual fields, it was not by incorporating irrigators into the larger structure of the 'machine', but rather by laying down bureaucratic (and often unenforceable) rules for non-wasteful water application.[12]

Failure to incorporate individuals effectively into the 'irrigating machine' in fact led to the assignment of a prominent place in irrigation structures to the 'community' of irrigators occupying the lands lying beyond departmentally controlled canal outlets. Given the technical constraints within which they operated, most engineers actually came to view their responsibility for maintaining the irrigating 'machine' as ending, basically, at the canal outlet. This did not mean that engineers were totally unconcerned with the distribution and use of water beyond the outlet. To oversee distribution, engineers often designed *warabandis*, or schedules of turns for water, which were intended to regulate the quantities of water (or, more accurately, the times of access to water) which were available to each field—and thus to each individual—on the watercourses attached to each canal outlet. But in practice such schedules were rarely rigidly enforced (nor carefully monitored). Indeed, official engineering law and practice empowered British officials to frame such warabandis only when communities of irrigators themselves specifically asked for help in preparing them. Whatever the contours of engineering theory, in practice, engineers thus delivered water not so much to individuals (though it was individual 'occupiers' who paid water charges), but rather to measured quantities of land (or *chaks*), which were attached to each outlet, and assigned water on the basis of calculations of duty and irrigation intensity. From this perspective, the success of irrigation was measured less by its role in delivering water to individuals to be put to maximum productive 'use', and more in terms of the total quantities of unproductive land—'wasteland'—that were brought under irrigation. Engineers thus commonly measured irrigation works by the gross areas of land brought under irrigation 'command',[13] even

---

[12] The Punjab Irrigation Department required, for example, that water be deployed into embanked fields (through the construction of *kiaris*, or small embankments) with the aim of limiting waste in irrigators' fields.

[13] The term 'command' was, like 'duty', a technical engineering term that metaphorically imputed human characteristics to water. The 'command' of a particular canal referred, in technical parlance, to the (measured) area of land that could be reached through gravity flow by water from that canal. The term thus suggested how control over water defined a structure of control over land.

as the local control and distribution of water was to an important degree left to the collective organization of communities of users.

Opening the maximum quantity of 'wasteland' to possible cultivation—and thus bringing this land within the structure of British revenue administration—had long been an overriding concern of Indus basin administration. In using this as a measure of the success of irrigation works, engineers were in some ways simply adapting to the political and social circumstances in which they operated. As one engineer put it, engineers had long recognized the importance of practical adaptation to the success of their craft; professional engineering was, after all, in the end nothing but 'a blending of theory and practice'.[14]

But the role of the individual producer and the local 'community' in Indus basin irrigation nevertheless remained a focus of considerable uncertainly and unease among Indus basin engineers. However important the role the local community came to play in organizing the use of water beyond the outlet, the idea of community control at this level had no formal, theoretical purchase within the technical metaphor of the irrigating 'machine'. In practice, the local community stood as a hinge at the heart of the system, facilitating on one level the actual delivery of water to the fields, but disrupting, on another level, the community of production—defined by a common commitment to the control of nature's waste—that linked the engineer and the maximizing individual producer in engineering theory.

The implications of this for the overall workings of Punjab's irrigation systems were substantial. But the significance of this lay not just in the practical difficulties in realizing the structure of engineering, but in the interface that this defined between the structure of irrigation theory and the structure of colonial political administration. Communities were, of course, in practice, highly varied. But if the local community

---

Indeed, the term operated on a hierarchy of levels, as the 'command' areas of the smallest channels were nested within the 'command' areas of larger distributaries and canal systems. These interconnections suggested how the control of flowing water defined also a system of nesting units of land, encompassed entirely within larger 'commands'.

[14] Note by E.S. Bellasis, Superintending Engineer, Derajat Circle, 15 August 1907. See Punjab Public Works Department, Irrigation, file no. 412 of 1909, PWD Secretariat, Lahore.

had no formal place in engineering theory, it had long occupied a critical place in the structure of colonial thinking about political control in the Indus basin. In administrative terms, the irrigation chak to which engineers delivered water in the canal colonies was largely synonymous with the *mauza*, or village estate, which held a central place in the politics of colonial revenue collection and administration. To analyse the impact of the community on irrigation, we thus need to analyse the important place that this vision of local community held within the structure of colonial administration, and how this, too, related to a vital set of colonial ideas about production, nature and the land. To analyse the development of colonial political theory too broadly would take us well beyond the scope of this essay. But to look at the local community as a central element in the structure of British rule—and how it related to a different set of ideas about nature and production from those fostered by the theory of professional engineering—we can do no better than to look once again, in a different context this time, at a single, critically important word: the term 'waste'.

Village 'Waste' and the Village Producer

To understand the distinctive meaning of 'waste' in the British revenue system one must begin with the primacy given to the village in the British revenue administration. The 'village' and the 'village community' defined the bedrock of the colonial social and property order. Individual agricultural producers and property holders were critical to the British property system, but they were almost invariably conceptualized by the British as being embedded in villages, and in British eyes villages were defined by the existence of village communities.[15]

Defining the meaning of 'village community', however, is hardly a straightforward enterprise; nor was it so for the British in the mid-nineteenth century. When the British first began to survey the land of the Punjab in the middle decades of the nineteenth century, they had found an immense variety of structures of social relationships

---

[15] This is not to suggest that landlords whose property encompassed many villages did not exist in Punjab. But the basic foundations of the property system, as it developed in the North-western provinces and in central Punjab, were shaped primarily by British thinking about the village, and later the 'tribe'.

and adaptations to the land. The presence of extensive forms of cultivation, linked to semi-pastoralism, was particularly important in many parts of Punjab. If 'villages' had an essential feature, it was that each village engendered, in the very particularism of its relationship to its physical and social environment, identities that were discrete from those of all other villages.

But the British nevertheless sought in the village a local frame that would serve the purposes of what James Scott has called, 'state simplification' (Scott 1995). Partly, the British achieved this through theoretical speculation about the evolutionary relationships that defined unifying *patterns* of variation in local social organization, patterns shaped both by relationships to nature and to previous states. This found a prominent place in many late nineteenth-century settlement reports, and laid the groundwork for much anthropological speculation about the general character of variation in local communities. But more important than this, the British themselves *gave* to villages a common form that essentialised the category in the administration of colonial Punjab—a form defined by maps. Whatever their variations, the one thing that *all* villages came to have in common under the British was that they were territorially bounded and mapped. The term 'village' in fact became synonymous administratively with a mapped territory (known technically as a mauza). This created the framework within which the term 'village community' came to have legal meaning within the colonial system—and it played an important role also ultimately in shaping the meaning of irrigation chaks.

The mauza or village estate became the local arena within which individual private property was defined, mapped and recorded—this was the realm in which individual producers resided. In this sense, it was an administrative frame that had no *necessary* connection to local community at all. Though the British sometimes made use of collective village responsibility in the collection of the revenue, the mapped village estate created a framework within which judiciable rights to individual property were virtually always clearly and separately recorded.[16] Each mauza's property owner was bound

---

[16] Joint revenue responsibility was conceived of as normal practice, but, as Douie noted, in reality it occupied 'a far more prominent position in our codes than in our practice' (Douie 1985: 61).

directly and individually to the state—both by a common interest in the enforcement of individual property law, and by a common commitment to the productive land use necessary for the payment of revenue. A nexus of law and agricultural productivity binding the individual property holder and the state together was in fact central to the 'public' identity of the state itself, and to the definition of the individual owner as producer.[17] It was in this sense that the law created a framework for the definition of the productive, maximizing individual who was theoretically critical to engineering theory.

And yet at the same time the recognition of the village as a vessel for local 'community' was also central to the British framework of administration. Recognition of the bonds of local community was vital to the political structure of the state, for this created the framework within which the British established structures of local leadership and 'representation'. But critical also to the structure of colonial rule was the grounding of local community in a conceptual arena that would not encroach on the contractual relations linking the individual and the state within the colonial revenue system. 'Community', as the British saw it, was thus grounded in a metaphorical field entirely separate from the realm of production—in the field of 'blood' and genealogy.

Critically for the structure of colonial power, this realm too was knowable by the British through careful administrative research and 'objective' framing. Just as the land of villages was mapped, the 'blood' of the village proprietors was also mapped through the recording of genealogies, which became a vital part of every settlement record. Genealogies were in fact often used to trace the village proprietors to a single ancestor or group of ancestors who had originally occupied the land and founded the village. 'Village by village', Clive Dewey writes, 'the Settlement Officers and their assistants traced the descent of rights and the descent of right-holders back to some mythical

---

[17] Many officials saw the ideas behind this notion as fully shared by Indian producers as well. See, for example, the comments of Sir Richard Temple in the 1880s: 'In an Oriental nation the land belongs to him who first reclaimed it, and to his heirs or assigns. The right thus originating in labour, industry and enterprise, descends by inheritance throughout the East. ...The people, regarding this property as the most precious of their material possessions...have clung to it with unsurpassing pertinacity' (Temple 1986b: 478–9).

founder...' (Dewey 1991: 25). Such stories of the original breaking up and settling of the land were central to the grounding of communities on the land. But the *essence* of community for the British generally lay not in the process of attachment to the land, but rather in the recorded genealogical tables themselves. 'A glance at them will tell the history of a village', wrote one settlement officer (Saunders 1873: 75). If history is a charter for community, then this was a very distinctive notion of 'history'. But it was one that supported the distinctive vision of 'village community' that the British were in the process of shaping. While the bonds of law and productivity bound the state and the individual, the legal existence of the community came to lie in a separate conceptual space—in the bonds of kinship.

The conceptual separation of local community from the realm of production was sustained by the colonial development of a dual system of property law. While individual rights of landed property were rooted in the law of contracts (and were based on state recognition of individual property rights in return for the regular payment of revenue), relations of community were regulated through a system of 'customary law', whose underlying principles were driven, as British legal theorists argued, by the dynamics of kinship. At the heart of customary law were a series of presumptions about the conveyance of property (primarily through inheritance) that were aimed toward the maintenance of patrilineal authority in the village, largely through the denial of virtually all landholding rights to women. While the British thus conceptualized the original establishment of property rights as rooted in a contract between the state and the landowner as a rational producer, they conceptualized customary inheritance law as rooted in the organic bonds of 'primitive' community. In his capacity as a member of the village community, the landowner was thus not a rational maximizer; to the contrary, he was a patriarch who acted only according to the logic of 'blood'.[18]

The complexity in this historic separation of genealogical community from the realm of production is suggested by the recent work of Richard Saumarez Smith, who has closely analysed one of the earliest British settlements in the Punjab. Smith has suggested

---

[18] The fullest discussion of the principles on which the British defined a system of 'customary law' in the Punjab is found in Tupper (1881).

that in many villages, issues of productivity and community were, at the time of the British arrival, often closely linked. In villages in Ludhiana District, Smith found that 'shares' in village assets were calculated originally in terms of 'ploughs', thus reflecting a system organized by 'the business of agricultural production, with shares based on the productive capabilities of individual members'. But British policy tended to shift the language of local community and of 'shares' in village assets from one based on productive participation in the village, to one based on recorded genealogy and descent. As they recorded them at settlement, the British used the definition of ancestral shares in the village largely to mark out a distinct community of village proprietors, that is, 'owners' (as distinct from 'tenants', who now had no shares in the village, whatever their actual contributions to the process of production). Shares thus carried increasingly small significance in terms of a community of village production; they were, rather, attached to individual proprietary holdings that were mapped on the land and heritable in perpetuity.[19] In order to map out clear individual rights to property, in other words, for purposes of establishing contractual revenue obligations, the British shifted the language of 'community' into an arena of 'blood' that was, at least in law and theory, entirely separable from the process of production.

But what, then, in British eyes, was the stake of the genealogically-based 'community' in the land and assets of the village? This is where the concept of 'waste' came to play a critical and central role in British thinking. As the British mapped the villages of the Punjab, they delineated distinctive categories of land that reflected the oppositions between individual, private property and the genealogically-based 'village community' that marked the British property system more generally in the last half of the nineteenth century. Critical to this was the demarcation of what was known as the village 'commons', the *shamilat deh*, a category of land widely referred to by the British as the village 'waste'.

In the mapping of villages, the delineation of individual property and the delineation of the 'village waste' were in fact inseparably linked. The first aim of British settlement officers when they mapped

---

[19] Of course, as Smith notes, local land controllers themselves may have viewed these processes in a variety of different ways (1996: 18–48).

Punjabi villages was to sort out the claims of villagers to land held in individual 'proprietary right'. This was, by definition, land that was potentially productive and assessable to British revenue (subject, in other words, to individual contract). The 'commons', as a legal category, basically represented that land which was left over.[20] It was thus, by definition, 'wasteland', that is, land on which claims to productive use (and thus to individual proprietorship) could not be, or had not been, effectively made.[21]

As a village institution, the extent of the 'commons' also depended on the external demarcation of the mauza (and thus depended on the definition by the British of the village as a mapped structure). In areas of the Punjab where uncultivated land was plentiful (which included large parts of the province at the middle of the nineteenth century), the regular British practice was to assign significant blocks of this 'waste' to village estates according to general formula. 'Where the waste was of small extent', Baden-Powell wrote, 'the whole of the adjoining area was included in the village-boundary as a matter of course; where it was extensive, each village received twice, and, in some cases, thrice, the cultivated area'. But whether defined in relationship to proprietary holdings, or to the external boundary of the village, the official marking out of the shamilat as commons, or joint share-held property, had far more to do with the legal distinction between production and waste, than with a history of actual common use.

'Commons' and 'wasteland' thus tended to become legally synonymous on village land in the Punjab. This, of course, did not mean that 'waste' held the same meanings for all. For the British, the association of the term 'waste' with common land was one with long historical antecedents in England itself. But in nineteenth-century

----

[20] As Chakravarty-Kaul puts it, 'The *shamilat* was apparently that waste which had not been appropriated by individual families descended from original settlers and had been kept in common for grazing "so long as it was not appropriated for cultivation"' (1996: 79–80).

[21] Cases where individual proprietors had laid proprietary claims to 'culturable waste', but paid revenue only on cultivated land, were thus viewed in early settlement reports as 'anomalies' that had to be explained and specially dealt with (Mackenzie 1861: 117).

Punjab, the term 'waste' subsumed a number of indigenous terms, for the indigenous cultural meanings attached to the oppositions between cultivated and uncultivated land were complex (Dove 1992). Uncultivated land in Punjab varied from *banjar jadid*, 'short fallows', that might have been cultivated relatively recently, to *jangal*, which signified barren scrub land, not subject to cultivated control (in revenue parlance, *ghair mumkin*, 'without possibility' of cultivation, which also included roads, the village site or sites, etc.). Though in much of western and southern Punjab, large chunks of shamilat were carved from *bar jangal*, in much of central Punjab village shamilat was constituted primarily from land referred to as *banjar qadim*, 'long fallows'. The term 'long fallows' suggested an opposition between village shamilat and cultivated, proprietary land that was far less sharp than that suggested by the term 'wasteland'. Such land was often vitally important to village production, used not only for grazing of plough and well animals, but also, in some cases, readily transformable to banjar jadid under pressure of increasing family sizes or in the event of greater availability of water. But all this nevertheless tended to be subsumed under the larger English rubric of 'waste'.

Many British officials, of course, knew fully well that 'wasteland' was not always without important uses; it was they, after all, who in their revenue records often explicated the nuances of indigenous terminology for 'wasteland'. But the logic of the binary distinction between proprietary land and 'wasteland' was in fact one that gained powerful saliency from the internal logic of the colonial property system. By classifying land as 'waste', the British marked it, in effect, as outside the realm of production and therefore, by definition, outside the realm also of individual property. And in so doing, they made the land available as an arena for the definition of a different kind of property—'community' property. Village 'commons' thus became the grounds on which the existence of a 'village community' was inscribed. Through the delineation of the 'commons', the shares of the proprietors in the village community as a whole were marked symbolically on the map of the village estate, and by classifying the commons as 'waste' the British made clear that the realm of community was in fact quite distinct from the realm of production. The labelling of the commons as 'waste', as a product of nature without productive use, in fact made possible the definition of the village 'community' itself as an organic, 'primitive', kinship-based construction, defining the 'communal' man, in effect, as the antithesis of the rational producer.[22]

In actual practice, of course, the role of the village commons and the village community in production was complex and highly variable, as Minoti Chakravarty-Kaul has demonstrated. In arid western Punjab (and in parts of southern and eastern Punjab as well), the use of common land was often intimately connected to the interactions between pastoralism and agriculture. In some Punjabi villages, the management of the commons was critical to the maintenance of individual household production and was closely integrated into community management of other productive resources. Private plots were often scattered in eastern and central Punjabi villages to equalize access to varying qualities of land, including the village commons. 'Collective management' of the commons, which was normally kept in relatively compact blocks, often went hand in hand in such villages with the collective village management of other productive resources, such as 'field channels of irrigation wells and ponds'. Income from common lands, whether from grazing fees from outsiders or from rents charged to kamins (village servants), supported collective village management expenses (Chakravarty-Kaul 1996: 80–92).[23] To suggest that British attempts to legally situate the shamilat on the 'waste' defined a form of 'commons' that had no relationship to production would seriously distort the realities of village life.

But the British were, in general, little interested in the administration of this collective realm, which was quite ancillary to their emerging

[22] The relationship of this to larger processes, by which modern communities have been marked as organic, and thus operating in realms distinct from those of production, would be interesting to pursue. Within many modern nations, for example, the demarcation of 'non-productive' land (in a market-based sense) as 'national' (as, for example, in national parks) has also provided a prime mechanism for inscribing ideals of community on the land in a world where individualism is linked to market-based production.

[23] See Wade (1988) for one of the best attempts to analyse the reasons (relating largely to issues of rational choice such as scarcity and risk) why levels of cooperative management of village resources in India, including the commons, may have varied significantly from village to village. See also Brara (2006) for a discussion of the tensions between state initiatives relating to local 'community' and a village 'public sphere' in Rajasthan.

vision of the village.[24] Many officials undoubtedly recognized that the commons was in some instances an important productive adjunct to household organization (particularly for agriculture depending on animal-powered wells), and 'rights' of access to the commons were often recorded in the *wajib-ul-arz* (the village 'record of rights'). These also became, at times, an issue of some importance in local conflict and in litigation in the British courts. But the structure of colonial law, as officials themselves noted, offered little to support the collective *management* of the commons.[25] That the commons were far more important to the British as a symbolic field for the inscription of community defined by ancestral shares was suggested by the fact that in many villages, areas of 'waste' were defined as 'commons' not only for the village as a whole, but for the many constitutive genealogical segments of villages (called *pattis* or *tarafs*) as well (Douie 1972: 61; Douie 1985: 263). Customary law, which was constructed largely in the language of 'rights', offered few legal remedies whereby the village community as a whole could take productive control of the commons and administer it for joint benefit. With increasing pressure to bring the commons into the realm of production, almost the only legal remedy that British law had to offer was partition of the commons into individual proprietary holdings. And ironically, while often

---

[24] This is why, as Wade (1988) notes, descriptions of these forms of collective village land management appear relatively rarely in British records.

[25] Though lawsuits could sometimes prevent unauthorized cultivation on the commons, or enforce rights laid out in the wajib-ul-arz, the law offered no standing to the village community to administer the commons in a corporate fashion. This is not to imply that villages did not sometimes effectively administer common lands in spite of this. But the basic legal situation was a product of the underlying structure of British law. The problems this engendered were sometimes noticed by British officials, often a bit disingenuously. As James Wilson wrote in the 1890s, 'A short act providing that common lands may be managed under rules drawn up with the consent of three-fourths of the recorded owners and of the residents in the village and with the sanction of the collector would lead to a diminution of partitions and be an immense boon to the agricultural community'. James Wilson, DC Shahpur, to S.S. Thorburn, Comm. & Super., Rawalpindi, 24 April 1896. Punjab Board of Revenue, file #171/36 ('Partition of shamilat lands of Mauza Mangowal Khurd, Shahpur'). Such legislation, of course, never occurred. More often, British officials simply blamed the lack of effective management on the inherent fractiousness of the villagers themselves.

precipitated by bitter conflict among the proprietors of the village (or between themselves and their tenants or *kamins*), partition by shares offered at least a symbolic reaffirmation of the idea that the ancestral proprietors in fact continued to embody the village community as a whole.[26]

While forms of collective village action and organization were thus common enough in the Punjab, as they were elsewhere (Brara 2006), the legal definition of local community had moved in another direction. The effect of British colonial policy in the Punjab was to shift the legal meaning of village community out of the arena of production, and into a realm of genealogy that was largely divorced from questions of production and management. Within this framework, community was defined, at least in theory, in relation to a conception of nature far different from that which defined the alliance of engineer and individual in emerging engineering theory. Community was inscribed on the land, at least in legal theory, only where the individualism of man's productive relations to nature was kept at bay (on the 'waste'), not through the act of conquering and subduing nature's inherent 'wasteful' tendencies. Whatever the attitudes of local villagers towards nature (and these were no doubt various), the structure of British power had itself defined large structures of integration that incorporated and organized community in sharply contradictory ways.

CONCLUSION

Contrasting colonial usages of the term 'waste' thus suggest, in the end, contradictions that were inherent in state efforts to incorporate local community organization into the structure of Punjab's newly

---

[26] The history of partitions, like all else to do with villages, was variable and complex. For a discussion, see Chakravarty-Kaul (1996: 121–37, 256–9). The common reliance, within the framework of customary law, on partition as the key legal instrument of proprietary control over the commons was suggested by the holding of the courts that the proprietary body could not oust a co-sharer who cultivated his portion of the commons except by partition (unless the encroachment was of the sort that would prejudice partition as a remedy). There were, however, some conflicting judgements relating to the circumstances in which an encroacher could be ousted (Rustomji 1929: 654–7).

engineered irrigation systems. In systems designed to control nature's 'waste', engineers sought to deliver water to maximizing individual water users and property controllers. Indeed, at the heart of engineering doctrine, as a historical development, was the notion of a moral community of engineers and producers, linked together by their perception of nature as a field whose 'waste' needed to be contained in the interests of promoting human happiness. In theory, Punjabi farmers were potentially as much a part of such a community as European producers; the very definition of property in the colonial system was in part predicated on the vision of the individual as a maximizing producer.

Yet, in spite of this, local 'communities' had, in practice, come to play central and disruptive roles in these systems. Recognizing the difficulty of delivering measured quantities of water to individual users, engineering doctrine came to emphasize the importance of delivering water to outlets beyond which lay 'communities' of water users. Some engineers conceptualized these local communities as part of the larger community of interests linking producers and engineers; indeed, some engineers saw the drawing up of warabandis as a step towards defining local communities of interest in production that were rooted in the common drive to minimize waste. And yet, the effort to incorporate such local communities into a state system of irrigation management ran up against another definition of community that was already firmly entrenched on the ground and linked to the political structure of colonial property. This was the village community—a structure defined by a very different definition of the term 'waste'. Within the property order of the British state, the local community was defined not in relation to a system of local production, but rather in relationship to genealogy—and it was associated pre-eminently not with productive village land, but with common land labelled as 'waste'. Whatever the actual roles of village institutions in matters of production, the 'village community' as a legal entity was conceptualized by the state as fundamentally non-productive and rooted in an entirely different conception of nature from that defining the mathematics of engineering. And given this structure, it is little wonder—whatever the important practical difficulties engineers faced with the pricing and delivery of water to individual villagers—that most colonial engineers avoided direct interference in village affairs. Efforts to incorporate local communities into the structure of irrigation thus proved problematic at best.

To detail the administrative problems engineers have encountered in the twentieth century in incorporating local communities into the massive, integrated irrigation systems of the Indus basin would take us well beyond the scope of this essay. Suffice it to say that these have been considerable.[27] Whatever the state's role in bringing large new areas under irrigation—and in increasing aggregate agricultural production—its inability to use engineering science to break through the power of local village communities and extend a technical system of irrigation control into the villages has sometimes been seen as a failure of development (Ali 1987). But it would be a mistake to see these processes as defined by the tension between development on the one hand, and indigenous community on the other. In assessing the colonial system, we must ask whether the contradictions that have led to these problems were not intrinsic to the very conception of development. The colonial property system laid the foundations for the extension of an engineering vision into the villages by defining a structure of landed property that was predicated on the existence of rational, economic producers. This was at the heart of effective state power and revenue collection, and it was also central to the process, as James Thomason put it in the quotation opening this essay, of 'developing the resources of the country'. But the very logic of this process demanded that the state relegate, for its own political purposes, the legal meaning of community to a very different realm— the primitive and non-productive realm of genealogy and 'blood'. Reflecting the imperatives of colonial rule, this too was a product of development.

[27] Given the emphasis on bringing water to a maximum quantity of 'wasteland', the Indus basin irrigation system has been significantly overbuilt, and many problems, such as increasing waterlogging and salinity, have been related to (though not entirely caused by) this fact. Within this structure, many analysts have detailed how serious problems have arisen in the interface between a bureaucratic structure of water delivery in the main system, and local control of village watercourses and on-farm water management. Problems with the local roles of patrilineages, *biradaris*, have often stymied efforts to extend efficient management into the villages. A discussion of this is found in Merrey (1983).

That two contrasting forms of community were predicated on two definitions of man's relationship to nature was not peculiar to colonial Punjab. It has been one of the consequences of modern development, generally, that these two forms of community, defined here through an analysis of the term 'waste' (and marked elsewhere, as in the United States, by the contrasting values attached to terms such as 'efficiency' and 'wilderness'), have simultaneously shaped modern history. Processes of development predicated on rational, market-driven, behaviour have simultaneously generated visions of community rooted in the common drive to control nature for purposes of production, and in solidarities rooted in identification with nature's fundamentally non-productive values—whether embodied in the village commons or in the national patrimony.

But the distinctive relationship between these in the Indus basin was a product of the structuring of colonial society, which brought them into uncomfortable juxtaposition. Irrigation planners have looked to local communities to play productive roles in irrigation management, even as the system of property has simultaneously pushed the concept of local 'community' out of the realm of productivity. The vision of land and water as 'resources', to be put to instrumental use by 'economic' men, was juxtaposed with the vision of land and water as symbols of 'nature', standing outside processes of production, and thus defining 'communities' outside the realms of economic rationality. Understanding how these contrasting visions of the environment—as 'resources' and as 'nature'—have come to be interrelated takes us to the heart of the processes of development, and to the contradictions they have entailed. Certainly, policy makers continue to deal with the legacies of this history as they seek to encourage 'grass roots' participation and the formation of local users' associations while rationalizing the operation of the Indus basin's irrigation systems today.

3

Contexts and Constructions of Scarcity*

Lyla Mehta

Introduction

Water scarcity is considered one of the most pressing problems confronting the survival of humankind in the next century. But what is it that makes water scarce? Is it the rapid dwindling of aquifers? Is it the billion-plus people who lack access to clean water? Clearly, water supplies are limited and finite, but does this make water scarce in absolute terms? By focusing on the case of 'water-scarce' Kutch in India and its relationship with the controversial Sardar Sarovar Project (SSP), this essay argues that access to, and control over, water is usually linked to prevailing social and power relations which influence how it is used or abused. The essay demonstrates that water scarcity can be constructed differently by different social and political actors, often to meet political ends. Through a detailed empirical and multi-sited examination of both actual practices and discourses around scarcity in the Kutch region of western India, the essay argues that

* See Mehta (2005) for a detailed treatment of scarcity in western India. Research was conducted in Kutch in 1995–6 for which funding was provided by the Overseas Development Institute, London. Subsequent research took place over short visits in 1998, 2000, 2002, and 2004. I am grateful to Annette Sinclair, Himanshu Thakkar and the Gujarat Institute of Desert Ecology for providing the rainfall data and helping with the analysis; P. Kaul for suggesting I read Herman and Chomsky (1988); and Oliver Burch for his help. Most of all, I express my thanks to the Sanghvi family, all my interview partners and my friends and quasi 'family' in the village 'Merka' where I conducted my detailed fieldwork. I will always be grateful to them for their continual cooperation, understanding, warmth, and inspiration.

scarcity is both 'real' and 'constructed'. The essay analyses the 'real' aspects of scarcity—dwindling groundwater aquifers, increased salinity—while also revealing the means by which scarcity is 'constructed' or 'manufactured' through political and policy processes. State discourses portray scarcity as natural (rather than human-induced) and chronic (rather than cyclical). The external 'essentialized' notions of scarcity generated by state discourse and state programmes are often quite different from local people's knowledge systems and livelihood strategies that allow them to adapt to the unpredictability and temporary scarcity of water. This essay begins by discussing the multifaceted nature of scarcity and then provides an overview of Kutch, its water resources and the links with the SSP. It then analyses the dominant discourses of scarcity and demonstrates what they obscure. The essay goes on to examine local responses to scarcity and ends with a discussion of how socio-political, discursive and institutional factors have successfully combined to naturalize scarcity in Kutch.

THE MULTIFACETED NATURE OF SCARCITY

From once being considered an abundant resource, water is increasingly seen as a 'scarce' resource, which needs to be managed judiciously. The statistics are well known: only 3 per cent of the water on earth is fresh and most of this is locked away in the ice caps of Antarctica and Greenland or deep in underground aquifers. As a result, only 0.3 per cent of global water is available for human consumption (Gleick 1993: 3). Water scarcity, as it is constructed in global declarations and debates, is often presented in absolute and monolithic terms, obscuring the complex nature of scarcity and its linkages with ecological, socio-political, temporal, and anthropogenic dimensions. Let us review some of them.

One, unlike other environmental resources such as forests and coal, water is a renewable resource, which means that its availability is constantly subjected to variation depending on its state in the hydrological cycle. Groundwater is the only exception to this rule, since it is less renewable than other water sources. Not only is water variable in form (solid, fluid, or gas), but it is also variable across time and space, depending on factors such as climate, season and temperature. These are the *biophysical* and *ecological* attributes determining water availability.

Two, water scarcity has *temporal* and *cyclical* dimensions. People living in arid and semi-arid regions have long recognized the temporal nature of water scarcity. Periods of dearth are interspersed by periods of abundance. Water availability, thus, is characterized by uncertainty in many parts of the world. However, while factors such as rainfall, vegetation and grass cover make water availability uncertain, it would be fallacious to see water scarcity as something that is constant and permanent. This is because supplies do become abundant in favourable seasons and climatic conditions. Thus, water supplies are relative to exogenous factors such as rainfall.

The third dimension is the *distributional* and *relational* aspects of scarcity. There is tremendous inequality in access to and control over water resources; scarcity is *not* felt universally by all. In water-scarce western India, irrigation pumps work twenty-four hours a day, while poor women find their drinking wells run dry. In arid parts of the world, people consume 10 litres of water per day (Mehta 2005) while an average American, by contrast, uses over 700 litres a day (Gleick 1993: 375).

The fourth dimension concerns the *anthropogenic* dimensions of scarcity. While water scarcity tends to be naturalized today, its anthropogenic dimensions are whitewashed. It is well known that the degradation of the Aral Sea and the Caspian Sea are largely due to human intervention. Furthermore, many of the silted up dams, broken hand-pumps and defunct water pipeline schemes are indicative of bad management practices and/or a failure to encourage or create supportive institutional arrangements to govern water supplies. In sum, it is wrong to conceive of water scarcity in absolute terms, but instead there is an urgent need to link water scarcity with socio-political, institutional and hydrological factors.

WATER SCARCITY AS SOCIALLY AND POLITICALLY CONSTRUCTED

...the whole [of] human development, at least up to now, has been a bitter struggle against scarcity.

Jean-Paul Sartre[1]

[1] Jean-Paul Sartre in Xenos (1989).

Scarcity is frequently considered a 'given' factor of human life and an existential reality. It is also one of the main premises of modern economic thought. Even some sociologists have been seduced by these ideas and see the combat against scarcity to be the basis of social action (cf. Balla 1981: 225). However, has it always been so? Nicholas Xenos in the work *Scarcity and Modernity* (1989) systematically shows how certain attributes of modernity have given rise to the universal notion of scarcity. Today, an unshaken belief in paradigms promoted by neo-classical economics makes scarcity out to be a ubiquitous and permanent feature of the human condition.

The etymological roots of the word 'scarcity' go back to the Old Northern French word *escarcté* which meant insufficiency of supply. Until the late nineteenth century, scarcity connoted a temporally bounded period of scarcity or dearth. Scarcity was experienced cyclically, dependent usually on poor yields. After the industrial revolution, which led to cataclysmic changes creating new needs, desires and the frustration of desires, the concept acquired a new meaning which culminated in its 'invention' in neo-classical economic thought of the eighteenth century (Xenos 1989: 7). From *scarcities*, which were temporally bound and spatially differentiated, came the scourge of *scarcity*, 'a kind of open-ended myth' (ibid.: 35) from which deliverance was sought. Scarcity, not *a* scarcity or *scarcities*, was essentialized and its simplistic universalization led to the obscuring of ambiguities and regional variations.[2] In modernity, the elusive twin of scarcity is abundance, making scarcity 'the antagonist in the human story, a story with a happy ending; vanquishing of the antagonist and a life of happiness ever after and abundance for all' (ibid.: 35).

Deliverance from scarcity could only take place, philosophers argued, via progress. Shades of this are still found in theories of modernization which promote unilinear paths from 'underdevelopment' to 'development'. Progress became the focus for social critics such as Marx and Mill whose theories argued that abundance was the pre-requisite for the full realization of human capacities. These models

---

[2] Modern economics is premised on human needs and their satisfaction: an increase in human needs leads to scarcity of goods; institutions such as property and markets mediate transactions with these scarce goods. In this way, the enterprise of economics is legitimized and the concept of scarcity is universalized (Xenos 1989).

continue to be 'evoked today by those who take refuge in the hope of
an abundant future to assuage their sense of the injustices of present-
day scarcity' (ibid.: 36).

In the international discourse on water resources management,
water scarcity is taken to be a given as also a starting point for policy
agendas (Postel 1994). Until very recently, the supply-oriented nature
of water resources management focused on meeting the ever-growing
and competing needs of industry, agriculture and domestic use. The
perversity of these needs, for example, growing water-guzzling sugar
cane in times of droughts or prioritizing cement plants over drinking
water schemes, is rarely questioned in state discourse. Even the recent
demand-oriented notion of water as an 'economic good' does not
question the universalized notion of water scarcity (see, for example,
Winpenny 1994). From being a 'free good' pillaged by free riders,
water is converted into an 'economic good' that needs to be managed
by dam builders and water bureaucrats.

It would be an ontological fallacy to deny that there is no such
thing as water scarcity or water shortage.[3] The ever-increasing length
of time spent by women on water collection and the visible decline
of groundwater reserves in aquifers are clear indications of *one* aspect
of the problem of water scarcity. There are, however, many other
intangible and ambiguous aspects of the problem leading to different
types of *scarcities* felt by a wide range of actors. Hence the responses
to 'scarcity' are also varied and there is a need to understand their
relational aspects. Over and above the understanding of the tangible
and physical evidences of the problem (that is dwindling water
levels), this essay also seeks to understand what scarcity means for
different actors. The focus is also on how certain actors in Gujarat
have constructed a naturalized and essentialized notion of scarcity.
In doing so, I follow Yappa's urgent plea to 'include the very intellect
that helped us to conceptualize' the problem in the first place (Yappa
1993: 225).

[3] See Matthew Gandy (1996) for the ridiculous dilemmas that emerge out of
the relativist trap in viewing environmental problems.

THE CASE OF KUTCH

The crescent-shaped peninsula of Kutch is the largest district in Gujarat and has an area of 45,612 square kilometres constituting 23 per cent of the state. Kutch is like an island as it is bound by the sea to the south and west, and by the Ranns (salt marshlands) in the east and north. It has nine *talukas* or administrative sub-districts: Bhuj and Nakhatrana in the north; Lakhpat and Abrasa in the west; Mandvi, Mundra and Anjar in the south, and Bachau and Rapar in the east. Apart from its very heterogeneous social and ethnic composition, the region has nine ecological zones (Gujarat Ecology Commission 1994).

Kutch has an arid to semi-arid type of climate. Temperatures range from 45 degrees centigrade in the summer to 2 degrees in winter. Humidity and evapo-transpiration are high throughout the year. In some areas, groundwater supplies are abundant, but increasingly the levels are dropping. Over-exploitation of the aquifer combined with seawater ingression has led to salinity in the water and soils and a sinking water table. The groundwater table sinks at a rate of a metre a year and, in two talukas in the district, falls under the over-exploitation category (ibid.: 14).

Rainfall is erratic and variable and averages about 350 to 370 millimetres. There is high regional variation, ranging from 440 millimetres in southern Kutch to 338 millimetres in western Kutch (Raju 1995: 10). It only rains a few days a year (fifteen on average) with significant intra-district variations. In official discourse, Kutch is considered drought-prone, with droughts taking place every two to three years.

Scarcity conditions in Kutch are often attributed to dwindling rainfall (Mehta 2001). However, this is a myth, both in Kutch as well as in other parts of the world (cf. Falkenmark et al. 1990). Rainfall data of the past sixty years, prior to 1997, indicates that while there have been erratic variations in the quantity of rainfall, there is no evidence to suggest that precipitation rates have changed. A t-test, comparing the rainfall in Kutch over thirty years (1968–97) with the previous thirty-year period (1938–67), revealed no significant difference ($t_{obt.} = -.28$, $p > 0.05_{2\text{-tail}}$). Inference tests using rainfall data for the talukas of Abrasa, Bhuj and Rapar over a longer period

(120 years) were conducted to compare rainfall differences between four thirty-year periods (1878–1907, 1908–37, 1938–67 and 1968–97). A repeated measures analysis of variance revealed no significant differences over these periods (Sinclair 1998).

Kutchi identity is moulded around water, or the lack of it. Villagers across the length and breadth of the district say that the lack of water is the cause of their misery, the depopulated villages and mass migration out of Kutch. Water scarcity is attributed to low rainfall, ever-decreasing rainfall and perennial droughts. There is a widespread belief in Kutch that due to the harsh climate, erratic water supply, declining groundwater sources and frequent droughts, the only solution is to get water from the rivers of Gujarat (Kutch Development Forum 1993). That is why all hopes are being pinned on the Sardar Sarovar Project (SSP) which is also made out to be Gujarat's lifeline (Raj 1991). It is also projected by many to be *the* only hope for Kutch.

THE POLITICS OF SCARCITY: KUTCH AND THE SSP

Plans to provide water for Kutch from the river Narmada have a long history and are no less complicated than the history of the Sardar Sarovar dam itself.[4] Though the project was conceived almost a century ago, actual work has been stalled due to inter-state conflicts such as the height of the dam, the extent of submergence and the sharing of benefits. Different committees were set up to resolve all these inter-state conflicts, including the Khosla Commission of 1965 and the Narmada Water Disputes Tribunal of 1979. Kutchis maintain that the government of Gujarat did not represent their interests adequately and was biased towards obtaining benefits for central Gujarat despite its more favourable water endowments. As a result, Kutch successively lost out in the several rounds of negotiations. From an original plan of three canals, the Narmada Water Disputes Tribunal sanctioned only one canal along the coast in 1979. Instead of allowing for the irrigation of 9.45 lakh acres of land in Kutch, only 95,000 acres of land were to get irrigation (Kutch Development Forum 1993). In

---

[4] It is not possible to present all the controversies of the SSP here. Please refer to Mehta (2001, 2005), Fisher (1995) and Morse et al. (1992).

this way less than 2 per cent of Kutch's area stands to benefit from the Kutch Branch Canal (KBC).

The hurdles of the past, however, are few compared with future chances of getting water to the region. Water can only enter Kutch after the Narmada main canal is constructed. Once diverted into the main canal, the water will traverse 500 kilometres before entering Kutch. Along the way the canal will cross major rivers such as the Mahi, the Sabarmati and the Banas and their valleys. Before entering Kutch, it will also cross the Little Rann. Here high evaporation is expected. The quantum of water entering into Kutch will almost be that of a small river. Consensus still has to be reached on whether the lift or gravity method will be used. Work is yet to begin on the proposed KBC as the alignment line has not been fixed. The present plan envisages a canal 200 kilometres long in Kutch, passing through a tiny coastal strip in eastern and southern Kutch. In this way five talukas stand to benefit: Rapar, Bachau, Anjar, Mundra, and Mandvi. Only two of these talukas, namely Rapar and Bachau, are considered to be drought-prone. The other three are richer in groundwater endowments and are considered to be part of the belt that has experienced the Green Revolution in Kutch. The industrial belt of Kutch in the Kandla-Gandhidham area is also located in the command area. Thus, the needs of industrial residents and rich farmers may be met more than those of needy farmers in other drought-prone areas. The SSP, if realized, may also intensify the existing class divide in the district. In short, the project of providing water from the SSP to Kutch continues to be embryonic and promises to be a protracted process. It is ironic that water-hungry Kutch should be used by the dam proponents to justify the project, given how unlikely it is that Kutch will benefit significantly from it. Recently, a pipeline brought Narmada water to Samakhiyari village in Kutch, some 600 kilometres north of the Sardar Sarovar dam. It remains to be seen whether work on the canals will continue and whether the dam will indeed assuage Kutch's water needs.

The propaganda machinery used by the state as well as decades of political promises have succeeded in 'manufacturing' perceptions or myths that reinforce the idea of SSP as bounty. In their book *Manufacturing Consent*, Herman and Chomsky (1988) describe the role of the media in mobilizing support for the special interests that dominate the state activity. In Gujarat, the state has manufactured one dominant perception of water scarcity, namely, the Narmada project as the magic bullet. In doing so, political and business interests all over the state are being served.[5] Additionally, the discourse on water resources management is overwhelmed by this one project. The focus on externally-supplied water has prevented water-harvesting schemes from gaining widespread acceptance in Gujarat. Officials of the Gujarat State Land Development Corporation (GSLDC) feel that their work is marginalized in water resources departments in Kutch and in Gandhinagar. Their efforts are stymied due to the state-wide obsession with the Narmada project. An official of the GSLDC in Bhuj said:

If all the 177 watersheds in Kutch would be developed, there would be no need for Narmada water. But our work is not taken seriously. Everybody is obsessed with the Narmada project, but what should the people do until the water comes? We lack human power, our offices are under-staffed and during scarcity years, all our work comes to a standstill because our schemes are converted to relief sites. In areas where we have worked, wells have been recharged and water conservation has increased. The need for relief has gone down. But this is a long and protracted process, which cannot take place overnight.

Villagers in the research village also echo these sentiments. Every year they watch helplessly as water flows unchecked into the Rann due to Kutch's topography. Due to the sharp gradient, all the ninety-seven rivers and streams of Kutch are non-perennial and have a high run-off rate. The limited rainfall flows off in streams and rivulets into the sea or the Ranns. Thus there is great potential for rainwater harvesting and catchment area treatment. However, in the late 1990s, Kutchis had largely bought into the grand narrative of the SSP as a 'water wonder'. They felt that it would solve all their problems and make up for the injustices of climate and history, especially the trail of broken promises made by politicians.[6] The widespread 'manufactured' nature

[5] For example, the Gujarat government has been promoting industries coming up along the 'Golden Corridor', largely situated in the SSP's command in Central Gujarat. It has attracted investments worth Rs 75,000 crores for this purpose (Desai 1995).

[6] I suspect that their experiences with shoddy resettlement and rehabilitation after the 2001 earthquake has probably further reinforced their sentiments of

of debates around the SSP also helped obscure the anthropogenic nature of scarcity to which I now turn.

THE ANTHROPOGENIC DIMENSIONS OF SCARCITY

While the actual volume of rainfall might not have changed, the severity of drought or scarcity is felt more acutely today than in the past. Scientists and local people maintain that the intensity of drought has increased (cf. Murishwar and Fernandes 1988). There are, however, several factors at play. The first factor is increasing *devegetation* which has certainly occurred due to increased commercial logging in the last five decades. Prior to Kutch's integration into the Indian Union, the Maharaos (rulers) had instituted a policy of afforestation. Areas known as *rakhals* were set aside, where tree cutting and grazing were prohibited. The rakhals were used as game sanctuaries, grass farms and for experiments at reforestation. Despite their elitist nature, the rakhals succeeded in experimenting with the types of trees suitable for Kutch's unique requirements and considerable forest cover was created (Rushbrook Williams 1958: 29). After 1948, institutional restrictions on rakhals ceased to exist and there was a boom in unchecked logging. Cut trees were smuggled out of Kutch into Gujarat for coal, resulting in serious loss of vegetational cover. The wild growth of ganda bawal (*Prosopis juliflora*) has also led to loss of grass cover and the undermining of indigenous tree species. Moreover, it is believed that ganda bawal neither attracts rain nor gives moisture to the soil even though it might conserve water within its own system. Bad water management practices have also played a role in vegetational reduction. The world-famous grasslands in northern Kutch, for example, have suffered considerably due to the damming of Kutch's northern rivers. The damming stopped the annual inundation and natural fertilization by the silt traditionally brought by the rivers. The grasslands are now dependent only on rainfall for their rejuvenation (Ferroukhi 1994: 41).

---

mistrust and resentment of Gujarat's politicians. Today the obsession with the SSP is less than what it was before due to the problems encountered with survival since the earthquake.

Another dimension to anthropogenic scarcity is the *overexploitation of groundwater aquifers*. Access to and control over groundwater in Kutch is marked by tremendous inequality. In my research village, higher castes such as the Rajputs and Jadejas comprise less than 30 per cent of the population but they control about 65 per cent of the land. They also own most of the wells in the village. Well ownership goes hand in hand with land ownership. Those who have access to land also control the water below it. The rich irrigators in rural areas (popularly known as 'water lords') are often responsible for depleting vast amounts of groundwater resources. They tend, however, to attribute declines in the groundwater to climatic change which again obfuscates the real problem: namely, rapidly increasing groundwater use. This can only dry out local wells and ponds and has far-reaching effects on biomass regeneration and the water recharging capacity of soils. Clearly, water extraction exceeds water recharging. Consequently, the water table is declining by about 1 metre every year in Kutch. Groundwater is Kutch's most precious yet most abused resource. Its control lies in the hands of powerful landed owners and irrigators for whom it is the most important form of material capital in their local communities (cf. Shah 1993; VIKSAT n.d.). These water lords overcome groundwater constraints by their willingness and financial ability to invest in annual or even monthly well digging, broadening and deepening operations. They are also successful at circumventing legislation and making the best of institutional loopholes.[7] The groundwater crisis, hence, is not just one of dwindling water levels, but instead a crisis of access and control over scarce resources. Irrigators in the region often tend to think short-sightedly. This manifests itself in their willingness to tap scarce water resources during droughts to grow water-hungry crops as the next sections demonstrate.

The above discussion should make it clear that the growing water 'crisis' in Kutch is largely human-induced. However, in popular discourse, the anthropogenic dimension of water scarcity is obscured.

---

[7] Gujarat was the first state to pass a groundwater law in 1976, which dealt with the regulation and licensing of tube well construction and control of groundwater use. Its implementation, however, has been difficult given the strong political opposition and because rights to use groundwater go hand in hand with land ownership (VIKSAT n.d.: 11). The skewed pricing of electricity contributes to uncontrolled rates of water extraction.

The culpability of large farmers, bad water management practices and state policies is denied. The story of 'dwindling rainfall' obscures the fact that water has been misused and regulations constantly circumvented. The power of the water lords remains unquestioned and their greed is exonerated. The water problem is seen as 'natural', something beyond human agency, even though rainfall and drought patterns are characterized by high uncertainty and variability. Projects such as the SSP are evoked as the only solution to set right what nature has ostensibly disturbed.

DIFFERENTIATED RESPONSES TO SCARCITY

I now turn to village-level experiences of water scarcity by drawing on findings from a village which I call Merka in eastern Kutch. The village is situated in the potential command area of the SSP. It is a medium-sized village with a population of 3,463. It has been declared a 'no source' village by the state, which means that existing water supplies in the village are not sufficient to provide water to its population. Water is, thus, supplied by the Gujarat Water Supply and Sewage Board either by tanker or by pipeline.

Merka is a multi-caste village. Caste is the basis for most social interactions and it also plays a crucial role in local water resources management practices. Merka's castes range from the erstwhile feudal lords (Jadejas) to Rajputs (warrior castes), pastoralists (Rabaris, Bharvads) and Dalits (Scheduled Castes). Sources of water comprise tanks around the village where rainwater is collected, wells with groundwater and *virdas* (holes) in the riverbed.[8]

In rural Kutch, the outcome of every year is uncertain. Periods of abundance are interspersed with periods of dearth and impoverishment. Rainfall is largely characterized by uncertainty and can be seen to be 'regularly irregular'. What are the institutional arrangements that deal with this uncertainty and scarcity? Livelihood strategies display a high degree of flexibility. Let me begin with dryland agriculture and pastoralism and the links between the two.

Dryland agriculture employs a wide range of risk minimization strategies such as the spreading of land assets over different land

[8] See Mehta (Forthcoming) for details on caste politics and water.

parcels distributed over a variety of soil types. Decision-making regarding field preparation is often an innovative response to an ever-changing environment. For example, if villagers sense a lean year, they are likely to plant drought-resistant crops. If the year appears promising, they invest in millets or cotton. Crop-related decisions are not just dependent on exogenous factors such as the rainfall. Personal need, practicalities and collegiality towards field neighbours are also important factors. Thus, agricultural practices are flexible responses to situations at a given time and given place. They are adaptations to the year, particular soil conditions and to highly specific contingencies arising within the social world. For example, it is usual to confer with field neighbours and collectively negotiate on crops to be grown in a particular vicinity. To borrow Paul Richards' useful analogy, all these factors make agriculture in Kutch an ongoing performance which is a 'sequential adjustment to unpredictable conditions' (Richards 1989: 41). Clearly of course, not all cultivators have uniform strategies. Large landowners with irrigation facilities enjoy the maximum buffer against uncertainty. By contrast, dryland cultivators and marginal farmers face the knocks of scarcity more.

The same resource base is also used by herders since the livestock-based economy has always been one of the most important sources of livelihood in Kutch. The district's semi-arid to arid type of climate encourages a vegetation of short annual grasses ideal for livestock rearing. The pastoralists are usually sedentary but, during lean years, the uncertainty of rainfall and forage availability in the village environs makes migration necessary. Those with large herds can afford to migrate for about 400 kilometres. Migration thus allows pastoralists with large herds to adapt to a variable and heterogeneous environment. Due to this mobility they can exploit and access different social and ecological patches across the range. One always hopes, quite literally, that the grass is greener on the other side. Each site has its own set of forage opportunities and restrictions. The water situation is always different, as is the reception from the host community. The institutional arrangements need to be highly flexible and entail constant decisions that respond to unexpected contingencies. Those with fewer animals (under 100) cannot afford to migrate and have to make do with locally available grasses.

Migratory pastoralism is possible only due to the wide support and social networks spread out over a wide area, indicating the embeddedness of institutions in wider social structures. These social networks include kinship ties amongst other pastoralists as also reciprocal relationships with farmers that have been built over several generations. The relationship between cultivators and pastoralists who use the same resource base has largely been synergistic. Landowners appreciated the manure provided by the pastoralists and they were allowed to pitch camp on fallow or harvested fields during their migratory routes. Recently, however, changes in agricultural patterns have made the relationship less symbiotic, with pastoralists losing out. State policies and interventions have tended to offer agricultural subventions to cultivators, leading to the introduction of double and triple cropping. The migration of pastoralists is actively discouraged with pastoralists being fined or areas being sealed off. Kutch has no state policies that foster pastoralists' rights to pastures. The diverse ways in which different social groups use the same land and common property resources is not appreciated. The institutional flexibility displayed by cultivators and pastoralists as they adapt their livelihoods to deal with uncertainty have been undermined, leading to a general worsening of ties between the two groups.

Of course, the diversity in livelihood strategies in drought-prone Merka is also shaped by people's occupational status and wealth assets. I now explore two different households' experiences of drought in 2000 in the course of a three-year drought cycle. I focus on a rich irrigator family with 100 acres of land and a labouring family with 5 acres of land.[9]

PROFILES OF TWO HOUSEHOLDS

Raghubhai, his sons and their families live in a majestic old house with a large courtyard. Together they own about 100 acres of land (spread across the village and under various names). The patriarch is one of

[9] For reasons of space I cannot provide ethnographic data on pastoralist households and coping strategies. For details on the livelihood strategies of a pastoralist family with moderate livestock and land assets and on pastoralist livelihoods more generally, see Mehta (2005).

the richest men in the village. About 20 acres of land are irrigated by four wells with saline water. Their prize is the 25 acres of land adjacent to a small check-dam from which they extract sweet water used to grow commercial crops such as cumin and castor. These activities have actively contributed to depleting the water in village communal tanks. Since this family is the patron of about twenty families spread out over the village in every quarter and caste, these activities do not meet with much resistance. The family has the financial clout to constantly deepen, broaden and extend their wells. This ensures good yields in a dry year.

The family grows subsistence crops such as *bajra* (pearl millet), *mug* (mung bean) and *tal* (sesame) in fields all around the village. In addition they grow fodder crops such as lucerne and *jowar* (sorghum) on irrigated fields in the dry months. In this way their cattle are assured of fresh green fodder. Cotton and cumin are their chief cash crops, grown on irrigated land. In good years, they can make about Rs 400,000 with a profit of about Rs 200,000. Cotton can grow with saline water from their wells. However, cumin cultivation is only possible with sweet water for which they use village communal tanks, often without permits.

This family does not suffer tremendously due to the drought. There is no change in their diet and milk continues to be drunk by all members, including women and girls. Even during the drought year of 2000–1, the third year of the drought cycle, their large land assets and irrigation facilities ensured a modest yield (3,000 kilos of grain and cereal which would last a year and 4,000 kilos of cumin). They somewhat managed to break even against their initial investment of Rs 250,000. Drought for this family means fewer yields and fewer profits, which means not having the cash to build a house or celebrate a wedding. In no way does drought entail misery or loss.

By contrast, drought means debt, hardship and a somewhat reduced intake of milk and milk products for the household of Kasiben and Khimjibhai, two Dalits. They have eight children and earn most of their money through seasonal labour and cultivation. Khimjibhai's father's land is shared between four brothers. It is so insignificant that Khimjibhai considers himself, for all practical purposes, to be landless. Against a payment of Rs 10,000, the family acquired land from a pauperized Darbar which they now cultivate in partnership with him.

They have two parcels of land—one is near the Rann and the other is close to one of the dams of the village.

They usually grow cotton and castor in one field and grains and cereals in another. In a good year, they can harvest about 400 kilograms of grains and cereals. They keep about eight months' worth and sell the rest. Unlike Raghubhai, their surpluses are not stored and no seeds are stored. Buying seeds can be difficult following a drought year. When the season is favourable they can earn about Rs 40,000 a year from agricultural activities, largely from cotton sales. In a bad year, their yields are very limited and last for barely a month or so. In 1995, Khimjibhai borrowed money (interest-free) from Raghubhai. In 2000, the three consecutive years of drought had taken their toll and Kasiben had pledged her jewellery to the moneylender against a loan of Rs 6,000.

In 2000–1, Khimjibhai and Kasiben reported that the first two rains were good but the last crucial shower failed. Hence the entire year was disappointing and there was no hope of any profits but Khimjibhai felt that he would break even. They also could not irrigate one of their fields near the dam because Raghubhai's family used up all the water in the tank. Since their relationship is one of patronage and dependence, they could not afford to be overtly critical.

The effects of drought are far more pronounced on this family and the periods of dearth are more extreme than for the large farmers. During drought periods, the pernicious trap of being indebted to the moneylender is a constant worry, the intake of milk produce is drastically decreased and the dependence on casual labour and relief is strong. But even this family does not compromise on food intake during the drought. They continue to eat pulses, grains and vegetables, largely purchased from the shop. Clearly, without relief work and other employment opportunities this Dalit family would encounter far more deprivation than it does currently.

These household profiles demonstrate two things: One, livelihood and drought-coping strategies in Merka are quite diverse and adaptable. Two, they are highly dependent on wealth and assets which explains the vast differences between the two families. Three, there is a high correlation between wealth and security. Secure livelihoods are maintained by large farmers who also have irrigation facilities which they enjoy, often to the detriment of poorer households' well being.

For example, their over-exploitation of the water in the communal tanks prevents the poor in the village from enjoying a minimum level of irrigation. By contrast, the Dalit family with its meagre assets experiences high insecurity. Their dependence on state-sponsored relief measures is very high. Thus, scarcity and drought mean different things to different resource users and their experiences and perceptions are largely linked with people's wealth, assets and social positioning.

I experienced drought in Merka in 1995–6, a semi-scarcity year, and in 2000, at the end of the three-year drought cycle. In 2000, Merka's rainfall was better than the Kutchi average and those with irrigation facilities were not doing too badly. But the three years of drought had visible manifestations: Unlike in 1995–6, people clearly seemed to be weighed down by fodder scarcity, low agricultural yields, debts and problems with ganda bawal. They also complained about the lack of liquid cash flow and few or no off-farm employment facilities.

But, the relative normalcy of drought, no matter how difficult and hard, was also evident. In response to my questions about drought, people would laugh: 'We are used to drought. Two years are bad and one year is good. This is our life. When it's bad we disappear away from the village. When the rains come, we race back. This is our home and we are happy here.' But this acceptance of the cyclical nature of drought and scarcity may not always persist. Even the highly adapted, flexible and diverse livelihood strategies of both cultivators and pastoralists will not always be able to withstand the problems of dwindling groundwater aquifers, depleted vegetation and soil degradation. There are limits to local resilience. I do not want to overly glorify 'adapting to and living with scarcity and uncertainty'. However understanding their dynamics will help planners and policy-makers overcome their 'dryland blindness' (Mehta 2005) and promote interventions that contribute to mitigating scarcity, instead of naturalizing it.

Largely, planners have not built on local people's coping strategies vis-à-vis scarcity. Instead of promoting dryland agriculture or agro-pastoralist occupations, they have neglected them. They do not view scarcity as a temporally bound phenomenon. Instead, Kutch is made out to be permanently drought-prone and cursed by scarcity. State-sponsored water interventions have not succeeded in mitigating scarcity. In fact, some of them have exacerbated the water problems in certain areas, making scarcity indeed ever-present and all pervasive. These flawed interventions arise because of the prevailing world views and experiences of policy makers—their dryland blindness—and because of institutional weaknesses in water management programmes. At one level, the people of Kutch imagine and experience scarcity as something that is cyclical, periodic and part of their lives. Increasingly, however, scarcity has become naturalized and all pervasive, due to a combination of discursive, socio-political and institutional factors. As long as this situation persists, scarcity and its accompanying 'scarcity and relief industry' will dominate life in Kutch.

DISCUSSION

This essay has argued that scarcity as a concrete period of dearth—either of water, milk or fodder, which is felt acutely by the human and livestock population in rural areas—has always been a part of Kutch. Scarcity is not permanent, but interspersed with periods of abundance and bounty. Several strategies, rooted in local knowledge systems and practices, exist to cope with seasonality and uncertainty, and rural livelihoods have adapted to the variable and uncertain nature of Kutch's rainfall. The coping strategies against scarcity are highly differentiated. The wealthy of the village tend to have the most options and can resort to a wider range of coping strategies than the poor. To a certain extent, social forms of differentiation such as caste and gender also legitimize the unequal access to and control over scarce resources.

Powerful discourses of scarcity have largely served the interests of the elites (for example, politicians, business constituencies and irrigators). They have obscured the fact that there is highly unequal access to and control over land and water resources in Kutch. They also succeed in essentializing scarcity in Kutch and making it seem 'natural', thus ignoring its anthropogenic nature. Scarcity is also used to legitimize the controversial SSP by evoking notions of its bounty and potential contribution to Gujarat's development. With respect to the large dam, there appeared to be unambiguous consent all over Gujarat that the SSP was the only way to mitigate the problem of water scarcity. However, this consent was largely 'manufactured' due to the socio-political processes discussed. Thus, there emerges the need to analyse water scarcity at two levels: at the discursive level and at the material level as a biophysical problem.

On the one hand, devegetation, dwindling groundwater aquifers, soil salinity and the general undermining of local strategies to cope with scarcity result in the rural poor experiencing the impact of drought more severely. These are 'real' manifestations of the biophysical problem of water scarcity and they are different from narratives of scarcity which have a 'manufactured' nature. Hence, it might be useful to distinguish between 'real' and 'manufactured' scarcity.

'Real' scarcity is a biophysical phenomenon with ecological and social dimensions (for example, dwindling aquifers, the depletion of water resources in a communal tank or a longer trudge for rural women). It is, however, usually cyclical given that periods of abundance are interspersed by periods of dearth. It is highly dependent on resource availability and exogenous factors such as rainfall and climate, which are variable and erratic. Real scarcity is relative to several hydrological, meteorological, agricultural factors and is also linked with social inequality. This complexity is obscured by 'manufactured' scarcity, which is a discursive construct. Scarcity is essentialized and universalized. Seen as permanent, the cyclical dimensions of scarcity are ignored. Scarcity is made out to be 'natural', thus ignoring the anthropogenic areas of culpability. The 'manufactured' nature of scarcity legitimizes controversial schemes such as the SSP and also unequal access to water and land resources.

Why is this distinction useful? This essay has demonstrated that environmental problems such as water scarcity are created and reproduced at both the discursive as well as at the biophysical levels. What is the nature of their interaction? The 'manufacture' of scarcity at the discursive level obscures several important aspects of 'real' scarcity. One, inequalities often shape access to and control over water. Two, water scarcity is not natural, but instead it is largely due to anthropogenic interventions, resulting from bad water management and land use practices. The naturalization of scarcity at the discursive level does not help mitigate the symptoms and causes of 'real' scarcity. In some cases, 'real' scarcity might be exacerbated due to the popular narratives (for example, water tables might continue to decline if the decrease in groundwater resources is attributed to climate change rather than to uncontrolled extraction). Furthermore, the 'manufacture' of scarcity might not result in the creation of solutions appropriate to local needs and conditions.

CONCLUSION

I have used the case of Kutch to highlight the multifaceted nature of scarcity and how it is socially and politically constructed to meet certain ends. This essay has largely focused on how scarcity has been used to legitimize the construction of large dams and to create a 'scarcity' industry. In the rest of the world, unlike in India and China, the rhetoric of large dams and scarcity may be on the wane but it is rapidly being replaced by a new mantra. Since 2000, we have witnessed new twists to currents in the water domain. The key issues that have emerged are cost recovery, the need to recognize water's economic value and the need for private sector involvement as a means to efficiently manage water and provide it to 'all' (Mehta 2003). Scarcity is used to justify these market-driven solutions too (ibid.).

In recent years, there has been much talk about a looming global water crisis. Against a growing alarmism around 'water wars', global and national agencies have been concerned with the causality and solutions to water scarcity. The usual suspects such as the World Water Commission, the World Bank and others have been warning us of a 'global water crisis' for a while, often drawing on the Malthus-influenced 'gloomy arithmetic of water' to highlight that half the world's population will live under conditions of severe water stress by 2025 (Mehta Forthcoming).

We are also currently halfway through the Millennium Development Goals process around water and sanitation and there is still much left to do. Without diminishing the importance of commitments to enhance access to water and sanitation to the billions who lack it, some questions beg to be asked. Does the rhetoric around 'water crises' and 'water scarcity' help to mitigate current water problems? Or, are important aspects merely obscured? The default position since the 3rd World Water Forum at The Hague is that more needs to be done: more money spent, new largely 'private' actors roped in, new institutions created. But the existing actors hardly resemble an effective cast and their understanding of the script is still somewhat shaky. Thus, we have ideological leaps preceding rigorous analysis, driving an industry of self-justification and, most dangerously, presenting 'evidence' that is only partially fact-based. There are powerful interests at stake, both financially (consider the emerging global market for water services especially in urban areas and the push towards water privatization by the World Bank and the International Monetary Fund) and developmentally in terms of poverty reduction (the billions who lack adequate domestic water and basic sanitation). Scarcity is used to justify new solutions such as market efficiency and water privatization. This is because scarcity is a concept that can provide meta-level explanations for a wide range of phenomena over which humans ostensibly have no control (Mehta Forthcoming). Luckily, such positions are increasingly being challenged through local level protests and more recently at the global policy level (UNDP 2006). It is now time to write the obituary for these generalized notions of scarcity.

4

Environmental Insecurities
Geopolitics, Resources, and Conflict

SIMON DALBY

It requires a very unusual mind to undertake the analysis of the obvious.
(Whitehead 1948: 5)

Nature is more civilized in a Pathfinder.

Nissan Corporation

RESOURCES, CONFLICT, AND GEOPOLITICS

At the largest of spatial scales, resources and conflict have long been a matter of geopolitics and struggles for the control of supplies of key materials. Oil in the Persian Gulf is the classic example that comes to mind from the period of the Cold War. The contemporary focus on conflict in the Gulf and in Central Asia continues a pattern related to petroleum supplies (Klare 2004). Whether one invokes the term 'resource war' or not, the relationships between violence and the supplies of vital materials is a persistent part of the pattern of international rivalries. The extension of the national interest to out-side national borders to ensure the supply of essential materials turns defence into intervention, national security into imperial ambition.

This is not a novel argument. In a more technocratic mode, similar themes were part of the debate about the limits to growth in the early 1970s and in the aftermath of the 'oil crisis' of 1973 and 1974 (Meadows et al. 1974). That scarce resources were a cause of conflict was accepted as common sense by the World Commission

on Environment and Development (WCED 1987) and in much of
the literature that followed. In light of a rising concern about ozone
holes, climate change, droughts, and tropical forest decline in the late
1980s in North America and Europe, these arguments appeared in
the terms of a discussion of 'environmental security'. Environmental
degradation might, some argued, become a cause of warfare as scarcity
drove desperate people to fight for the remaining resources.

The assumption that environmental degradation might cause
conflict and, on the largest scale, warfare between states, became an
important part of the discussion of security after the demise of the Cold
War. It triggered considerable scholarly debate and empirical research in
various places but despite numerous case studies, arguments continue
about both the relationships between environment and conflict and
whether these issues are usefully discussed in terms of environmental
security (Kahl 2006). In this 'environmental security' debate, the
empirical link between environmental change and violence was more
often assumed than demonstrated. It was also assumed that linking
the environment and conflict in this manner was a suitable focus for
policy prescription.

The dominant formulations of these matters in the global North
in the last decades have drawn on fears of conflict over scarce
resources to formulate interventionist policies. In some cases fears
of spreading conflict have been used to formulate policies that focus
on the stability of particular states as a foreign policy on the part of
the United States (Esty 1999). At first glance, and viewed from the
affluently appointed office suites of the policy makers in Washington,
the term environmental security seems eminently sensible. But once
one probes a little into its conceptual assumptions, the construction
of environment in terms of security quickly becomes problematic. It
also, not surprisingly, becomes the site of a political argument about
the nature of threats and precisely who is insecure and why. Critics
have forcefully argued that using concerns about security to raise an
alarm about deleterious environmental trends in many places has not
necessarily produced appropriate policy thinking (Deudney 1999a).
Neither environment nor security it turns out is simple; neither can be
invoked without terminological and political difficulties. Juxtaposing
environment and security compounds the political and conceptual

difficulties although it presents interesting possibilities for critiquing both (Dalby 2002).

Discussions of environment and security are ineluctably part of the larger constructions of geopolitics, and as such need to be examined in this discursive context. The argument in what follows emphasizes the large-scale geographical premises of the environmental security discourse. It is possible to analyse all this in terms of critical linguistic approaches to political discourse as has been done elsewhere (Broda-Bahm 1999). It is also relatively easy to trace its historical antecedents in terms of the two-century-old debate about Malthus (Ross 1998). Both of these themes appear below, but in what follows I look more specifically at the taken-for-granted contextualizations of the debate, the usually unquestioned geographies in the discourse. These geographical specifications of security are usually unquestioned because they appear to be so obvious. To rethink the modern assumptions of autonomy, separation and threat on which security discourse operates, requires, in Alfred North Whitehead's (1948) terms from the epigraph to this paper, 'unusual minds'. Such rethinking also requires revisiting the historical legacy of empire and its reinvention in the current patterns of global urbanization.

ENVIRONMENT AND CONFLICT

In reading the literature on environmental security that has appeared in the last twenty years, basically since the publication of the WCED report (1987), a number of themes have become clear. The initial policy discussion took for granted that environmental degradation was a widespread problem, and that it was one that post-Cold War security planners ought to take seriously. The social science literature has long suggested that matters are much more complex, but that has not stopped the repeated reinvention of discourses on environmental threat. Nonetheless, as the debate has progressed, the calls to examine the complexity of the issues and to investigate specific contexts have become more prominent (Dobkowski and Wallimann 2002; Matthew et al. 2002).

First, there was an initial concern to identify environment as a threat in terms that were broadly similar to the formulations of a

Cold War security discourse. Whether this was in the United States, or in the Soviet Union, where environmental security became a matter of considerable importance in the final years of the Gorbachev administration, instabilities and disruptions to society as a consequence of environmental problems were the dominant theme (Mathews 1989; Myers 1989). Once again, external threats to the political order of modernity structured the discussion; policies determined at the centre would monitor and hopefully contain threats.

Second, there was substantial literature in social science trying to formulate an appropriate empirical validation of the basic contention that environmental matters cause social threats. Thomas Homer-Dixon's teams of researchers, who became known as the Toronto School, posited a series of complex links between environmental scarcities and social responses which, when coupled to other political factors such as weak states with inadequate capacities for resource management, appropriate infrastructure provision or conflict resolution, would likely lead to overt conflict (Homer-Dixon and Blitt 1998; Homer-Dixon 1999). Homer-Dixon's attempts to construct matters in conventional American social science terms or, more specifically, to establish a plausible series of causal links between environmental scarcity and conflict, met with objections from other scholars who charged that the case was made on the basis of highly selective case studies. Arguments that establishing plausible causalities was a key scholarly task clashed with calls for comparison cases and null hypotheses while discussions of the purposes of all of this in terms of the formulation of policy advice added to the confusion (Diehl and Gleditsch 2001; Levy 1995).

Third, in Europe, the Swiss Peace Federation sponsored a large project which included several case studies which looked at violence and environment in various places. Drawing on more broadly conceived intellectual traditions than the empirical methods of the North Americans, the Environment and Conflicts Project (ENCOP) linked environmental conflicts to development problems and the spreading influence of commercial societies. Most explicitly, Gunther Baechler (1999) drew on Karl Polanyi's (1957) formulations of The Great Transformation to suggest that poverty-ridden marginal lands in mountainous regions and the more remote areas of Africa, on the margins of ecological zones, were the most likely locations for environmental conflict. But there were other dimensions to the relation of environment and conflict too, not least the damage done to specific environments and local peoples by the dislocations of major development projects. The struggles by indigenous peoples to protect rainforests and other lands from oil wells and mining corporations are part of this larger pattern (Baechler and Spillmann 1996).

Fourth, in the late 1990s the environmental scarcity leading to conflict argument, and neo-Malthusianism more generally, was tackled quite directly by some researchers interested in the emergent research in political ecology. Challenging the high profile dystopias of journalist Robert Kaplan (1994; 2000), and some of Thomas Homer-Dixon's (1991, 1994; Homer-Dixon et al. 1993) earlier arguments, the political ecology literature focused much more on the political economy of resources and, in particular, the complexity of local resources intersecting with the global commercial economy (Peluso and Watts 2001). Showing how local power structures, gendered access to farmland, traditional modes of subsistence agriculture and fishing were overlain with new modes of resource extraction, this literature challenged the arguments about scarcity in the neo-Malthusian formulations. Although some of the authors might be guilty of too hastily dismissing Homer-Dixon's arguments, and especially of overlooking the importance of 'structural scarcity', 'resource capture' and 'ecological marginalization' as crucial parts of the sequence that frequently leads to violence, what this critical literature has made very clear is that the complexities of the global economy have to be factored into local struggles, and that this has to be done with considerable care to ensure that the specifics of local circumstances are incorporated into the analysis.

Fifth, in the late 1990s an apparent counter-argument suggested that resource shortages were *not* correlated with conflict. The converse, it was suggested, was the case (Le Billon 2001a; Renner 2002). More specifically, the argument emerged that 'greed' rather than 'grievance' was the motivation behind some of the persistent and violent conflicts in the poorer parts of the world (Bannon and Collier 2003). Civil wars were clearly tied into the struggle to control the rents from resource streams that were being exported to the global economy. Controlling resources, whether timber, diamonds or oil, was the way to getting rich quick, rather than following the painful and

slow routes of economic development. Elite rivalries and the promise
of wealth are, so goes the argument, powerful incentives to initiate
hostilities, especially where tribal or other particularistic loyalties can
be mobilized (Jung 2003). But these wars were not largely about either
subsistence lands or the politics of agriculture. They might overlap
with the politics of marginal populations that concerned some of the
ENCOP researchers, but the resources that were in some cases the
cause of the fighting were 'lootable' and hence easily removed and
smuggled or traded illegally (Le Billon 2005).

The discussion of these contemporary resource wars in some ways
connects back to earlier debates on resources and conflict, but the
link to contemporary civil wars also connects to the larger matters
of development, failed states and the international political economy
of the arms trade. The links between resources, environments and
conflict are clearly numerous, and their construction in political and
academic discourse is unlikely to follow any single formulation. Nor
is there now any reason to think that conflict and resources can be
connected by a unidirectional causation.

Questions of Definition

The sheer diversity of the terrestrial contexts in which conflict might
occur, and the multiplicity of materials that might be considered
resources by many diverse cultures and economies, makes generalization very difficult. More complex still are the ecological contexts
within which environmental conflict supposedly occurs. Work done in
Africa in the 1990s suggested that at least some of the environmental
changes that have alarmed observers in recent decades are cyclical
fluctuations rather than signs of irreversible human destruction (Stott
and Sullivan 2000). Simple degradation explanations frequently do not
take history or ecological complexity into account, nor the specifics of
particular environments, much less the micro-level contestations of
property relations, gender and cultures that are crucial to explaining
either crises or everyday practices (Mackenzie 1998). But empirical
generalization is precisely what social science promises to provide and
what policy makers seek in justifying various courses of action.

The early literature assumed that conflicts occur due to the absence
of supplies of key resources. Michael Klare (2001) updated the argument

in his suggestions about likely scenarios for future conflicts. Besides oil, scarce water is the focus of conflict in a number of situations, not least the Middle East where many studies have examined both the potential for conflict and the possibilities of peacemaking as a result of cooperative arrangements for resource management. On the other hand, the counter-argument that resource wars focus on abundance and struggles for control over resource rents suggests that the opposite situation is more likely to cause conflict. Abundance is understood here as the problem, not scarcity. This is particularly the case with oil where the geopolitics of south-west Asia, the American invasion of Iraq in 2003, and the ongoing military conflicts in the region are tied into control over the flows of petroleum from the region to the global economy (Klare 2004).

But a few moments' reflection on these contentions, and especially the implicit assertion that they are by definition mutually exclusive, suggests both that matters are not well defined and that questions of the appropriate scales and contexts have been ignored (Dalby 2007a; Diehl and O'Lear 2007). Resources are not just resources; renewables and non-renewables have different qualities. Contexts matter too; the exploitation of oil reserves is different in many ways from the use of marginal farmland. Subsistence activities are likely to have different social dynamics from the large-scale commercial exploitation of mineral raw materials. These matters need to be clarified if the debate about environmental causes of conflict is to offer useful generalizations.

Thomas Homer-Dixon's (1999) analysis suggested that scarcities were a factor in political violence, but did not assert that all scarcities were alike or that all caused political violence. He deliberately set aside the notion of security because it was ill-defined; acute violence is easier to identify than insecurity. While Homer-Dixon's models are complex, his focus is on supplies of agricultural land and water, the basic ingredients of food production. He concluded that environmental violence was likely to be small scale, diffuse and mostly on a sub-national scale albeit with the ever-present possibilities of international dimensions where displaced populations crossed state boundaries. He pointed clearly to the importance of structural scarcities, situations where elites used a crisis to increase their control of resources and so marginalize further the poor and dispossessed. He also argued that control over resources in the urbanizing slums of Southern states pits newly arrived migrants against established residents within the same ethnic or national groups leading to intra-ethnic disputes rather than ones that polarize on prior allegiances. Gunther Baechler's (1999) analysis suggested that marginal populations close to major ecotones were especially vulnerable and were likely to end up in conflict situations as the pressure of numbers and expanding modern property arrangements pitted nomads and farmers against each other in the grasslands of Africa and in the more remote mountainous areas where traditional cultures and ways of life are interacting with encroaching modernity.

On the other hand, the argument that resource abundance is likely to cause violence is obviously valid in some cases. Violence in Nigeria is related to the complex politics of oil extraction and the disruption of Ogoni environments where the local population does not reap any of the benefits of oil wealth (Watts 2004). As the scriptwriters for the James Bond film, *Die Another Day*, and more recently, *Blood Diamond*, have noted, smuggled diamonds from conflict areas are part of global politics (Le Billon 2007). Violence is related to the control of diamonds, gold and many other minerals. It is certainly part of the history and current politics of the exploitation of petroleum. But the definitional issue here is important. It is possible to argue that these resources are being fought over because they are scarce; they are by definition a resource precisely because they are not ubiquitous. And yet the violence is happening in places close to their production—at mine sites, oil wells, pipelines and export routes that are geographically proximate to the conflicts. It is precisely these facilities where the resource is geographically abundant that are the locations of military activity (Le Billon 2005).

There is a simple matter of scale here that needs to be worked into the picture because both abundance and scarcity are part of any political economy; diamonds would not be valuable if they existed in all soils and were available to all by the simple expedient of using a shovel for a few minutes. If there is violence over the control of oil supplies where these are abundant, it is because they are in demand, and hence relatively scarce elsewhere. But conflicts have specific geographies in places where modernity is less established than in the more peaceful parts of the world where the resources exported from the conflict zones are consumed. Many of the weapons, and some of the funds to keep warfare going, do come from these distant places. If the geography of warfare ever did, it now no longer conforms to simple matters of blocs and states (Jung 2003). The political economy of violence in the 'new wars' of the post-Cold War world spills over boundaries and frontiers, linking resources and diasporic communities through complex, long distance political economies (Kaldor 2007).

SCARCITY, ABUNDANCE, AND SCALE

The question of scarcity and scale is crucial here. The suggestions in both the Toronto model and the ENCOP framework are that marginal populations are vulnerable and that struggles may turn violent in local situations. The scale here is local, although of course displaced populations may have disruptive consequences far from the initial sources of scarcity. But it is clear that there is more than a simple notion of Malthusianism at work in these writings. In some places the scarcity of agricultural land, water supplies and pasture is aggravating the political tensions that plague marginal populations. Problems of what Baechler calls 'maldevelopment' or, in a closely analogous way, 'structural scarcity' in Homer-Dixon's schemes, are related to violence, especially in situations where states are not capable of an effective government that resolves property and rural power issues.

Indeed, and this point is important in the ENCOP formulations of the causal pathways from environment to conflict, in many cases the imposition of centralized state resource projects often either cause or aggravate matters precisely because of the forms of property enclosure involved which dispossess subsistence farmers and disrupts nomadic modes of living. Structural scarcity, in Homer-Dixon's terms, is enhanced as marginal populations lose their access to subsistence. The neat lines of property and park boundaries that are the modern state's mode of rendering problems legible and manageable frequently cause disruption and resistance that is then defined as environmentally-caused violence (Scott 1998). But nonetheless, the fact that environmental disruptions are sometimes related to political violence seems unavoidable. But so too does the conclusion in both the Toronto School and the ENCOP analyses that this violence is likely to be sub-national and diffuse.

Clearly, abundance and scarcity are geographically as well as politically located. In this sense the 'abundance or scarcity' as a source of violence argument is misconceived. Both are clearly related to violence in some circumstances; but the issue is under what circumstances and at which geographical scale (Diehl and O'Lear 2007). It is not clear that the forms of violence and the political arrangements that lead to polarization, mobilization and overt conflict are necessarily likely to be similar; the literature on the new resource wars suggests that overt violence in the form of civil war may result from competing attempts to gain control over resource rents. There is little evidence of an exactly analogous form of violence in the case of struggles over agricultural land or nomadic grazing lands. In the case of some commercially exported foodstuffs (shrimp 'farms' may be the best example), violence is related to the export trade and dispossession of traditional uses of land and water are involved; but the case studies do not suggest violence on the scale of civil wars analogous to diamonds in Sierra Leone, timber and oil in Angola, or oil in the Sudan (Stonich and Vandergeest 2001).

Indeed, attention to the ecological and political-economic specificities suggests that environmental security is not an appropriate way to think about resource wars at all. Clearly, insofar as minerals and petroleum are not 'environmental', in the sense of being renewable parts of active current ecosystem processes, they can be excluded from discussions of environmental matters as a cause of conflict. But their extraction and, crucially, their consumption, has environmental consequences that may be disruptive of ecosystem processes both in terms of local effects and at the biospheric scale. Environmental disruptions are part of modernization; the removal of populations in the way of dams, highways and other infrastructure, not to mention parks, game reserves and golf courses for tourists, is part of the process of urbanization and the expansion of commercial modes of economy into rural societies. Violent opposition to such changes is not unusual; those who face dispossession are not always likely to appreciate all the benefits of urban progress (Evans et al. 2002; Gedicks 2001).

Constructing the relationship between violence and resources thus needs a much more nuanced geographical imagination in order to incorporate the general assertions of causality into the practical realities in different places. Abundance and scarcity may be concepts that matter in terms of discussing the largest scale and the most abstract dimensions of the human condition. But practical relevance to either detailed scholarly research, or policy advice for states or international agencies, requires a much more specific focus on particular contexts and the geographical connections between resource extraction and exports to the urban markets of the global economy. Only some of these resources, however, are 'renewable' and then, strictly speaking, appropriately called 'environmental'.

WATER WARS?

The causal link between environmental scarcity and political conflict is exemplified in the debate over water. It is widely claimed that water is the most obvious environmental resource over which conflict seems likely and that water wars will be the wars of the future (Ashton 2002; Dimitrov 2002). Supposedly, states vying for control over specific rivers will fight to secure access to supplies of fresh water. But once again, this hypothesis needs to be qualified by geographical specificity. In only a few cases are the strongest states located downstream on contested rivers. Both Israel and Egypt are in this situation. In 2002, Israel threatened Lebanon over the construction of water works on rivers that flow into Israel from Southern Lebanon (Fisk 2002). As Israel has long made clear, and as Palestinians aspiring to farm on the West Bank of the Jordan have repeatedly discovered to their cost, water is at a premium. In the case of Egypt, as Michael Klare argues (2001), the state may well have a powerful incentive to promote subversion and civil dissent in Ethiopia, to prevent the emergence of a developmental state and the building of dams on the Blue Nile in the upstream nation.

But empirical research into the matter suggests that, notwithstanding the few cases mentioned here, 'water wars' are rare and generally unlikely (Gleditsch et al. 2006; Lonergan 2001). Indeed, the research argues that cooperation is more likely in many cases as the benefits to all parties are clear. So too are the pitfalls of conflict that might destroy shared infrastructure essential to both sides. The contrasting case, in Michael Klare's (2001) discussion of Egyptian antagonism to Ethiopia, and the diversion of water supplies to irrigation projects in Ethiopia, emphasizes that Ethiopian development itself is a danger to Egypt. But few states are so tied to the waters of one river that such extreme dynamics unfold. In the case of India and Bangladesh, a similar geography determines the potential conflict dynamics, but difficulties over water have usually generated bilateral cooperation despite security problems on other matters (Swain 2002). Likewise, Turkey, Iraq, and Syria have considerable potential for conflict given the fact that the headwaters of the Tigris and Euphrates lie in eastern Turkey but flow into Syria and Iraq. Conflict here has been threatened, and tensions over Kurdish issues are sometimes intense, but overt hostilities concerning the Anatolia dam projects in Turkey have not broken out. In many other instances, the classic case being the Colorado in the southern United States, upstream states are stronger and there is little the downstream state, in this case Mexico, can do about reduced water supplies. But note that, in the case of south-western United States, the conflict concerning the expropriation of water supplies has long been mainly within the United States and about agricultural and urban appropriations at the cost of small-scale users and local ecologies (Leslie 2000). Mike Davis (2002) goes so far as to call the contemporary expropriations by a rapidly growing Las Vegas 'environmental terrorism' to emphasize how the surrounding region is effectively being re-plumbed to supply water for leisure pursuits that are completely ecologically inappropriate in the middle of a desert.

The long term possibilities of climate disruptions and environmental changes altering weather patterns and exacerbating shortages or excesses of water loom over these discussions. Greater precipitation in some places may in fact alleviate the potential for conflict, by either increasing river flows and hence irrigation possibilities, or improving agricultural productivity by watering fields directly. It might also cause more unpredictable rainfalls and droughts. The important point here is that such variability will follow from 'global' consumption of carbon fuels and the production of greenhouse gases far more than they will flow from Southern actions. Scarcities may be caused by actions far from the scene of the most acute political and economic disruptions. But while pollution is a huge problem in many places, especially in the growing cities of the South, it is rarely a direct cause of political conflict. There have been important exceptions, not least the struggles in Eastern Europe in the 1980s, where environmental destruction was a mobilizing theme for opponents of Soviet rule.

Nonetheless, empirical discussions of environmental change and water repeatedly suggest that cooperation is far more likely in the case of water issues. A recent example of the attempts to resolve difficulties in the case of Lake Victoria suggests a stark alternative to the resource war scenarios. The need to curtail over-fishing and the importance of remediation has encouraged cooperation; conflict arguments due to scarcity have not been common in the region and they have not influenced policy prescriptions. Indeed, following Jon Barnett's (2000) pointed argument, Canter and Ndegwa (2002: 58) suggest that the Lake Victoria case bears out the criticism that the environment-conflict thesis 'is largely a conceptual lens invented by Western analysts with particular northern security interests rather than empirical deductions'.

IMPERIAL FORMULATIONS

But 'Lake Victoria' is in the middle of Africa! Which, given its name, just might suggest that imperial history matters in these discussions. If one stops and thinks about the relevant scale for discussing resource issues and conflicts in temporal terms rather than just in spatial terms then longer perspectives for thinking about resources and history have to be considered. More specifically, the violence in the 'wild zones' of the South can only be understood in a context that includes discussions of the legacies of imperialism updated to incorporate the post-Cold War remapping of rural and peripheral dangers to the American metropole (Ó Tuathail and Luke 1994). European imperialism had dramatic impacts on the natural ecologies of many parts of the globe that it touched. In Richard Grove's (1997: 183) succinct summary:

Colonial ecological interventions, especially in deforestation and subsequently in forest conservation, irrigation and soil 'protection', exercised a far more profound influence over most people than the more conspicuous and dramatic aspects of colonial rule that have traditionally preoccupied historians. Over the period 1670 to 1950, very approximately, a pattern of ecological power relations emerged in which the expanding European states acquired a global reach over natural resources in terms of consumption and then too, in terms of political and ecological control.

The processes of crop and animal introductions and the extension of the market in grains to a truly global market, connected by railways and steamships, produced a global division of production and globalized vulnerabilities to famine and poverty in a manner that led to the emergence of an underdeveloped Third World by the early part of the twentieth century. Economic arguments about comparative advantage were coupled to the naturalization of disaster in the South as the product of a cruel nature to portray famine and political violence as a regrettable part of life for those who were unfortunate enough to not (yet) reap the benefits of European civilization. The emergence of meteorology as a global monitoring system provided a form of knowledge that suggested the inevitability of famine and disaster in regions that were far from the European experience in many ways (Davis 2001). Lack of civilization on the part of non-Europeans could in part be explained by environmental matters. Environmental determinism has long structured discussions of planetary politics in these terms; in this sense too much of the current debate is not new (Deudney 1999b; Lipschutz 1997).

In the nineteenth century, however, the expropriation of wealth from the South and the enrichment of the North in the process was sometimes also a matter of direct physical violence. Colonial wars were wars of conquest, as were the wars that Americans were involved in, despite their periodic claims to being an exceptional power not given to European-style colonial escapades (Boot 2002). Not only were subject peoples forced into the commercial economy by the necessity to earn currency to pay the new European taxes, but also their lands and resources were sometimes simply plundered. Violence in the attempts to control resources at the beginning of the twenty-first century in central Africa has been eerily prefigured by the violence of the Belgian conquest, the dispossession of native peoples, and the wholesale looting of ivory and rubber in the nineteenth century (Hochschild 1998). In this sense, at least the resource wars of the contemporary period are all too familiar.

The geopolitical viewpoint, the view from the think tanks in Washington and, all too often, from the academic classrooms in North

America, is one of tame zones of prosperity threatened from without by spreading violence caused by indigenous environmental factors. This notion of wars in the periphery, as with their imperial predecessors over the last few centuries, relies on a geography that separates that periphery from the affluent civilization. Instead of acknowledging imperial exploitation, Northern policies promote modernization, the taming of wilderness and the pacification of the uncivilized as bringing peace and prosperity in the long run for all. As Ó Tuathail (1997: 42) pithily puts the matter: 'In sum, modern geopolitics is a condensation of Western epistemological and ontological hubris—an imagining of the world from an imperial point of view'.

But, and this is the crucial point for thinking about how environment is constructed as a causal agent in discussions of conflict, imperial formulations of resources, markets and populations as matters for administration have frequently remained salient in the aftermath of formal decolonization. Now that local political forces administer the parks, forests and rivers, the populations and their participation in commercial markets, the pattern of empire is reproduced in the supposedly post-colonial states (Neumann 2001). Calling these processes either development or globalization invokes temporal or spatial designations that occlude the continuing importance of the patterns initiated centuries ago in the growth of European power. What are called effective states in current development discourse are all too frequently states that are effective at the extraction of resources for the global economy. The extraction of resources to fuel the global market, and the disruptions of local peoples and rural ecologies in the service of development, follow an imperial pattern. This historical geography needs to be remembered. Its codification in numerous 'scientific' modes of resource evaluation, even its formulation of 'environment' as something potentially hostile in need of management, comes from this legacy of imperial knowledge (Grove 1995).

More generally, the historical pattern of development and the appropriation of resources are connected to the rapid urbanization of humanity. The twentieth century was notable for the huge expansion of population and its movement into the urban areas. We are now an urban species and have wired and paved the planet to move food, timber, oil, electricity, minerals and all sorts of commodities from rural areas into these burgeoning cities. In a way loosely analogous to earlier imperial arrangements, the flow of commodities inevitably disrupts traditional forms of economic life. Just as wheat flowed from Africa to Rome, so now does oil flow from the Middle East to other parts of the new imperium.

The Roman Empire built roads to facilitate communications and so too do modern states. Indeed, it is possible to argue that such an infrastructure provision is a key part of both state structures and the commercial culture of the automobile. The promotion of the privately owned automobile is a major part of the function of states (Paterson 2007). Car ownership is understood as a matter of status in numerous developing states while the resulting pollution and congestion problems are ignored much of the time. The latest gas guzzlers in North America, the rather inaptly named Sports Utility Vehicles (SUVs), are presented to would-be buyers in tropes of conquering nature, of civilizing nature in Nissan Corporation's terms, a matter of being able to go anywhere regardless of obstacles (Paterson and Dalby 2006). SUVs are sold with the dream of universal mobility and freedom in a world without boundaries—an imperial subject if ever there was one.

RETHINKING ENVIRONMENTAL GEOPOLITICS

Where environmentalism has frequently been based on assumptions of stability, of a relatively fixed arrangement of resources, habitats and biota, the contemporary science of ecology suggests that a more flexible series of arrangements is necessary. The humid fallacy, to extend Mike Davis' point about the conceptual failures of Americans who assume that the relatively stable and predictable climatic regime in New England ought to apply in Southern California (Davis 1999), is not useful for understanding climate, especially in areas where El Niño effects are a predominant forcing factor (Davis 2001). Understanding that flexibility and adaptability are essential to the flourishing of both societies and ecologies is necessary, but such understanding runs counter to many states' attempts to fix, render legible and administer all manner of phenomena in terms of standards, fixed boundaries, and property. Asking how the fluid and flexible is to be administered, how flows rather than fixities might become the focus of governance, are matters that need consideration, not least because they directly challenge the modern geopolitical imagination.

Knowledges that look to universal explanations of the relationships between environment and conflict are usually urban and modern knowledges, ones that take an imperial view of matters for granted. Combined with satellite imagery and modes of monitoring statistics compiled by states and international agencies, and the assumptions of the inevitability of economic development in terms of the expansion of carboniferous capitalism, these formulations of the resource and environment problematique inevitably downplay the rural, the contextual and the disruptions inflicted on traditional peoples by modernization. They do so also within a state cartography, one that draws lines between places, ensuring that civil wars 'over there' are not usually a matter of responsibility 'in here' in the cities of the metropoles (Dalby 2007a). But as the literature on resource wars now makes clear, the consequences of modes of extraction in distant places is tied into violence, dispossession and environmental destruction in many places.

Putting this geography of resource extraction back explicitly into the picture changes the terms in which it is possible to construct both 'resources' and 'conflict'. It also suggests the need for political innovation in the metropoles to facilitate less ecologically destructive modes of living. Above all, such thinking challenges the taken-for-granted geography of danger as external to the modern spaces of prosperity. It requires a shift away from an understanding of environment as the external context of humanity to recognition of a life within a changing biosphere. This necessity to rethink the geopolitical imagination is now accentuated by the growing realization that the largest disruptions of environment are likely to come as a result of greenhouse gas emissions and climate disruptions (Flannery 2006). This is not a matter of peripheral dangers to modernity, but the environmental insecurities in the peripheral parts of the global polity are now more clearly understood as a result of the global economy and its modes of consumption of fossil fuels in particular (Pirages and DeGeest 2004).

In short, the geopolitical contexts of the invocation of a problematique of environmental security matter (Dalby 2007b). The implicit geographies within the environmental security discourse are crucial to the construction of environment as a threat. and to the knowledge practices and policy prescriptions that follow from these constructions. In thinking about these things, scale is an important dimension: claims to abundance and scarcity are part and parcel of all these discussions, but specific geographies matter much more than abstract generalizations about local and global. The geographies of specific places, and of the connections across the apparently obvious spaces specified in the discourse of environmental security, are, as this chapter argues, crucial to understanding how resources and conflict are coupled as well as to how one might now think differently about environmental threats and insecurities.

5

Investing in Nature around Sylhet*
An Excursion into Geographical History

DAVID LUDDEN

Nature may exist outside society, but natural *resources* derive from social investments that give nature social life (Appadurai 1986). Modernity has so invested nature with national identity that national maps seem to contain natural environments eternally (Gadgil and Guha 1992). But national maps do not adequately describe nature's social geography; they merely represent one brand of modern territorialism impressing itself on nature. Territorialism comes in many forms, however, and it is not the only social force invested in nature: mobility is equally important. Focusing more attention on the diversity of territorial claims to nature and on mobility's investment in natural environments is critical as globalization increases the power of mobile social forces over natural resources.

* I presented an earlier version of this paper at the SSRC Conference on 'Resources: Conceptions and Contestations', Kathmandu, 3–12 January 2003. Many thanks to the participants for useful papers and discussions, especially Amita Baviskar, Bina Agarwal, Michael Watts, Tania Li, and Anna Tsing. Research for this paper depended on sabbatical funding from the American Institute of Bangladesh Studies, American Council of Learned Societies, John Simon Guggenheim Memorial Foundation, and University of Pennsylvania. For research assistance, I thank Brooke Newborn and Richard Mo. For essential material, I owe special thanks to Sirajul Islam, M. Mufakharul Islam, Pritam Bhattacharyya, and the staff at the Bangladesh National Archives, particularly its Director, Sharif Uddin Ahmed. For many useful ideas, I thank Bela Malik, Thomas Mathew, Taj Hashmi, Manzurul Mannan, Samia Huq, and Jukhruf Binth Junaid. For help with all aspects of my work, I thank Dina Mahnaz Siddiqi.

When we put geography in motion and keep the temporality of space in view, we see that nature's social assets live inside geographies defined simultaneously by mobility and by shifting forms of territorialism. Natural things become resources inside any place because social forces that make nature productive move in time and space. The term 'globalization' refers to a geographical expansion of the spaces of mobility within which social forces operate, but such spatial mobility is a very old feature of natural resource environments. Nature may begin its social life in places of territorial dominion, but natural resources typically live mostly in realms of mobility, where nature's elements move from hand to hand, place to place, and from one physical state and social identity to another, as, for instance, forests fall from land where water, seed, soil, and labour generate plants that become crops, food, cuisine, and commodities which finance families, communities, businesses, and governments.

Such transformations of nature occur at intersections of territorialism and mobility during the continuous reconstitution of natural resource environments. Conflicting attachments to nature emerge at these intersections and animate social life in local farming communities as well as in regions, cities, and states (Ludden 1999, 2002, 2003a). The basis for conflict over resources is that people living in each territory exert proprietary power over resources inside that territory, and they invest their assets to generate proceeds for people inside their territory; while mobile folk move resources from place to place, investing assets locally to carry proceeds away into the realm of mobility, and into other territories. Transactions between mobile and territorial interests in natural resources increase social wealth but also pit people against one another, as for example in fraught relations between nomads and farmers, shifting and sedentary cultivators, and merchants and artisans. Relationships between empire and nation and between nation and globalization are of this kind: a complex of fraught interactions between people who operate across territories and people in each territory who covet mobile assets but fight for territorial closure so they can put assets from the wider world to work for themselves on their own ground.

Combining productive powers and reconciling conflicting interests of territorialism and mobility has long been the specialty of elites who produce most of our historical records; they typically live in central territorial sites, spread their influence across networks of mobility, enrich themselves at intersections of territorialism and mobility, and endeavour to accommodate conflicting claims to resources with various combinations of coercion, adjudication, patronage, and persuasion. The geographical reach and provenance of such resource elites has changed countless times, over centuries; their territorial domains have had shifting, mobile geographies.

From Mauryan times onwards, mobility has reshaped natural resource environments in southern Asia, and in the second millennium of the Common Era, its spatial scale increased dramatically, as Turks, Afghans, Mongols, and Persians reshaped territories across Asia, and as Europeans reshaped territories across the Americas, Africa, and Asia, while mobile folk in South Asia reshaped territories across the subcontinent. In the eighteenth century, as much as half the population in South Asia may have comprised mobile artisans and workers, peasants colonizing new land, itinerant merchants, nomads, pilgrims, shifting cultivators, hunters, migratory service workers and literati, herders, transporters, soldiers, people fleeing war, drought, and flood, and camp followers supplying troops on the move. All this mobility entailed widespread conflict and a huge expansion of commercial activity, commodity production, and global connections (Ludden 1999).

In South Asia, territorialism began its modern ascendancy with expansive conquests by armies of British imperialism (Kolff 1989), but territorial boundaries of the rigid sort that national states define only emerged, as in most of the world, after 1945. Only then did all the histories of all peoples in the world, for all times, appear in a cookie-cutter world of national geography. But the force of mobility did not decline. Quite the contrary, lower transport costs, bigger populations, and increasing inequality accelerated and expanded mobility. National boundaries became the legal and cultural norm, but did not contain mobility; they rather constituted new instruments of territorial power over mobility. Today, new complexities of old tensions between mobility and territorialism appear as features of national territories, where people strive simultaneously to enforce closure, control nature, exclude and subdue aliens, move in and out of territories, bring in and take out resources, move and settle in other places, change and mix territorial identities, and expand claims to resources across territories.

Natural resource environments thus occupy multiple and shifting geographies, which national mapping mentalities obscure, and which we can explore only by abandoning the idea that any form of territorialism can ever contain mobility so as to establish spatially exclusive rights over natural resources. Territorial wealth depends on mobility that territorialism cannot control, and mobility is always at work transforming territory in ways that territorial authorities never comprehend. In the simplistic legal frame of modern states, natural resources are national resources, fixtures of rigidly defined state territories: nature's national identity supersedes all others. But nature's social life cannot be circumscribed realistically in this manner, because various kinds of territorial and mobile social forces always constitute nature's social life in practice. Natural resource environments appear more realistically in their elaborate social complexity at shifting historical intersections of mobility and territorialism.

Productive Powers: Creating Sylhet

One strategic site for exploring these intersections surrounds the city of Sylhet, in northeast Bangladesh. In its vicinity, many territorial transformations have occurred in expansive geographies of mobility where people and resources have travelled widely and combined forces locally to invest in nature. The city itself inhabits a low mound of land in the floodplain of the Surma River (S. Rahman 1999), where population density is like that of Bangladesh generally, while the wider Sylhet region is much less densely populated, at about 70 per cent of the national figure (Rashid 1991: 431–2). This is because the Sylhet region includes thinly populated mountains and lowland depressions (haor) that flood very deeply and extensively for half of every year.

Nature is on the move in Sylhet. Tectonic shifts continue to lift highlands and deepen haor depressions (Alam et al. 1999). Seams of natural gas seep through tectonic folds (Huq 1999). Thumping earthquakes periodically destabilize the land and water's established pathways (Rashid 1991). Shifting waterways scour the land under annual floods and gouge haors deeper (Islam 1985: 1–4). Though two named rivers, the Surma and Kushiara, officially define Sylhet lowlands, they are merely the biggest of many moveable rivers descending from Meghalaya, Tripura, Manipur, and Assam (Bagchi

1944; Chakrabarti 2001:17–21; Strickland 1940). Forty miles upstream from Sylhet town, the region's two major rivers split from the Barak River in Assam; and a hundred miles downstream, they meander, split, and recombine before joining the Meghna, which then joins the Brahmaputra, whose main course shifted in the 1780s to send its confluence with the Meghna a hundred miles south (Rashid 1991: 55ff).

Dense tropical jungles originally covered the land around Sylhet. Amidst massive annual flooding and the highest rainfall in South Asia, lowland societies have navigated Sylhet's overflowing geography at strategic elevated sites, where inundated fields meet habitable land hacked out of forest (Ludden 2003c). Nature's topography is thus itself a critically important natural resource. Sylhet's urban site typifies the lowlands by being partly natural and partly constructed. Eighteenth-century District Records indicate that embankments protecting Sylhet were built, rebuilt, strengthened, and lengthened repeatedly to prevent land from washing away.[1]

Here, as in most old agrarian spaces in southern Asia, sanctity marks venerable sites of continuous social investment in the land (Ludden 1985: 15–41; Ludden 1999: 66–76). Upriver in Cachar, a cult site for Kapilasram (or Siddheswar) retains the memory of an ancient river goddess who was eventually overshadowed by Siva. Such overlays occurred as migratory settlers transformed local territory, in the case of Kapilasram, as Bengali Brahmans established Siva's local authority (Bareh 1987). In the Dimasa language of the local people in Cachar, 'Dimasa' means 'sons of the river' (Bhattacharjee 1987) and the Khasi people in the nearby hills worship many river gods, among whom, goddess Kupli reigns supreme.[2] Kapileswar perhaps came to life

---

[1] Bangladesh National Archives. Sylhet District Records, volume 293, pp. 145–6, 12 December 1784. Citations hereafter in this format: SDR293.145–6: 12Dec84. Firminger (1917) contains reprints of many SDR texts. SDR293.155: 8Apr85 reports expense of Rs 2,000 for renewing banks of the rivers 'Surma, Coosearah, and Munnoo', saying, 'These banks have received no repairs for these last 15 years and were totally swept away in different places for the extent of many miles'. Similar events occurred along the Gomati, where river embankments built around 1710 broke in 1783 (S. Islam 2000: 62, 94–5, 97–9).

[2] The Kupli (or Kapili) River drains Manipur, running north into the Brahmaputra. See Pakem (1987: map facing p. 244).

at an old Kupli cult site, where a social stratification of cult practices emerged as high caste settlers worshiped Siva, while other locals venerated the site but not Siva (S. Chaudhuri 1985: 31–46).

Kapilasram seems to encode the incorporation of an old Khasi site by immigrant Siva-worshipping Bengalis. This cultural change would have been part of a very long, complex set of transformations that affected groups now called 'tribes' in South Asia. Like many other such groups, the Khasis once occupied the lowlands (Ludden 2003c); in their case, up the Ganga basin into Bihar and down to the old Ganga delta. The Khasis specialized in shifting rice cultivation. Ancient Khasis had pioneered rice farming in Vietnam's Red River delta, and when conquered by the Vietnamese, they moved up the Red River, to Yunnan, into China, and across northern Burma, into Assam and the Ganga basin (Ludden 2003b). As Gangetic agrarian societies extended their territorial domains eastward, from Mauryan times onwards, people like the Khasis enriched agrarian cultures based on permanent farming that eventually forced all the Munda language speakers, including Khasis, to submit, assimilate, or move into the uplands, which became their refuge (Bareh 1987: 263 ff).

Over many centuries, lowland territorialism compelled and informed expansive tribal territorialism at higher altitudes. In 1600, groups like the Koch, Khasi, and Garo still occupied many places in the deltaic lowlands, but facing unprecedented pressure to submit to the Mughals, most then retreated into the mountains (Islam 1985: 6–9). After 1500 and again after 1800, the accelerated expansion of sedentary agriculture drove shifting cultivators out of the plains generally and increased violence between contending interests on the land, confining tribal societies to the hills and producing new political forms in the mountains and plains alike (Ludden 1999: 133–40; Ludden 2003c). All these connected trends continue today (Chaudhuri 1993; Raghavaiah 1979).

Siva's overshadowing of the river goddess in Cachar represents one local moment in the advance of lowland territorialism, which produced Bengali societies on moving eastern frontiers of Gangetic cultures, by pushing permanent farms into places inhabited by shifting cultivators, who lived in the highlands and lowlands, who moved freely among forests and fields, mountains and plains, and who hunted and fished without settling down permanently anywhere.[3] Such mobile lifestyles remained well adapted to the environment's watery vacillation, but animist cults and non-Aryan practices (including matrilineal kinship) stigmatized shifting cultivators as primitive aliens in the eyes of Hindu, Muslim, and European lowlanders who invested in nature inside expansive territories of sedentary agriculture, urbanism, state revenue, and permanent territorial authority.

Sylhet town (*Srihatta*) became a centre of lowland territorialism after the tenth century CE. Before then, copper plate inscriptions indicate that land around the Kushiara was instead the more densely populated part of the region, because Kamarupa kings had granted large tracts of land there to immigrant Brahmans and supporting castes to attach this region to Assam (*Khanda Kamarupa*) (Imam 1999: 173–202; Chakrabarti 2001: 158–9). In the thirteenth century, the Afghans conquered Sena rajas downstream in Bengal, inducing more Hindus to move east into Sylhet (Islam 1985: 9), and Sylhet town's site on the Surma then became a fortified centre for the local rajas. In the fourteenth century, the town received the sanctity of Shah Jalal, who arrived from Turkestan with 300 *dervishes* (mystics), conquered the local rajas, and introduced Islam. In 1346, Ibn Batuta met Shah Jalal and described his commanding stature, ascetic celibacy, yogic discipline, and miraculous deeds (Dunn 1986: 254, 255, 263). The first Arabic inscription to mention Shah Jalal, dated 1506, comes from a 'blessed building' that perhaps housed Sufis visiting his tomb, which soon became a pilgrimage site (Chaudhuri 1999; Eaton 1993: 73–7; Karim 1992: 8, 58, 270–3; Karim 1985: 129–133). Shah Jalal's spirit still pervades Sylhet, where some say it makes the land the richest in Bangladesh (Gardner 1995: 75–6).

In 1345, Ibn Batuta travelled the Meghna and saw 'water wheels, gardens and villages such as those along the banks of the Nile in Egypt'. He wrote that, 'For fifteen days we sailed down the river passing through villages and orchards as though we were going through a mart' (Eaton 1993: 258). He did not describe market towns, as he did routinely elsewhere, though marketplaces thrived

[3] Lowland fishing tribes included Kaivartas. See Eaton (1993: 278, n78, citing Gupta 1931).

a thousand years earlier at the confluence of the Meghna and the old Brahmaputra, in Wari-Bateswar and Bhairav Bazar, northeast of Dhaka, where archaeological data suggest trade with Gangetic and Indian Ocean ports (Chakrabarti 2001: 62–66). Fourteenth-century Sylhet would thus seem to have no big market towns, though its saint from Turkestan and visitor from Morocco show it did have wide connections. Mobility would change the land more dramatically in centuries to come.

The Mughals brought with them unprecedented force for change (Karim 1997: 35). Sylhet became a Mughal frontier town on river highways leading up to the lands of the unconquered Khasis, Dimasas, Ahoms, and others. When the Mughals conquered Orissa and Bengal, the Afghans fled up the Meghna and became powerful around Sylhet. A Mughal fleet sailed to Sylhet, and in 1612, the Mughals conquered the Afghans, but peoples ensconced in the highlands, including the Khasis, Garos, Ahoms, and Dimasas, did not succumb (Nathan 1936: 110–11, 158–66, 171–3ff).

The Mughal conquest invested nature with a new cultural politics. Local Afghans escaped the Mughals into forested hills and *haor* depressions, where high caste Hindus had escaped the Afghans three centuries earlier (S. Islam 1985: 8). Myriad escape routes made most land around Sylhet impossible to conquer, until the British finally succeeded, after 1791 (see below and Ludden 2003c). Well into the nineteenth century, however, highbrow lowlanders considered Sylhet a wild frontier, and lowland rulers supported settlers who would use the weight of demography to civilize the land. A seventh-century inscription described Sylhet as 'outside the pale of human habitation, where there is no distinction between natural and artificial; infested by wild animals and poisonous reptiles, and covered with forest out-growths' (Niyogi 1967: 42; Eaton 1993: 258). The Kamarupa kings gave tracts of forest to the Brahmans to civilize. A millennium later, the Mughals gave forests to Muslims and Hindus. In the eighteenth century, Nawabi Faujdars fought to defend nawabi grantees of forest land who strove to bring Sylhet more firmly into the ambit of Bengali Muslim culture (Eaton 1993: 259–65). Meanwhile, the rajas in Cachar and Jaintia embraced Hinduism and patronized the Brahmans who expanded mixed Hindu-tribal polities and mixed tribe-and-caste societies around the Barak Valley. In Cachar, Hindu rituals elevated

Bodo rulers over Dimasa subjects and enabled high caste Bengalis to mix among tribal masters, neighbours and servants, in the manner of oil on water (Bhattacharjee 1987: 177–211).

NATURAL ECONOMY: COMMERCIAL SPACES

Over the centuries, local territories of natural resource utilization diversified along a topographical continuum running from the highest highlands, where shifting *jhum* cultivation prevailed, to the lowest lowlands, where farmers grew *boro* rice, planted in December–January, when fields would dry out enough to plant, and harvested before floods would arrive in June. In 1800, forest still covered much of the land, roughly in proportion to altitude. Permanent agriculture expanded and contracted, in fits and starts; and expansion only gained a firm upper hand in the nineteenth century.[4] Farmers facing recurring flood calamities routinely abandoned old farm sites to colonize new land. The 1780s brought the worst floods in local memory, which destroyed farm investments in years when the Tista River shifted its course and joined the Brahmaputra, changing its course as well. (M.A. Islam 1997: 706). The 1790s brought floods and earthquakes that demolished the lowest farmland behind the eighteenth-century market town of Ajmiriganj, spawning endemic malaria, which stymied new colonization until 1900 (Islam 1985: 6–21).[5]

Nature's topography defined economic geography. In the late eighteenth century, farming communities in the lowland floodplains grew almost nothing but *boro* rice, which they consumed with locally abundant fish. There were no large market centres, let alone major cities, by the standards of lower Bengal, no weavers exporting cloth, and no locally resident rich merchants, let alone portfolio-capitalists.[6]

[4] Areas completely out of cultivation in 1800 and substantially under cultivation by 1900 covered most of Chittagong and Noakhali, all the Sunderbans, most of the Barind, and all the Haor basin (S. Islam 1997: 19). For similar ups and downs in Dinajpur, see Martin (1838: 815).

[5] For more detail on the late eighteenth-century floods and their impact, see Ludden (2003a).

[6] By contrast, in 1789, for example, the Collector at Murshidabad borrowed Rs 41,192 from seven Indian bankers to make good his revenue payment to Calcutta (Mohsin 1997: 217).

Hundis were so hard to find that early Company Collectors had to ship revenues on armed boats to Dhaka.[7] No European Company ever made a major commercial investment in the Surma basin. Yet markets thrived here as supply and demand met in countless small transactions with very little input from urban commercial networks that pervaded lowland Bengal (Datta 1990, 2000). The rulers of Sylhet collected taxes only in cash. Specialists in fishing, horticulture, hunting, mining, trade, transportation, crafts, finance, and administration all bought rice in local lowland markets that thrived amidst the flood-induced uncertainty of local harvests. In 1790, Sylhet District had over 600 named marketplaces (*hat, ganj,* and *bazaar*) (Datta 2000: 208), and long-distance commodity chains passed through them, up and down the Meghna, to and from Dhaka, Narayanganj and Bakarganj (near Barisal), and up and down the Barak Valley, to and from Manipur, Assam and Burma.[8] In the late eighteenth century, as the number of markets increased in Bengal generally (ibid.: 207), Sylhet town became a more active regional market, to which the Manipur and Tripura rajas built a new jungle road from Manipur, in the 1790s (van Schendel 1992: 135–7).

Many commodities drawn from nature carried Khasi social identities from the mountains into the lowlands. Khasi merchants brought goods from Assam through high river ports at Pandua and Jaintia.[9] The Khasis sold mountain *jhum* rice in Jaintia. In high valleys and on low slopes, they grew areca nut, betel, turmeric, and fruits to sell in the plains, along with wax, ivory, and cloth. The mountain Khasis also specialized in iron mining and smelting, and they would denude whole forest tracts to stoke their blow-bag iron furnaces, with

[7] SDR294.112:15Nov85. See S. Islam (2000:71).

[8] James Rennell describes the natural basis of this trading environment: 'The Kingdom of Bengal, particularly its Eastern Tract, is naturally the most convenient for trade within itself of any country in the world; for its rivers divide into just a number of branches that the people have the convenience of water carriage to and from every principal places [sic]'. 'An Unpublished letter of Mr. Rennell' published in *Bengal Past and Present*, September 1933, quoted in Chaudhuri (1997: 36).

[9] See R. Lindsay 1858 in A Lindsay 1858, III: 174–5ff; and Ludden 2003c. General accounts in SDR293.126–9:24Sept84; SDR297.48:29May88; SDR297.54.12May88; and SDR300.56–7: 2Sept90.

cowhide bellows, before moving on to exploit new fuel wood sites. Khasi iron,[10] steel, and metal tools travelled lowland rivers routes, along with their gold, silver, other metals, and ornaments (Bareh 1987: 264–7).[11] The Khasi quarries behind Sunamganj provided the finest quality limestone (Ludden 2003c).

Elephants and ivory also travelled down from the mountains,[12] as salt and rice moved up.[13] Aloe wood and China root appear as Sylhet products in the *Ain-i-Akbari* (Habib 1982: Map 11B). Timber, sandalwood, cane, ivory, rubber, cotton, and silk came from Cachar and Manipur (Bhattacharjee 1987: 186, 194; van Schendel 1992: 137). Cotton came from Tripura (Islam 2000: 49–52). Sylhet's first resident Collector, Robert Lindsay, dramatized the commercial value of the mountains by buying limestone and burnt lime in the mountains to sell in Dhaka, Calcutta, and elsewhere. He even, once had four sea-going ships built on the mountain tops with local timber and then had them filled with mountain products and sailed on the flood to Bakarganj, where his agents sold forest products and bought rice to sell in Madras.[14]

Lindsay's ships would have returned to Calcutta or Chittagong with a ballast of cowry shells, Sylhet's only coin at the time.[15] Though cowries had served most everyday commercial purposes in Bengal

---

[10] SDR312.141:7 April 00: Loads of iron ore in 'immense quantity … is extracted and brought down by [Khasis] for sale and compose a principal article of their traffic with the natives in Sylhet'.

[11] SDR297.48: 29 May 88. SDR297.54.12 May 88.

[12] The Company Collector in Sylhet, Robert Lindsay, reported that, 'at least five hundred elephants were caught annually', in the decade he lived in Sylhet (1778–88) and describes the *khedah* hunting techniques (R. Lindsay 1858: 190–7). Elephants suffered about 50 per cent mortality in captivity. SDR291.24–5: 15Oct78 reports that of 217 elephants caught that year, only 112 survived. SDR291.18Jul78 reports that 106 elephants died of 221 caught in the months from *Kartik* to *Baishak*. Abul Fazl describes hunting elephants in *khedah* during the Mughal times (Allami 1927: 295).

[13] SDR291.8–9: 2Dec77; SDR291.18Jul78.

[14] SDR292.57: 29Mar83.

[15] SDR295.108:30Oct87: ' …there are not 500 Rupees in circulation through-out the district and the few that make their appearance are bad Arcots …'; SDR297.44:17May88: ' …there is not above 6 or 700 Rupees to be found in Sylhet and these are bad Arcots … no copper coins of any Species passes through

before Mughal times (Hussain 2003: 271, 290–4), by the eighteenth century, their role in Bengal as a whole was much diminished, with each region having its own monetary identity designed in mobile geographies of commodity exchange. In 1787, for example, most coins in Rangpur markets were French Arcot Rupees, minted in Pondichery, and Narainy Rupees, minted by rajas in Cooch Behar, though in nearby Mymensingh, English Arcot Rupees prevailed, because Rangpur did heavy trade with Cooch Behar and Chandranagore, while Mymensingh sold its rice in Calcutta. Specific coins also attached to individual commodities, as in Dinajpur, where merchants used Sonaut Rupees to buy rice and other grains, while they used French and English Arcots to buy ghee and oil, and used only French Arcots to buy hemp and gunny. In general, the locally dominant metal coins of Bengal came from far away, most of all, from Arcot and Pondicherry (Mitra 1991: 70–90). Likewise, cowries had come mostly from the Maldives for perhaps a millennium (Hussain 2003: 291; Maloney 1980: 112, 126, 137, 417).

Sylhet depended entirely on cowries until after the 1820s. These tiny shells served as the cheapest coin all around the Indian Ocean and in coastal Southeast Asia and Africa (Hogendorn and Johnson 1986; Perlin 1993: 152–63, 270; Wicks 1992: 28–72). Eighteenth-century Bengal was still a major cowry market, but of all Bengal regions, only Sylhet had virtually no metal coins, and no commercial coins other than cowries. Sylhet people imported almost nothing from downstream, except cowries that the merchants brought from the Maldives, stored in Dhaka and Calcutta, and carried to Sylhet in boats that returned with rice and upland products.[16]

Sylhet was unique in Bengal as cowry country. One explanation was surely political: the weakness of regional states. English observers believed however that the reason was poverty, that Sylhet people could only afford the cheapest coin. But because barter trades flourished alongside cowry exchange, it can be said that cowries functioned to bridge the gap between barter and commerce in local markets. Cowry

---

the District. The Revenues are paid in Cowries and all mercantile transactions are carried on through the same currency'.

[16] SDR293.126–131:24Sept84.

country had a southwestern borderland, around Habiganj,[17] where silver rupees circulated, indicating that Sylhet cowry country coincided with the spatial dispersion of markets that most intimately connected the hills and plains along with their distinctive yet intermingled set of cultural groups. The repeated depiction of Sylhet as a 'mountain region', from the fourteenth century onwards,[18] reinforces the idea that mountains and lowlands contained a diverse yet coherent economic space where cowries articulated a distinctive kind of market territory.[19] Cowry country was a cultural domain of spatial mobility, expressing itself in its coinage and embracing mountains, valleys and lowlands, and Muslim, Hindu and tribal societies around Sylhet.

EMPIRE, ETHNICITY, AND NATION: TERRITORIAL POWER

From the Bengal perspective, cowry country was a violent, turbulent, unruly frontier. In 1765, Sylhet—which had been a *faujdari* (military district) of the Bengal nawabs (Firminger 1969: I, cxii)—suddenly became a frontier district of Bengal Presidency, under the East India Company Raj. Despite a large area and population, Sylhet was poor revenue territory for the Company,[20] as we can see by comparison with nearby districts in northern Bengal, where, in 1783, the Dinajpur zamindar spent more on religious events than the Sylhet District paid revenue (Datta 2000: 171), and in 1785, the Rajshahi zamindar's monthly tax (*kist*) exceeded Sylhet's entire annual tax assessment (*jamma*) (Mahmood 1970: 28). Yet the Company increased Sylhet

[17] SDR300.106: 30Dec90; SDR301.64: 29July91; SRD301.82. 11Oct. 91.

[18] Abul Fazl treats Sylhet only as a mountain region: 'In the Sarkar of Sylhet there are nine ranges of hills. It furnishes many eunuchs'. He goes on to list only the mountain products of Sylhet: Suntarah, orange, China root, Aloe wood, Bhangraj, and tamed birds (Allami 1927: I, 136–7).

[19] The financial integration of this territory into the political economy of Bengal Presidency involved Company efforts to convert Sylhet cowry revenues into Sicca Rupees, which necessitated large cowry exports to Dhaka and Calcutta until the 1790s. These efforts began when Collector Lindsay took the entire Sylhet cowry revenue into his own hands to finance commercial ventures that made him rich and reduced Sylhet cowry exports somewhat in the 1780s. See Ludden (2003c) and SDR293.126–131: 24Sept84.

[20] 1783 area and revenue figures for Bengal districts are in Firminger (1969: II, 403). 1822 area and population figures are in GoI (1961: 71).

taxation as much as possible. The nawab's regime had collected 3,50,000 Kahans of cowries in Sylhet, all spent locally, mostly on the army, which remained standard practice until 1776, when Sylhet's jamma rose to 8,00,101 Kahans of cowries. By 1783, it had risen to 9,36,000 Kahans.[21] State tax demands on Sylhet thus tripled in eight years after 1775, a much higher increase than in Bengal Presidency as a whole.[22]

Sylhet revenue collections stagnated below 70 per cent of jamma until 1788, when they began a steep climb, approaching 100 per cent by 1790.[23] This increase came with the expansion of Company authority over farms that became tax-paying private property. In 1784, 'upwards of 4,000 independent proprietors of the soil' paid land taxes;[24] in 1795, 26,000;[25] and in 1798, 27,000.[26] In 1785, remittances to Calcutta began a steady climb,[27] and in the 1790s, with the addition of Habiganj, Sylhet District began to look like a moneymaker for the Raj, though still a small one compared to other Bengal districts.[28]

In Sylhet, as in Chittagong (Serajud-din 1964), Company revenue came from small village landlords, not big zamindars, merchant magnates, or big *jotedar* tenants, who dominate the agrarian history of Bengal (Bose 1993; Datta 2000; Ray 1979;Taniguchi 1996). Even the smallest Sylheti landowners rarely tilled their own land, but rather employed tenants and labourers. To secure assets against any calamity, locally dominant families held land in several places and combined various sources of income, including commerce, thus

[21] SDR295.122–30: (n.d.)Nov87; SDR299.34: 5Nov89.

[22] SDR294.53:31May84; SDR293:24Sept84; SDR293.156:1May85; SDR295. 122–30: (n.d.)Nov1787. Index values for Bengal Presidency jamma are 100 in 1767, 137 in 1776, and 164 in 1784 (Datta 2000: 334). Revenue demand on Rajshahi zamindari increased only 18 per cent from 1765 to 1784 (Mahmood 1970: 28, 32, 34, 42).

[23] SDR293.156:1May85; SDR306.21–5:19Aug94.

[24] SDR293.99–100: 4Apr84; SDR294.143: 27Jun86 says the number is 5,000.

[25] SDR306.126–7: 8Sept95.

[26] SDR294.143:27Jun86 and SDR309.51–5:12May98.

[27] SDR304.9: 20Apr93.

[28] The first available district budget, in 1794, shows a total annual expense of Rs 1,31,144, and a total jamma of Rs 2,90,554, leaving a balance of Rs 1,59,410, which at the current exchange rate, translates into 8,36,900 Kahans, more than the Sylhet jamma in 1776, now available for remission. SDR306.21–5:19Aug94.

becoming central figures in local markets and revenue operations. For tenants and labourers, mobility remained an always-open option. Most tenants were *paikasht* or non-resident tenants, who received no occupancy rights but did receive agricultural and subsistence inputs from landowners who needed to attract them to clear and cultivate land (Datta 2000: 93–99). Landless workers also lived mobile lives. Some would have come from tribal societies that moved among hills and plains and merged with lowland societies at the lowest ranks. Seasonal migrant workers often came from far away to bring in the harvest and return home with boatloads of rice, as many still do today (Islam 1985: 31–2).

In 1798, the statistically average Sylhet (revenue) village held a tiny population of about seventy people in four landed estates (talukas), each estate embracing one extended family, it dependents and servants.[29] Local farming territory expanded in compact areas scattered across the land, as dominant families spread their influence and vied for land and labour. Many such families held the title of Chaudhuri, which the Mughals used to denote sub-zamindari authority and which spread among Sylhet gentry to become a family name. Mughal governors anointed few if any major zamindars, one of whom an early Collector called the 'only true zamindar' in the Sylhet District, because he had received a Mughal *jagir* for protecting Mughal territory against Khasi incursions.[30]

Unconquered Mughal opponents still exercised considerable power in Sylhet in the eighteenth century, when Sylhet remained a frontier of Gangetic imperialism, as it had been for centuries; and like other such regions in Asia, it has retained a frontier legacy ever since (Giersch 2006). Eighteenth-century Sylhet was still an 'in-between space', a region of mingling and transition at intersections of Bengal and Assam and of southern and eastern Asia (van Schendel 2002). Sylhet's cowry coinage symbolized separation from Bengal and attachment to mountain regions stretching to Yunnan, where cowries

---

[29] Collectors often asserted that the typically Sylhet landholding represented a single joint family. SDR297.126: 5Sept88; SDR300.141–4:24Oct91. Statistical averages are calculated from data on populations in 1789 and 1808 in Rahman (1999: 115, 117); and on villages in SDR300.141–4:24Oct91; and talukas (estates) SDR309.51–5:12May98.

[30] SDR299.72–4:15Jan90.

also circulated (Hussain 2003: 291–4). The Khasis with ancient roots in Southeast Asia ruled Sylhet's northern mountains, the Cachar rajas with their mixed tribal and Hindu heritage held the eastern upland Barak Valley, and comparable Tripura rajas ruled the southern mountains. The Mughals had kept them all at bay in part with arms and land grants, but the Mughal presence in Sylhet consisted mostly of thousands of local patriarchs who acquired the title of Chaudhuri as they bowed to the Mughals to boost their local authority.

By 1778, when the Company's first resident Collector, Robert Lindsay, arrived in Sylhet, Chaudhuri had become a Sylheti family name that fused the personal identity and official state rank of local elites who were expanding their investments in farming as the Company arrived and as rulers based in the hills were also extending their authority in the plains.[31] The new British imperial domain, based in Calcutta, derived from the Mughals and nawabs and likewise lacked effective power in the mountains, focusing on the lowlands. In the nineteenth century, the British Empire expanded into the uplands more extensively and effectively than any predecessor, and here as throughout Asia, thorough conquest of mountains by lowland imperialists became a topographical signature of modernity, one that independent national states re-inscribed afresh in the twentieth century (Giersch 2006; Ludden 1999).

The Company's early steps in Sylhet consolidated power over agrarian revenues in the lowlands by pushing back the highland rulers who challenged Company authority in the plains. Collectors settled borders with Cachar, Jaintia, and Tripura by transacting with established rajas,[32] who had long experience with lowland empires. But the Khasis in the northern mountains posed a more difficult problem: they had never submitted to Mughal or nawabi authority; they were scattered across land north of the Surma (Pakem 1987: 261–306 and facing 244); and they had spawned a mixed population of Bengali

[31] This is one of many examples of naming practices in South Asia (see also Sethu Pillai 1950), of fusing folksy local and official state forms and functions, contra Scott et al. (2002).

[32] All these borders were fuzzy in practice: '… the lands of the Rajahs of Chachar and Jointah are blended with those of this District; indeed, the Rajah of Jointah possesses lands adjacent to the town of Sylhet' (SDR308.150:22Feb98). For Tripura, see S. Islam (2000: 1-30).

Khasis who lived low on the mountains and in the plains and whose leaders defied the Company and Khasi rulers alike.[33]

In cowry country, at the confluence of mountains and plains, resource environments looked very different to lowland rulers and to Khasi peoples, each invested in their own way in nature's productivity. For the British, as for the Mughals, nawabs, and Bengali farmers, nature's bounty appeared as an attribute of geographically circumscribed spatial domains of territorial authority. Such agrarian territorialism had changed spatial form many times over the centuries (Ludden 2002, 2003c), but retained from medieval times onwards a cultural attachment to royal authority. By contrast, for the Khasis, however, Khasi territory had a purely ethnic identity: nature was attached to Khasi families, wherever they lived. Thus, at the same time as the British sought to fix boundaries around their state territory, Khasi territory travelled and dispersed with Khasi settlements here and there across the landscape. The Khasi rulers in the hills presumed authority over the Khasi communities living in the lowlands where the Company claimed exclusive authority over all the land and inhabitants. These conflicting visions of territory by contending mobile enforcers of social power over geographical space produced serious conflict.

In 1789, following many skirmishes, the mountain Khasis and Bengali Khasis attacked Company settlements, and the Collector summoned troops to push the Khasis into the hills. This accomplished, the Collector declared an absolute boundary at the base of the hills and prohibited any Khasis from owning land in the plains, to vitiate future claims by Khasi rulers to Company land. Hill trades hence came under strict regulation. In 1791, a new border thus came into being to separate the Bengalis from the Khasis; in 1947, it came to separate India and Pakistan; and, in 1971, it came to separate India from Bangladesh, and Meghalaya from Sylhet.[34]

The hills and plains and all their natural resources thus acquired official ethnic identities enforced by imperial states, and later, by national states. The hill Khasis became aliens in the Bengal plains, which the state proclaimed as Bengali. By 1797, Bengali farmers had

---

[33] SDR297.164:18Dec88; SDR298.7:20Dec88.

[34] Ludden (2003c) has a detailed account of these events.

bought titles to all the land expropriated by the state from the Bengali Khasis,[35] who became extinct as an ethnic group and faded from history when mixing Khasi and Bengali families disqualified the new family from owning land on either side of the border. The border that kept the Khasis and the Bengalis apart also confirmed separate Khasi authority in the mountains (in what became Meghalaya) where few lowlanders would ever settle. By contrast, in the adjacent mountains of Cachar and Jaintia, where eighteenth-century peace treaties normalized relations between rajas and the Company, borders remained open and lowland settlers swarmed into upland farming frontiers in the nineteenth and twentieth centuries. The highland Khasi resistance to empire in the eighteenth century thus effectively imbued nature with a lasting Khasi ethnicity that remains intact today.

In the nineteenth century, the imperial territorialism of British India also moved south into the Sylhet mountain frontiers behind Maulvi Bazar and Habiganj, where English-owned tea estates took the land of the forest peoples. These mountains stretch into the plains east of the Meghna, running across Tripura, Manipur, the Chittagong Hill Tracts, and into Burma. Mountain societies remained mobile, as their land fell into the hands of Bengali colonizers. Ethnic conflict over land ensued, along with complex cultural mixing and tense ambiguities of political authority (GoP 1970: 328–31). Like the Khasis, people from Tripura in the south continued to live, settle, work, and move across the uplands and lowlands, as they became official aliens in the plains; but unlike the Meghalaya mountains, and like Cachar and Jaintia, Tripura's frontiers in southern Sylhet remained open for lowland territorial expansion.

The uphill march of lowland territorialism accelerated after 1800, 1880, and 1947 (Ludden 1999: 130–40), under expansive national state regimes run by the British, Indians, Pakistanis, Bangladeshis, and Burmese. More and more Hindus, Muslims, Christians, and Buddhists from the lowlands turned mountain land into their own private property. Hill peoples thus became minorities in the hills adjoining southern Sylhet in Tripura and the Chittagong Hill Tracts (Adnan 2004; Bhattacharyya 1991), as at the same time, the hill people became aliens in the plains. After 1947, the borders

[35] SDR308.27–8:15Sept97.

between the hills and plains became harder and more aggressively protected by national regimes (Ludden 2003b). The northern Sylhet border with Meghalaya became rife with conflict between security forces drawn into struggles by old trades between mountains and plains that continued to operate—now illegal, but licit (Abraham and van Schendel 2005)—across the 1791 boundary, now a border between India and Bangladesh. Reflecting life on the ground in these borderlands, a group of Khasi organizations submitted a petition to the Indian government, in 2001, seeking official permission to carry on their trades without harassment across the border of Meghalaya-Sylhet, saying their trades had continued 'from time immemorial' at 'our simple Hat markets', which account for a much larger volume of cross-border trade than recognized in official statistics, which classify all this trade as 'smuggling' (Kakoty 2005).

Modern territorialism thus acquired two contrasting identities inside Sylhet. On the one hand, state power and private property rights are firmly in control. Investments in nature occur in peaceful, harmonious environments, as indicated by this tourist image of Sylhet from the 'Visit Bangladesh' website:[36]

Nestled in the picturesque Surma Valley amidst scenic tea plantations and lush green tropical forests, Sylhet is a prime attraction for all tourists visiting Bangladesh. Lying between the Khasia and the Jaintia hills on the north, and the Tripura hills on the south, Sylhet breaks the monotony of the flatness of this land by a multitude of terraced tea gardens, rolling countryside and exotic flora and fauna. Here the thick tropical forests abound with many species of wild life, scented orange groves and luxuriant pineapple plantations spread their aroma around the typical hearth and homes of the Manipuri Tribal maidens famous for their dance.

On the other hand, struggles continue inside and across state borders that mark the domains of unfinished conquest by investors and states. The Sylhet-Meghalaya border was a site of conflict during the war in 1971, when the term 'infiltrators' that is so prominent today in India was standard state vocabulary in East Pakistan.[37] Borders marked by

[36] http://www.betelco.com/bd/sylhet/sylhet.html
[37] For Sylhet news of infiltrators in 1971, see http://www.profile-bengal.com/mnapril30.html. The term 'infiltrator' is used today in a manner that blurs the distinction between migrants crossing borders without state authorization and active enemies of the state moving across borders. See, for example, recent news

Khasi ethnicity have remained contested since 1971. Most notably, in 2001, Indian and Bangladeshi border patrols fought skirmishes over control of the village of Pyrdiwah, claimed by Bangladesh for Sylhet but lying in the East Khasi Hills district of Meghalaya (van Schendel 2005). In 2002, Bangladesh Forest Department officials and 'bands of local miscreants' forcefully evicted from forests in Sylhet's Moulvibazar Zila twenty of a thousand Khasi families who had cultivated betel vines there for generations. This eviction (one among many) killed one person and injured several others, as part of an effort to create an eco-park as a tourist attraction.[38] Sylhet's Tripura border is even more troubled, and is now being fenced with intimidating barbed wire by the Indian government, amidst daily accounts of violence.[39] For instance, on 2 February 2002, *Frontline* reported that:

Ethnic violence in … Tripura and Assam claimed 56 lives within a span of 10 days in mid-January. The victims were Bengalis and Hindi-speaking Biharis and the killers were tribal extremists belonging to the National Liberation Front of Tripura (NLFT) and the National Democratic Front of Bodoland (NDFB). … The tribal militants in Tripura, who belong to either the NLFT or the All Tripura Tiger Force (ATTF), have persistently followed a policy of ethnic cleansing. They want Bengalis to move out of the State where the tribal people once formed the majority community. Militant tribal leaders know that they cannot achieve this objective, as Bengalis now constitute over 60 percent of the State's population. … Extremists in Tripura enjoy an operational advantage as the State is surrounded on three sides by Bangladesh.

---

coverage of 'Bangladeshi infiltrators' in Jammu and Kashmir (http://timesofindia. indiatimes.com/articleshow/855373.cms) and in Assam (http://news.webindia123. com/news/articles/India/20070712/711258.html).

[38] *Daily Star*, 25 July and 5 August 2002, omits mention of the eco-park, which appears in Hossain (2001: 147).

[39] More than forty 'major incidents of violence' have occurred on this border between 1992 and 2005. See http://www.satp.org/satporgtp/countries/india/states/ tripura/data_sheets/majorincidents.htm. For extended treatment of border issues, see van Schendel (2005). For detailed analysis of the conflict in northeast India, see Baruah (2006). Reports about events on the Bangladesh side of the border appear almost daily in the *Daily Star*. 9 May 2003 was a typical day when Tripura rebels were said to have killed twenty-one Bengalis on the Tripura borders of Comilla District, Bangladesh, where 'tribal militants charge that Bangalee settlers have changed the demographic makeup of Tripura, turning the indigenous population into a minority'.

They have their hideouts in Bangladesh where they find easy shelter when under pressure from the security forces.

TERRITORY AND MOBILITY: FORM AND CONTENT

Modern state borders are thus features of state politics and weapons in political struggles inside and among states. The mapped borders of Sylhet District remained officially stable after 1820, except for a small subtraction of eastern land that went into the Cachar District of Assam at partition in 1947 (Islam 2002; Ludden 2003b). But mobility across Sylhet borders has reconstituted Sylhet's territorial substance dramatically, as Sylhet moved four times among modern state jurisdictions. Its internal character changed in each new context, as it formed a part, in succession, of Bengal, Assam, Pakistan, and Bangladesh. During these migrations, it retained a single name endowed with shifting political identities.[40]

In its century as part of Bengal Presidency (1765–1874), Sylhet was a space of moving frontiers and stable base of operations for expansive British imperial power, which spread into Burma and up to China, while the Raj created a bordered, mapped territory, called 'Sylhet', which had never existed before. In this context, a mixed flow of immigrants arrived, including tea plantation workers, whose English employers captured Sylhet's southern hills and then led Sylhet District into an Assam 'planters' raj', in 1874 (Guha 1977).

After 1874, Sylhet lay in Assam, until 1947, except for five years in the hotly contested and still poorly understood Province of Eastern Bengal and Assam. In its Assam phase, lowland Sylhet's cultural composition remained an elaborate mix of Hindu and Muslim elements, which became more identified politically as Muslim over time. Sylhet people classified in the 1871 Census as Hindus and Muslims each respectively comprised about half the population; and Brahmans numbered 6 per cent of the Hindu population (M.M. Rahman 1999: 105–7), which is a higher proportion than we find in most Hindu majority regions of British India.[41] Hindu Sylhet was

---

[40] In this respect, it is like Assam, whose form, content, and political affiliations have shifted during the course of its incorporation into India. See Kar (2004); Ludden (2003b); Misra (2000:62).

[41] In 1931, Brahmans comprised 3 per cent of the census population in Madras

more Brahmanical than most of Hindu Bengal and boasted of rich
Sanskrit scholarship (Mandal 1999); and its influence was such that
the leader of the Sylheti language movement, Moulvi Abdul Karim,
printed books in a Siloti Nagri font at his Islamia Press (Shiby 1999).

Sylhet's Muslim population began to increase proportionately after
1808, when an estimated 2:3 ratio of Muslims to Hindus implies that
the Muslim proportion increased by one-third in the next six decades,
to produce a 1:1 ratio in 1871 (M.M. Rahman 1999: 115). During its
Assam phase, the Muslims increased proportionately in each decennial
census (ibid.: 108; Schwartzberg 1992: 93–4). Immigration was the
reason. In 1911, people reportedly born in Mymensingh composed
31 per cent of the population of the Assam valley (including Sylhet),
and they numbered 63 per cent in 1931 (M.A. Islam 1997: 706). In
the inter-war decades, this migratory mobility acquired new territorial
meanings. In 1931, the Assam *Census Report* called Muslim Bengalis
'invaders' and the Assam Congress resolved to move Sylhet out of
Assam (Chaudhuri 2002). The Partition Plan produced a Sylhet
referendum, after which, a truncated Sylhet District, identified as
Muslim, entered East Pakistan (Islam 2002).

After 1947, vast immigration transformed Sylhet's population.
In the decade after the first good post-partition census, in 1961, its
population grew by 37 per cent; and after 1971, by 22 per cent (GoB
1996). A hundred thousand Muslim Bengalis moved out of Assam into
Sylhet's *haor* basin, where land remained open for new colonization
(Islam 1985: 16, citing Dass 1980). In 1951, the proportion of Muslims
reached 68 per cent, and rose faster thereafter with each census (M.M.
Rahman 1999: 108).

The Sylhet region now has a profoundly Muslim territorial identity
inside Bangladesh, but Indian scholars still typically identify Sylhet
with Assam, not only because of Sylhet's medieval and colonial
locations—which also inform Sylheti identity inside Bangladesh
(Imam 1999: 186ff)—but also because more than a million Sylhetis,
mostly Hindus, live in east and northeast India, where Silchar is their
cultural capital and where their mobile sense of homeland travels

Presidency and 5 per cent in Bombay Presidency (GoI 1933). In the Tinnevelly
District of Madras Presidency—about the same size as Sylhet and 98 per cent
Hindu—the Brahmans formed 3.5 per cent of the 1881 population (Ludden
1985: 25).

across India and through Assam, skirting Bangladesh.[42] Mobility and fluidity typify Sylheti identity. Its migratory propensities, in Bangladesh, South Asia and abroad, have generated various cultural geographies, and the US-based founders of CyberSylhet.com, for example, treat 'overseas Sylhet' as virtually meaning 'global Bangladesh'.[43]

Yet despite its territorial fractures and spatial mobility, Sylheti identity has a coherently ethnic character. Meanings of being Sylheti rest in part on language, for Sylheti differs markedly from standard Bangla (Morshed 1999). A Sylheti literary movement, which began in 1860, has revived in recent decades,[44] and Sylhetis seem much more likely than other South Asian migrants in England to receive education only in their native language (Burholt 2004: 391). Sylheti identity also depends critically on family, lineage, descent, and marriage networks, which typically separate Hindus and Muslims. In Bangladesh, Sylhetis have a reputation for being 'clannish', the word I hear most often when Sylhetis in Dhaka describe their culture as one based on strict marriage strategies, tight extended families, and strong kin networks.[45] Migrant Sylhetis in Birmingham are much more likely than Punjabis or Gujaratis to live in households composed of several generations (ibid. 2004: 390). Sylheti families also promote a specific pattern of gender relations. In Sylhet haor communities, where many Muslim women from other districts work outdoors in agriculture, Sylheti women maintain *pardah* by working indoors and rarely, if at all, in the fields (Islam 1985: 26). In Birmingham, gender differentials in education, employment, and other measures of personal status are much more pronounced among Sylhetis than Gujarati and

[42] As indicated by a recent *yatra* from Kanyakumari to Silchar by authors of a rich Sylheti cultural website: http://personal.vsnl.com/syhlleti/yatra.htm.

[43] 'CyberSylhet.com is a premier portal for Bangladeshis living in the United Kingdom, and Bangladeshis around the world'. See http://www.cybersylhet.com/modules.php?name=About_Us.

[44] See http://sylheti.org.uk.

[45] Sylheti marriage advertisements, formerly posted on http://www.sylhetcity.net, include the following two: 'Bride wanted for a Muslim male. He has a good job, business and lives in his own house. Bride should be attractive, educated and religious. Must be from a Sylheti Sunni family background'; 'A bride required for an attractive Sylheti Muslim male. Groom is postgraduate from Bangladesh. Elder brother is willing to pay for the return fare and other necessary expense'. Now other Sylheti websites serve marriage ad functions, e.g., http://www.sylheti.com/.

Punjabi immigrants; and though many more Sylhetis have little or no education, and speak no English, Sylheti women are much more likely to be completely uneducated and conversant only in their native language (Burholt 2004: 291). In Bangladesh, Sylhet stands out as the district where men are most likely to be opposed to birth control and family planning (M.A. Islam et al. 2004: 4). Religious piety is another pronounced feature of Sylheti identity, for Hindus and Muslims alike; in Bangladesh, Shah Jalal represents the spiritual heart of Sylhet, and Sylhetis identify most intensely with his legacy.

Sylhetis in Bangladesh are deeply invested in Sylhet land, giving it a strong ethnic identity. Underground natural resources in Sylhet, such as natural gas, are Bangladeshi national resources, but Sylhet's natural environment is profoundly Sylheti. Tourist advertisements, like the one above, represent a unique landscape, where plans for an eco park on a national forest land brought the expulsion of Khasi residents, and where the exotic image of 'Manipuri maidens' mingles with the smell of pineapple plantations. Also in Sylhet, international conflicts on the border with Meghalaya have a definite local flavour—as well as international significance—and often evoke the 1791 war that divided Sylhet from Meghalaya. For instance, the *Daily Star* reported on 20 August 2002 that 'Two Bangladeshis were kidnapped and shot dead by Indian Khasia (tribesmen) aided by the [Indian Border Security Forces] near Bichhakandi border under Gowainghat upzila Sunday night.... [when the] two Bangladeshis ...were returning home after working in the Bichhakandi stone quarry near the border...' (Ludden 2003c; van Schendel 2005).

INVESTING IN NATURE: LOCAL TERRITORIALISM

The social identity of natural resources in Sylhet thus depends on the particular history of proprietary power over nature in the region. Under British Rule, local landed families controlled agrarian Sylhet. Recording, adjudicating, and protecting private property rights became the main function of government. The government never meddled in the affairs of the local estates. The Bengal Rent Act of 1859 had no impact. When Sylhet moved into Assam, it escaped later Bengal tenancy reforms. Local Sylheti territorialism became a constituent of modern governance and also of Sylhet regional identity, which

though distinctive, also reflects a broader pattern, because all across
the land that became Bangladesh, British authority attached itself
to intimate powers wielded by the local gentry, Hindu and Muslim
(Islam 1989). Trends after 1947 nationalized this pattern. In 1951,
zamindari abolition in East Pakistan multiplied private property
rights and produced new forms of tenancy (Siddiqui 1997). The
1945 Famine Commission's conclusion that requisitioning rice for
public distribution lay beyond the state's capacity in Bengal proved
prophetic when state requisitions in East Pakistan produced intense
local opposition, stoked violence against Hindu traders, and helped
to kill the Muslim League in the 1954 elections (Famine Commission
1945; Kamal 1988). In the Pakistan context, Bengali visions of what
Bangladesh meant developed inside distinctive local environments and
institutions of proprietary power and political authority. The localism
of the agrarian power structure remains a potent feature of political
life in rural Bangladesh as a whole (Adnan 2007; Riaz 2005).

In Sylhet, such local authority has a distinctively Sylheti idiom.
Locality is in general, of course, a place of belonging, and also a domain
for investment. Being well placed in local society provides key people
with privileged access to networks of connectivity that expand their
opportunities in wider worlds of mobility (Baviskar 2007b). In Sylhet,
these local intersections of mobility and territorialism take shape in
social spaces composed of Sylheti *gushti* (patrilineages).

Agrarian territory in the Haor Basin epitomizes Sylhet. A haor is
a deep radial depression that fills up to the brim and often overflows
with the monsoon, and dries up sufficiently for boro rice cultivation
between January and May. Farming communities occupy natural
ridges and built-up land around haor lakes, lapped by deep waters
that cover *haors* from June to December. There are countless haors
in Sylhet, but the western Haor Basin is entirely covered with haors;
it is deeply flooded annually by meandering branches of the Surma
and Kushiara. During the monsoon it looks from the air like a vast
sea dotted with islands, which is how Robert Lindsay described Sylhet
under flood in 1784 (Ludden 2003c: 19). In this region, investments
in agriculture have been hard to secure and large tracts remained
open for new colonization as late as 1950 (Islam 1985: 5).

On haor lands, compact enclaves (*bari*) of related families (gushti)
formed settlements where local Sylheti landlords held sway before land

reforms in 1950, and where locals reproduced landlordism thereafter, as the land filled up with immigrant settlers. Communities established residential sites based on their common place of origin; occupational and religious groups also formed mini-territories on haor ridges. As in most of agrarian South Asia, micro-ethnic partitions of local agrarian territory occurred as the region attained an over-arching ethnic identity defined by the cultural affinities of the major landowning groups (Ludden 1999: 140–5, 190–216). Today, distinctive haor social identities appear as Bengali Muslim, in the frame of Bangladesh, and Sylheti, in the frame of Sylhet.

Nature's topography articulates inequality among *gushti* in the Haor Basin. Higher, wider ridges are wealthier and more populous. Lower lands that extend across deeper, wider haor lakes host more precarious, poorer communities filled with seasonal migrants who still come by water from afar to harvest boro crops. On the widest, richest haor ridges, wealthier families live on higher land and are less vulnerable to flooding. Upwardly mobile families buy higher, more profitable farmland, just below the haor ridge; and they live in higher, drier residential sites, atop the ridge. Poorer and downwardly mobile families can buy more land at lower prices for housing at the lowest edge of the ridge, nearest the lake, where their homes feel the lapping of the floods; and they can also buy farmland more cheaply farther out in the haor lakes, where floods come sooner, lands produce less, and work is harder and less profitable (Islam 1985).

Another typically Sylheti form of territorialism prevails in and around the towns of Sylhet, Sunamganj, Moulvibazar, and Habiganj, where local investments stand out as big, fancy, brightly painted houses. These houses belong to families in gushti whose men went to London, generations ago—some as early as the late eighteenth century—originally as workers on ships, and who eventually opened restaurants.[46] Early twentieth-century British immigration laws restricted Sylheti immigration to relatives of earlier settlers, which fostered a Sylheti monopoly of the London 'Indian restaurant' business. Today, Sylheti Londoni families have created a mobile

---

[46] One early Sylheti overseas migrant, Syedullah, described his travels and displayed his cooking skill when he arrived at Robert Lindsay's home in Scotland, sometime before 1825 (R. Lindsay 1858: 215–17).

territory of business activity, anchored simultaneously in Sylhet and London, composed of Bangladesh and UK citizens (Gardner 1995). In recent decades, these transnational locals have been most active in organizations devoted to making Sylheti language, literature and regional identity more publicly visible.[47]

Like others who have built family business domains in South Asia, London Sylhetis invest meticulously in marriage, religion, and other social activities to enhance their family status, cultural capital and business assets that include dependable partners, financiers and employees. Young Sylheti women, born and raised in London, travel to their family's home village in Sylhet to marry selected men from appropriate families. When immigration officials allow, the husband joins his wife in London to work in his father-in-law's restaurant, while his wife, typically more educated and always more Westernized, follows other suitable occupations. In time, sons-in-law may attain UK citizenship, which might allow a rupture with the in-laws. But the independence of London brides can cause even more difficult problems. Should daughters marry men who are not of their parents' choice in Sylhet, family struggles might ensue in which parents seek redress for the loss of honour and prospects, and as UK citizens, dissident Londoni brides can enlist the help of the British High Commission in Dhaka to return independently to England (Siddiqi 2002).

Better-off Londoni families typically address legal dilemmas by using local police and courts, while the less well-endowed often resort to informal village mediation hearings, called *shalish*, a distinctive local institution in Bangladesh. Conflicts over land and other property pre-occupy about half of all shalish mediations where local men of authority, convened ad hoc and case-by-case, sit to hear troubles and make a judgement (Rahman and Islam 2002: 146). Its informality makes the shalish difficult to historicise, but a new phase clearly began in 1993, when one Sylheti shalish issued a fatwa to punish a woman and her father for her 'illicit' marital union, by caning him and stoning her, after which she committed suicide.[48] Similar events elsewhere spurred public campaigns to reform the local shalish in

[47] See http://sylheti.org.uk/.
[48] Personal communication, Hameeda Hossain and Dina Siddiqi. For more on fatwas, see Siddiqi (1998).

conformity with Bangladesh national law. In this, as in many other contexts, localism is being construed as anti-modern by national and international reformers whose circuits of mobility converge on universities, law courts and capital cities in Bangladesh and abroad, and who face not only entrenched local authorities but travelling crusaders who strive to construct, justify and defend local shalish traditions in pan-Islamic cultural terms (Riaz 2005; Siddiqi 2002).

CONCLUSION

Investments in nature in Sylhet today operate simultaneously in local, regional and national territories, and in trans-territorial spaces of globalization. Mobility has been reshaping natural resource environments for a very long time, and is still reshaping the Bangladesh context of life in Sylhet in myriad ways. Activists, researchers, and officials travel the country to bring Sylhet localities into the national project of development, to reform local shalish procedures, and to alter gender relations, and to spread the word of Islam. Packed airplanes fly Sylheti families to and from London. Villagers flock to cities and to Persian Gulf states to remit funds to support their families. International capital and commodity flows engaging Sylhetis in town and country sustain a Bangladesh Readymade Garments industry that benefits American consumers. The US government has been trying for years to force Bangladesh to export natural gas from Sylhet to India, to profit US oil companies. Goods and people move massively across international borders. The Indian government decries Bangladeshi 'infiltrators'. The Indian military pushes Bengali Muslims into Bangladesh. Tripura rebels find refuge in mobile spaces that defy national maps and comprise a real human geography of another kind. Tales abound of how rampant mobility generates everyday conditions inside territories of natural resource control. Yet the ideas, information, and academic disciplines that we typically use to comprehend transactions between mobility and territorialism constantly redraw the black-and-white lines of national geography. History in Sylhet indicates a rather more complex, diverse spatial reality, composed of many grey areas and shifting, overlapping spaces. By exploring the grey areas, we can better analyse modern structural transformations and discontinuities, which take shape at shifting intersections of mobility and territorialism.

The practical lesson is this: the mobility that characterizes globalization today operates simultaneously in many spatial and temporal registers; it forms many geographies, which coexist, conflict, and complicate one another, and have done so for a very long time. In the modern world of capitalism, investments move from place to place to garner returns, dividends move into the hands of people 'in the loop' of capital accumulation (Smith 1984), and spaces of power and belonging mutate accordingly (Ong 2006). The biggest winners are certainly the rich folks in rich countries and in rich urban neighbourhoods. But many local families in rustic environs like Sylhet are also 'in the loop'. In countless localities, the mobility of people, assets and state power work inside shifting territorial forms of capital accumulation (Ludden 2006a, 2006b, 2006c). In this real-world context, national politicians and intellectuals who work in shifting spatial domains spanning local and global geographies would do well to abandon the idea that static national maps represent the reality of natural resource environments. They might be well advised in fact to abandon the idea that any legal definition of territorial sovereignty could ever maintain effective dominion over nature.

6

Economies of Violence*
More Oil, More Blood

MICHAEL WATTS

Blood may be thicker than water, but oil is thicker than either.

Perry Anderson (2001:30)

Oil, more than any other commodity, illustrates both the importance and the mystification of natural resources in the modern world.

Fernando Coronil (1997: 49)

The annals of oil are an uninterrupted chronicle of naked aggression, genocide and the violent law of the corporate frontier. Iraq was born from this vile trinity. In their own way, the awful spectacle of oilmen parading through the corridors of the White House, the rise of militant Islamism across the Koran belt, and the carnage on the road to Baghdad, all bear out the dreadful dialectics of blood and oil. Paul Wolfowitz's recent confession, to the Asian Security Summit in Singapore in early June, that the Iraq war was driven not by the fiction of weapons of mass destruction but by the 'simple fact' that the 'country swims on a sea of oil'[1] is consistent at least with the last eighty years of US foreign policy (Painter 1986). But there is another oil story in train, bearing all the hallmarks of the long, ugly history of petrolic violence. Two years ago, Vice President Dick Cheney

* I am grateful to Oronto Douglas, Ike Okonta, Von Kemedi , Amita Baviskar, and Donald Moore for their suggestions and assistance.

[1] George Wright, 'Wolfowitz: Iraq War was about Oil', *Manchester Guardian*, 4 June 2003.

predicted that Africa would become the fastest growing source of oil for the American market (as much as 25 per cent of US imports by 2015) and it is hardly a surprise to learn that where oil reigns supreme the military are sure to follow. The *Wall Street Journal* reported several weeks ago that the Pentagon, in the most radical deployment of American forces since the end of the Cold War, will move troops from Germany to the Caucasus and West Africa to 'protect key oil reserves'.[2] More oil, more blood.

Protection demands, of course, keeping the oil flowing by working hand-in-hand with a phalanx of African dictators and political psychopaths on the one side, and super majors like ExxonMobil and ChevronTexaco on the other who, citing confidentiality agreements, refuse to disclose the fees, royalties and other services (paramilitaries and security forces among them) made to the phalanxes of well-placed African *nomenklatura*. Such is the scale of the decrepitude and venality—$300 million in Equatorial Guinea, billions in Nigeria over the last two decades—that the British Government is in a trans-Atlantic tug of war to have oil majors disclose their payments for leases and concessions, a proposal fiercely resisted by American Big Oil and the Bush administration. In a separate proposal, George Soros calls for mandatory reporting as a prerequisite for listing of oil companies on the world's stock exchanges.[3] In the last year, a raft of new reports inventory the appalling record of oil-based economies in relation to corruption, economic growth and poverty alleviation.[4] Oil, as Anderson says, is thicker than blood or water.

ANOTHER OIL STORY

A year before the events of 11 September 2001, the US Department of State in its annual encyclopaedia of 'global terrorism' identified the Niger Delta—the ground zero of oil production in Nigeria—as a breeding ground for increasingly militant 'impoverished ethnic groups' for whom terrorist acts (abduction, hostage taking, kidnapping and

[2] Ike Okonta, 'Nigeria and the World', *This Day*, 22 June 2003, Sunday editorial.

[3] Gal Luft, 'Africa Drowns in a Pool of Oil', *Los Angeles Times*, _ July 2003.

[4] See Gary and Karl (2003); also see Christian Aid (2003); Global Witness (2004); Renner (2002); Ross (2001a).

extra-judicial killings) against foreigners were legion.[5] The Central
Intelligence Agency (CIA) concurred (CIA 2000), laying emphasis
on the catalytic effects of 'environmental stresses' in the oil-rich
southern delta on 'political tensions'. At this time, Nigeria—the
thirteenth largest producer of petroleum (and which provides 80 per
cent of government revenues, 95 per cent of export receipts, and 90
per cent of foreign exchange earnings)—was providing almost 14 per
cent of US American petroleum consumption.[6] At about the same
time, the Petroleum Finance Company (PFC) presented to the US
Congressional International Relations Committee Sub-Committee
on Africa a report of the strategic and growing security significance of
West African oil whose high quality reserves and low cost output—
coupled with massive new deepwater discoveries—required, in the
view of PFC, serious attention and substantial foreign investment.
In the wake of the Al-Qaeda attacks, and on the larger canvas of
the crisis in Venezuela and the Iraq war, West Africa has emerged
as the site of 'the new Gulf oil states'.[7] Indeed, by January 2002, the
Institute for Advanced Strategic and Political Studies was providing
a forum for the Bush oil-administration to declare that African oil is
'a priority for US national security'.[8] In the last year, Africa's black
gold—in Gabon, Sao Tome, Angola, Equatorial Guinea—and its ugly
footprint are rarely off the front pages. Oil and blood, as Jon Anderson
put it, are ubiquitous.[9] With the additional *frisson* of terrorism: the
'nightmare', as the *New York Times* noted, of 'sympathizers of Osama
Bin Laden sink[ing] three oil tankers in the Straits of Hormuz'.[10]

The mythos of oil and oil-wealth has been central to the history
of modern industrial capitalism. But in Nigeria, as elsewhere, the
discovery of oil, and annual oil revenues of $40 billion currently, has
ushered in a miserable, undisciplined, decrepit, and corrupt form of
'petro-capitalism'. After a half century of oil production from which
almost $ 300 billion in oil revenues have flowed directly into the

[5] See http://www.state.gov/s/ct/rls/pgtrpt/2000.
[6] See http://www.eia.gov/emeu/cabs/nigeria.html.
[7] Servant, *Le Monde Diplomatique*, 13 January 2003.
[8] See http://www.iasps.org.
[9] Anderson, J., 'Blood and Oil', *The New Yorker*, 14 August 2000, pp. 46–59.
[10] *New York Times*, 14 October 2001: III, 1

Federal exchequer (and perhaps $ 50 billion promptly flowed out only to 'disappear' overseas), Nigerian per capita income stands at $ 290 per year. For the majority of Nigerians, living standards are no better now than at independence in 1960. A repugnant culture of excessive venality and profiteering among the political class—the Department of State has an entire website devoted to the so-called 419 fraud cases—confers upon Nigeria the dubious honour of sitting atop Transparency International's ranking of most corrupt states. Paradoxically, oil-producing states in the federation—the Niger Delta—have benefited the least from oil-wealth. Devastated by the ecological costs of oil spillage and the highest gas flaring rates in the world, the Niger Delta is a political tinderbox. A generation of militant 'restive' youth, deep political frustrations among oil-producing communities, and pre-electoral thuggery all combine to prosper in the rich soil of political marginalization. The massive rigging of elections across the delta in the April 2003 elections simply confirmed the worst for the millions of Nigerians who have suffered from decades of neglect.

The Middle East historian Robert Vitalis (2002) has recently suggested that the rapid, complete and irreversible rise of American dominance in Saudi Arabia can shed much light on why 'the Niger Delta is currently in crisis'. And indeed it is. Since 12 March 2003, mounting communal violence accounting for at least fifty deaths, and the levelling of eight communities in and around the Warri petroleum complex, has prompted all the major oil companies to withdraw staff, to close down operations and reduce output by over 750,000 barrels per day (almost half of national output). President Obasanjo has dispatched large troop deployments to the oil-producing creeks, prompting Ijaw militants, incensed over indiscriminate military action and illegal oil bunkering in which the security forces were implicated, to threaten the detonation of eleven captured oil installations. The strikes on the offshore oil platforms—a long-festering sore that rarely reaches the media—were quickly resolved but nobody seriously expects that the deeper problems within the oil sector will go away. Relatively new to delta politics, however, are a series of assassinations, the most shocking being the killing of Chief Marshall Harry, a senior member of the main opposition party and leading campaigner for greater resource allocation to the oil-producing Niger Delta. Fallout from the Harry assassination has already become a source of tension in his native oil-producing state of Rivers where supporters of the main opposition party, the All Nigeria Peoples Party, and another opposition grouping of activists and politicians, the Rivers Democratic Movement, have linked the ruling party to the assassination. With good reason, the business-as-usual character of the gubernatorial election victories across the oil-producing states, has led some to believe that Nigeria is another Colombia in the making (Cesarz et al. 2003).

The strategic significance of Nigeria is incontestable. One of every five Africans is a Nigerian; Nigeria is the world's seventh largest exporter of petroleum and a key player in African regional security, most recently in Sierra Leone. Nigeria is an archetypal oil nation. Three quarters of government revenues, and almost all export earnings, flow from black gold. A long-time member of the Organization of the Petroleum Exporting Countries (OPEC), and the fifth largest supplier of oil exports to the US, Nigeria pumps oil much coveted for its 'lightness' and 'sweetness', yielding more gasoline and diesel than the 'sour' crude from the Middle East. It is also home to a vast Muslim community. Since the oil boom of the 1970s, political power has shifted from the conservative Sufi brotherhoods to well-organized modern Islamist groups like the Yan Izala founded in 1978. Shari'a law, of a dogmatic and literalist sort, has been adopted and implemented in twelve of the populous northern states, amidst considerable political acrimony and international censure. At least 350 people were killed in four days of terrible rioting in northern Nigeria triggered by protests against US military action in Afghanistan, including particularly bloody clashes between Muslims and Christians in Kano, Kaduna and Jos.

Olesegun Obasanjo's presidential victory in 1999, in the wake of the darkest period of military rule in Nigeria's forty year post-Independence history, held much promise. An internationally recognized statesman and diplomat, imprisoned during the brutal Abacha years, he inherited the mantle of a massively corrupt state apparatus, an economy in shambles, and a federation crippled by longstanding ethnic enmity. Committed to reforming a corrupt and undisciplined military—the largest in Africa—and to deepening the process of democratization, Obasanjo was confronted within months of his inauguration by militant ethnic groups speaking the language of self-determination, local autonomy and resource control (meaning a greater share of the federally allocated oil revenues). In an incident widely condemned by the human rights community, some 2,000 persons were slaughtered in Odi, Bayelsa State, after federal troops were dispatched in response to clashes between local militants and the police. Obasanjo has consistently refused to apologize for the murders and there has been no full inquiry. In 2002, the military was involved in yet another massacre, this time in the Middle Belt, in Benue and Taraba States, the most serious communal conflict since the clashes preceding the outbreak of the Biafran civil war in 1967. On President Obasanjo's watch, over 10,000 have perished in ethnic violence. He has failed miserably to address the human rights violations by the notoriously corrupt Nigerian security forces. Early in his tenure, Obasanjo did retire a number of senior officers and embark upon an anti-corruption campaign, aided and abetted by the US's role in 'retraining' the Nigerian armed forces. President Clinton committed foreign assistance to 'reprofessionalize' the Nigerian army in 1999, including the equipping and training of seven battalions at a cost of over $ 1 billion. During the Bush's imperium, the presence of 200 Special Forces in Nigeria, including on-site training grounds in some of the most sensitive areas of the Muslim north, has generated enormous suspicion and now vocal opposition. Not unexpectedly, a number of powerful Nigerian constituencies see a beleaguered and corrupt Obasanjo regime as simply another miserable US oil colony.

The *zeitgeist* of oil—its mythic and spectacular qualities in relation to the modern—is an essential expression of contemporary hydrocarbon capitalism. Oil's fetishistic appeal was not lost on the great Polish journalist Ryszard Kapucinski who, in his reflections on oil-rich pre-revolutionary Iran, sardonically observed that, 'Oil creates the illusion of a completely changed life, life without work, life for free.... The concept of oil expresses perfectly the eternal human dream of wealth achieved through lucky accident...In this sense oil is a fairy tale and like every fairy tale a bit of a lie' (1982: 35). It is this lie, one might say, that currently confronts West African oil producers, and Nigeria in particular.

A RESOURCE CURSE?

In virtue of the geo-strategic significance of oil to contemporary capitalism—and to US hegemony in particular—relations between natural resources (and oil in particular) and economic growth, democracy, and civil war have emerged as an object of substantial scholarly attention (operating under the sign of 'resource politics'), not least by economists and political scientists.[11] The International Monetary Fund (IMF) and its stenographers have posited a strong association between resource-dependency, corruption and economic performance. Sachs and Warner (1995) argue that one standard deviation increase in the ratio of natural resource exports to Gross National Product (GNP) is associated with a decrease of just over 1 per cent in the growth rate (irrespective of the endogeneity of corruption, commodity price variability and trade liberalization). Leite and Weidmann (1999) believe that for fuels the figure is 0.6 per cent and due 'entirely to the indirect effect of corruption' (p. 29). For Michael Klare (2001), writing from a very different vantage point, oil is a dwindling, key-strategic resource that will necessarily be generative of inter-state conflict (see also Homer-Dixon 1999).[12] This is a line of argumentation developed by Paul Collier (2000), who, in his work with the World Bank, uses resource dependency as a way of thinking about rebellion (especially in Africa), with oil posited as central to the *economics of civil war*. It encourages extortion and looting through resource predation (at least up to the point where 26 per cent of GDP is dependent on resource extraction). And the feasibility of predation by states or rebel groups determines the risk of conflict. For Collier, the risks are greater because of resource dependency than ethnic or religious diversity. Oil is a 'resource curse'. Ross elaborates on this claim seeing oil in terms of its *rentier effect* (low taxes and high patronage dampen pressures for democracy); its *repression effect* conferred by direct state control over sufficient revenues to bankroll excessive military expenditures and expanded internal security apparatuses; and a *modernization effect*, namely the 'move into industrial and service sector jobs render them less likely to push for democracy' (2001b: 357).[13] This comes terribly close to a sort

[11] Economists typically distinguish direct (so-called Dutch Disease) effects in which resource booms lead to recession, and indirect effects through rent seeking and institution building.

[12] For an elaborate critique of this position, see Peluso and Watts (2001).

[13] Ross (2001b) provides a shopping list of the consequences of oil: limited backward linkages, inelastic demand, labour extensive, subject to boom and

of commodity determinism confirming perhaps Coronil's point that oil, more than any other commodity, 'illustrates both the importance and the mystification of natural resources in the modern world' (Coronil 1997: 49). But if oil hinders democracy (as though copper might liberate parliamentary democracy?), one needs to appreciate the centralizing effect of oil and the state in relation to the oil-based nation-building enterprises that are unleashed in the context of a politics that pre-dates oil.

Much of the resource curse analysis runs the risk of imputing enormous powers to oil (without grasping its specificity), conflating petroleum's purported Olympian powers with pre-existing political dynamics, and, as in the case of Collier, misidentifying a predation-proneness for what is in fact the dynamics of state and corporate enclave politics (Leonard and Strauss 2003). What is striking in so much of what passes as 'resource politics' is the total invisibility of both transnational oil companies (which typically work in joint ventures with the state) and the specific forms of rule associated with petro-capitalism. My analysis charts the relations between oil and violence, but does so through examining how forms of governable (or non-governable spaces) are created through the analytics of 'authoritarian governmentality' (Dean 1999) growing out of the soil of petro-capitalism. Rather than see oil-dependency as a source of predation or as a source of state military power, I explore how oil capitalism produces particular sorts of enclave economies and particular sorts of governable spaces characterized by violence and instability. To do so, the qualities of oil in relation to predation matter (oil and diamonds are after all very different sources of predation: see Le Billon [2001b]). But so do the powers of transnational oil companies, the character of what I call 'the oil complex', and the ways in which oil as a territorially based and nationalised commodity can become the basis for making claims. Unlike the work of Collier and others, I seek to trace the varieties of violence engendered by oil, to elaborate the ways in which

---

bust cycles, subject to rent seeking and so on. At the very least one needs to be clear how oil differs from other commodities (in order to be able to distinguish what is peculiar to oil as opposed to extraction in general), and to be able to distinguish what is it about the resource (and not the political context into which it is inserted) that can explain the so-called 'paradox of plenty' (see Gary and Karl [2003] as a case in point).

resources, territoriality and identity can constitute forms of rule (or unrule), and understand the genesis of economies of violence that emerge from differing sorts of governable (or ungovernable) spaces.

BLACK GOLD AND THE NIGER DELTA

The Niger Delta is a vast sedimentary basin constructed through successive layers of sediments dating back 40–50 million years to the Eocene epoch. A classic arcuate delta covering almost 70,000 square kilometres, the Niger Delta is also endowed with very substantial hydrocarbon deposits. Crude oil production currently runs at almost two million barrels per day, roughly 90 per cent by value of Nigerian export revenues. Nigeria is not only the largest producer of petroleum in Africa and is among the world's top ten oil producers but, in the wake of September 11 and the current Middle East crisis, it is being pursued by the Bush Administration as a major supplier for the US market.

The contemporary geo-strategic significance of the Niger Delta has emerged from an astonishing ethnic and linguistic complexity, and from a recent history of economic and political irrelevance. There are five major linguistic categories (Ijoid, Yoruboid, Edoid, Igboid and Delta Cross), but each embraces a profusion of ethno-linguistic heterogeneity. The establishment of the Nigerian colony and the imposition of Indirect Rule in the early 1900s marked an end to the brief period of commercial vitality associated with the commercialization of palm oil across the region in the nineteenth century. For most of the first half of the twentieth century, the delta was an economic and political backwater. In the gradual transition to Independence in the 1950s, the so-called ethnic minorities voiced their concerns to the departing British administrators that their interests in a Nigerian federation dominated by three ethnic majorities (the Hausa, the Yoruba and the Ibo) were to all intents and purposes invisible. What was true at the moment of imperial departure only became more so as the postcolonial period got under way.

The onset of commercial petroleum production in the heart of the delta in 1956—discovered in Oloibiri in current Bayelsa State— seemed to hold out the promise of rapid development for the ethnic minorities. But instead, the presence of transnational oil companies in

joint ventures with the Nigerian State (through the Nigerian National
Petroleum Company [NNPC]) produced enormous environmental
despoliation and a crisis in extant forms of livelihood. By the 1970s
and 1980s, a number of ethnic communities had begun to mobilize
against the so-called 'slick alliance' of oil companies and the Nigerian
military. Most famously, the Movement for the Survival of the Ogoni
People (MOSOP) led by Ken Saro-Wiwa challenged Shell for its
environmental despoliation and human rights violations and the
Nigerian state for its unjust control of 'their oil'. Saro-Wiwa and the
MOSOP leadership were executed by the Nigerian military in 1995,
but since that time the Niger Delta has become a zone of intense
conflict as more oil-producing minorities (for instance, the Adoni, the
Itsekiri, the Ijaw) clamour for compensation and for the recognition
of their claims for resource control. As I write, substantial coverage in
the world press has been devoted to a group of Delta women who have
occupied Chevron oil refineries, demanding company investments
and jobs for indigenes.[14]

I want to make three important points about oil in Nigeria. The
first is that oil capitalism operates through what I call an 'oil complex'
(comparable in, say, Venezuela or Gabon or Indonesia) involving a
statutory monopoly over mineral exploitation (the 1969 Petroleum
Law in Nigeria, reinforced by a number of key laws including the
1978 Land Use Decree), a nationalized oil company (NNPC) that
operates through joint ventures with oil majors who are granted
territorial concessions (blocs), the security apparatuses of the state
(and the companies) to ensure that costly investments are secured,
the oil-producing communities, and an apolitical mechanism (in
Nigeria called the 'derivation principle') by which federal oil revenues
are distributed to the states (Anugwom 2001; Ibeanu 2003). This
oil complex, rather than a laundry list of oil-attributes *a la* Ross, is
key to understanding the relations between oil and violence. The
second is that this oil complex matters profoundly to the character
and dynamics of Nigerian development. Oil is, of course, a biophysical
entity (a subterranean fluid capable of being pumped and transmitted);
it is also a commodity that enters the market with its price tag, and
as such is the bearer of particular relations of production. And, not

[14] *New York Times*, 13 August 2002.

least, oil harbours fetishistic qualities: it is the bearer of meanings, hopes, expectations of unimaginable powers. Not unexpectedly, oil is a constant in the popular Nigerian imagination (see Watts 2000), resplendent with all manner of brilliant and unctuous qualities. The third point is that Nigerian petro-capitalism contains a sort of double-movement, a contradictory unity of capitalism and modernity captured in the fact that oil production in Nigeria has always been a joint venture, currently with fourteen transnational companies, in which joint operating agreements determine the distribution of royalties and rents. On the one hand, oil has been a centralizing force that has rendered the state more visible and globalized, underwriting a process of secular nationalism and state building. On the other, a corrupt and undisciplined oil-led development, driven by an unremitting political logic of ethnic claims making, has fragmented and discredited the state and its forms of governance. It has produced a set of conditions that have compromised and undermined the very tenets of the modern nation state. Coronil (1997) refers to this conundrum as 'the Faustian trade of money for modernity', which in Venezuela brought 'the illusion of development'. In Nigeria, too, the double movement brought illusion and produced forms of governable spaces that questioned the very idea of Nigeria, spaces that generated forms of rule, conduct and imagining at cross purposes with one another, antithetical to the very idea of a coherent modern nation state that oil, in the mythos of the West, represented.

ECONOMIES OF VIOLENCE AND GOVERNABLE SPACES

Government, for Michel Foucault (2000), referred famously to the 'conduct of conduct', a more or less calculated and rational set of ways of shaping conduct and securing rule through a multiplicity of authorities and agencies in and outside the state, and at a variety of spatial levels. In contrast to forms of pastoral power in the Middle Ages from which a sense of sovereignty was derived, Foucault charted an important historical shift, beginning in the sixteenth century, towards government as a right manner of disposing things 'so as to not lead to the common good…but to an end that is convenient for each of the things governed' (2000: 211). The new practices of the state, as Mitchell Dean (1999: 16) says, shape human conduct by 'working through our desire, aspirations, interests and beliefs for definite but shifting ends'. It was Foucault's task to reveal the genealogy of government, and the origins of modern power, the fabrication of a modern identity. The conduct of conduct—governmentality—could be expressed as pastoral, disciplinary or as biopower. Modern governmentality was rendered distinctive by the specific forms in which the population and the economy were administered, and specifically by a deepening of the 'governmentalization of the state' (how sovereignty comes to be articulated through the populations and the processes that constitute them). What was key for Foucault was neither the displacement of one form of power by another, nor the historical substitution of feudal by modern governmentality, but the complex triangulation involved in sustaining many forms of power put to the purpose of security and regulation (Foucault 2000: 219).

On this theoretical canvas, I seek to explore the relations between two interrelated aspects of governmentality.[15] One is what Foucault explicitly refers to as relations between men and resources (in my case, people and oil in the Niger Delta) as an expression of his complex notion of the governance of things. As he put it:

On the contrary, in [the modern exercise of power], you will notice that the definition of government in no way refers to territory: one governs *things*. But what does this mean? I think this is not a matter of opposing things to men, but rather of showing that what government has to do with is not territory but, rather, a sort of complex composed on men and things. The things, in this sense, with which government is to be concerned are in fact men, but *men in their relations, their links, their imbrication with those things that are wealth, resources, means of subsistence, the territory with its specific qualities, climate, irrigation, fertility, and so on; men in their relation to those other things that are customs, habits, ways of acting and thinking and so on; and finally men in relation to those still other things that might be accidents and misfortunes such as famines, epidemics, death and so on....*What counts is essentially this complex of men and things; property and territory are merely one of its variables (2000: 208–9).

---

[15] Some of these Foucauldian ideas have already been productively deployed in the understanding of nature and resource management—what one might call 'green governmentality'—and the relations between nature and nationalism. See Braun (2000).

The other aspect of governmentality that I use is taken from Rose's notion of 'governable spaces' as they emerge from the analytics of government detailed above. For Rose, governable spaces and the spatialization of government are 'modalities in which a real and material governable world is composed, terraformed, and populated' (1999: 32). The scales upon which government is 'territorialized'—territory is derived from *terra*, land, but also *terrere*, to frighten—are myriad: the factory, the neighbourhood, the commune, the region, the nation. Each of these governable spaces has its own topology and is modelled, as Rose puts it, through systems of cognition and remodelled through government practice, in a way that frames how such topoi have emerged: the social thought and practice that has territorialized itself upon the nation, the city, the village or the factory. The map has been central to this process as a mode of objectification, marking and inscribing, but also as 'a little machine for producing conviction in others' (ibid.: 37). But in general it was geography that formed 'the art whose science was political economy'.[16] Modern space and modern governable spaces were produced by the biological (the laws of population which determine the qualities of the inhabitants) and the economic (the systems of the production of wealth). Governable spaces necessitate the territorializing of governmental thought and practice but are simultaneously produced as differing scales by the cold laws of political economy.

The Nigerian oil complex can be grasped in territorial terms, taking as my cue Nikolas Rose's point about enclosures:

Governmental thought territorializes itself in different ways.... We can analyse the ways in which the idea of a territorially bounded, politically governed nation state under sovereign authority took shape.... One can trace anomalous governmental histories of smaller-scale territories...and one can also think of these [as] spaces of enclosure that governmental thought has imagined and penetrated...how [does it] happen that social thought territorializes itself on the problem of [for example] the slum in the nineteenth century?' (Rose 1999: 34–6).

I want to think about the genesis of differing sorts of governable spaces in Nigeria as part of a larger landscape of what Dean calls 'authoritarian governmentality', that is to say an articulation of generalized uses of

[16] Rhein quoted in Rabinow (1989: 142).

the instruments of repression with bio-politics. As he says, 'it regards its subjects' capacity for action as subordinate to the expectation of obedience' (Dean 1999: 209). I want to root these spaces and forms of power in the logic of petro-capitalist development, that is to say a particular sort of extractive development which is generative of differing sorts of scale, or the 'politics of scale' as Neil Smith (1992) calls it. My analysis conversely charts the relations between oil and violence, but does so through examining how forms of governable (or un-governable) spaces are generated by the baneful twins of authoritarian government and petro-capitalism. To do so, I will turn briefly to governable spaces, and to three in particular that I shall refer to as the space of chieftainship, the space of indigeneity, and the space of the nation state.

The Space of Chieftainship

The Nembe community[17] in Bayelsa State stands at the originary point of Nigerian oil production. In the 1950s, the Tennessee Oil Company (a US company) began oil explorations there but oil was not found until much later when Shell D'Arcy unearthed the Oloibiri oil field in Ogbia. Subsequent explorations led to the opening of the large and rich Nembe oil fields near the coast in Okpoama and Twon-Brass axis. Currently, the four Nembe oil fields produce approximately 150,000 barrels of high quality petroleum through joint operating agreements between the NNPC, Agip Nigeria, and Shell. If Nembe is the ground zero of oil production, it is also a theatre of extraordinary violence and intra-community conflict, the result of intense competition over political turf and the control of benefits from the oil industry. The violence can be traced back to the late 1980s when the Nembe Council of Chiefs acquired power from then king, Justice Alagoa Mingi IX, to negotiate royalties and other benefits with the oil companies. The combination of youth-driven violence and intense political competition has transformed Nembe's system of governance

---

[17] Nembe in its macro-usage refers to six towns (Bassimbiri, Ogbolomabiri, Okpoama, Odioma, and Akassa) that are among the sixteen towns that comprise Nembe Kingdom. For the purposes of this essay, however, Nembe town refers to Ogbolomabiri only.

and set the stage for further challenges to the traditional authority of chieftainship (see Human Rights Watch 2002; Kemedi 2002).[18]

Oil became commercially viable in the 1970s, but to grasp its transformative effects on Nembe politics and community—that is to understand its genesis as a distinctive governable space—requires an understanding of chieftainship in the Niger Delta. Indirect rule in the colonial period certainly left much of the delta marginalized and isolated, but it also, in the name of tradition, built upon and frequently invented chiefly powers of local rule which in the Nembe case were grafted onto a deep and complex structure of kingship and gerontocratic rule. To understand the dynamics of Nembe as a governable space one must recall that land lay in hands of customary authorities (notwithstanding the fact that the 1969 Petroleum Law granted the state the power to nationalize all oil resources). Land rights and therefore claims on oil royalties were, from the outset, rooted in the *amayanabo* (king), and derivatively the subordinate powers, namely the Council of Chiefs and the Executive Council. Historically, the Nembe community possessed a rigid political hierarchy consisting of the amayanabo presiding over, in descending order, the chiefs (or heads of the war canoe houses[19]) elected by the entire war canoe houses constituted by their prominent sons. Although the chiefs were subservient to the amayanabo, they acted as his closest advisors, supporting him in the event of military threat and, in turn, were responsible for electing the amayanabo from the Mingi group of Houses, or the royal line. The current Nembe Council of Chiefs is the assemblage of the recognized Chiefs of Nembe 'chalked' by the king.[20]

---

[18] The data for the case study was collected during a visit to the Niger Delta in January and February 2001. I also rely on the assistance of Von Kemedi and his work (Kemedi 2002) and the Nembe Peace Commission (Alagoa 2001).

[19] The war canoe houses were the units of the kingdom's defence forces. A war canoe house consisted of the head of the house and a formidable number of able-bodied men who were responsible for defending the house and the king.

[20] There is a long running dispute over kingly authority that has spilled over into the establishment of local government areas (LGAs). In this essay I do not address the conflicts between Bassambiri and Ogbolamabiri (two contiguous towns) over the authority of their respective paramount chiefs, and disputes over LGA territory (and hence access to oil rents).

Accordingly, in 1991, the Nembe monarch's ineffectiveness in dealing with the oil companies led to a radical decentralization of his powers to the Council of Chiefs, headed by Chief Egi Adukpo Ikata. Insofar as the Council now dealt directly with Shell, and handled large quantities of money paid by the oil companies, competition for election to the Council intensified as various political factions struggled for office. By 2000, the Council had expanded from twenty-six to ninety persons. Coeval with the evisceration of kingly powers, the deepening of the Council mandate, and the expansion of the Council members, was a subtle process of 'youth mobilization'. In an age-graded society like the Nembe Ijaw, youth refers to persons typically between their teens and early 40s who, whatever achievements they may have obtained (university degrees, fatherhood and so on), remain subservient to their elders. Central to any understanding of the emergence of a militant youth in Nembe town was the catalytic role, played by a former company engineer with Elf Oil Company named Nimi B.P. Barigha-Amage. He deployed his knowledge of the oil industry to organize the youths of the Nembe community into a force capable of extracting concessions from the oil companies, in essence, by converting cultural organizations into protection services. Chief Ikata was quick to exploit the awareness and restiveness of the youths to pressure Shell into granting community entitlements. A pact between Chief Ikata and the young engineer was in effect instituted; the engineer supplied the youths with information regarding community entitlements, and the chief deployed his knowledge of military logistics to organize the shutting down of flow stations, the seizure of equipment and sabotage (Alagoa 2001; Human Rights Watch 2002).

Armed with insider knowledge of the companies and an understanding of a loosely defined set of rules regarding company compensation for infringements on community property, Barigha-Amage pushed for the creation of youth 'cultural groups' which gradually, with the support of some members of the Council of Chiefs, intermediated with oil companies and their liaison officers, and manipulated the system of compensation in the context of considerable juridical and legal ambiguity. Liaison officers, colluding with community representatives, invented ritual or cultural sites that had ostensibly been compromised or damaged by oil operations, for which monies exchanged hands. As the opportunities for appropriating company resources in the name of compensation became visible through the success of the cultural groups, other sections of the youth community began to organize, in turn, around clan and familial affiliations. In 1994, for example, a group called 'House of Lords' (*Isongoforo*) was created by a former university lecturer, Lionel Jonathan, and a year later, in 1995, Mrs Ituro-Garuba, wife of a well-placed military officer, established *Agbara-foro*. Inevitably, with much at stake financially, and control of the space between community and company in the balance, conflicts within and among youth groups proliferated and deepened. In turn, growing community militancy spilled over into often-violent altercations with the much-detested mobile police ('Mopos') and local government authorities. The regional state and governor attempted to intervene as conditions deteriorated but a government report, on which such action was predicated, was never released for political reasons. A subsequent banning of youth groups had, as a result, no practical effect (Human Rights Watch 2002).

Slowly, the subversion of royal authority, the strategic alliances between youth and chiefs, and the growing (and armed) conflict between youth groups for access to Shell resulted in the ascendancy of a highly militant Isongoforo. In an environment of rampant insecurity and lawlessness, the occupation and closure of flow stations, and tensions between the companies, the service companies and the local security forces, the Isongoforo was provided 'stand by' payments by the companies (that is to say, it was hired for protection purposes), even as it colluded with the community liaison officers to invent compensations cases. The Isongoforo occupied the centre of a new governable space, which it ruled through force rather than any sense of consent or customary authority. This quasi-mafia was funded by the large quantities of monies that it commanded from the companies, and by the arms which it controlled. This volatile state of affairs collapsed dramatically as local resentments and struggles proliferated. In February 2000, a 'People's Revolution' overthrew Isongoforo, ostensibly precipitated by the humiliation of the Council of Chiefs at the hands of Shell (backed by the intimidating Isongoforo forces). The chiefs now orchestrated the occupation of flow stations and undermined the powers of Isongoforo by recruiting and supporting other youth groups. By May 2000 Isongoforo had been sent into exile but it was promptly replaced in the wake of Barigha-Amage's return as High Chief of Nembe, by his own 'cultural group' *Isenasawo/ Teme*. Teme instituted a rule of terror and chaos far worse than its predecessors. It too proved unstable in the context of excessive youth mobilization and split into two factions, which subsequently produced two 'counter coups' and much bloodshed. A government Peace Commission was established in January 2001 in a desperate effort to bring peace to one of the jewels in the oil-producing crown (Alagoa 2001; NDWC 2000).

Much of this later violence (after 1996) could not be regulated by the state authorities because of its concurrence with the 1999 elections in which some of the key youth leaders were expected to deliver votes for the incumbent gubernatorial race. In the creation of what, in effect, was a sort of vigilante rule, there were complex complicities between chiefs, youth groups, local security forces, and the companies. Plans to occupy oil flow stations (for purposes of extortion) were often known in advance and involved collaboration with local company engineers; youths were *de facto* company employees providing protection services, and the local compensation and community officers of Shell and Agip produced fraudulent compensation cases and entitlements. Nembe, a town with its own long and illustrious history and politics, had become a sort of company town in which authority had shifted from the king to warring factions of youth who were in varying ways in the pay of, and working in conjunction with, the companies. The Council of Chiefs stood in a contradictory position, seeking to maintain control over revenues from the companies and yet intimidated and undermined by the militant youth groups on whom it depended. In the context of a weak and corrupt state, the genesis of this power nexus bears striking resemblances to the genesis of the Mafia in nineteenth-century Sicily (Blok 1974).

What I have described is the displacement of a specific form of power (chieftainship) by a governable space of civic vigilantism, a thickening of civil society that does not necessarily imply the basis of the kind of governance put forth by Granovetter, Putnam and others (see Putnam 2000)—that is, the self-organizing networks that arise out of the interactions between a variety of organizations and agencies. Civic powers have expanded by overthrowing a territorial system and a gerontocratic royal order. Youth mobilization—whose political affiliations and ambitions in any case were complex because they reflected an unstable amalgam of clan, family and local electoral loyalties—had thrown up an identity and subject that was indisputably revolutionary, representing an unholy alliance between civic organizations (presenting themselves as cultural organizations) and private companies. Rule in Nembe is a realm of privatized violence, a form of consent by a form of force. Government here turns on what Foucault (2000: 208–9) calls 'men in their imbrication with wealth and resources'—the government of men and things, as opposed to territory. It is institutionalized through forms of calculability, *techne*, and visibility that emerge from the legal and company dispositions to regulate local populations backed by the forces of repression. The governable subject is de facto a sort of employee, and rule is a Gramscian 'war of position'. Culture serves as the form by which company rule is experienced—violent youth groups—but in a way that renders the space increasingly *ungovernable*.

The Space of Indigeneity

The Niger Delta is a region of considerable, even bewildering, ethno-linguistic complexity. The eastern region, of which the delta is a part, is dominated statistically by the Ibo majority, but there is a long history of excluded ethnic minorities in the delta dating back at least to the 1950s when the Willinck Commission took note of the inter-ethnic complexity of the region. Throughout the colonial period prior to arrival of commercial oil production, there had been efforts by various minorities, who saw themselves as dominated by the Ibo, to established Native Authorities of their own. In the 1960s, prior to the outbreak of civil war, two charismatic local figures, both Ijaw—Nottingham Dick and Isaac Boro—declared a Delta Republic, a desperate cry for some sort of political inclusion that lasted a mere twelve days. The ill-fated Delta People's Republic of 1966 was the forerunner of what is now a prairie fire of ethnic mobilization by the historically excluded minorities—now tagged as 'indigenous' in order to capture the political and legal legitimacy conferred by the International Labour Organization of the United Nations (ILO169) (see Brysk 2000; Nelson 1999). The paradigmatic case in the delta is of the struggle by Ken Saro-Wiwa and the MOSOP. Their case reveals a rather different sort of governable space, one marked by ethnic subjects and indigenous territory.

The Ogoni are typically seen as a distinct ethnic group, consisting of three sub-groups and six clans dotted over 404 square miles of creeks, waterways and tropical forest in the northeast fringes of the Niger Delta. Located administratively in Rivers State, a Louisiana-like territory of some 50,000 square kilometres, Ogoniland is one of the most heavily populated zones in all of Africa. The most densely settled areas of Ogoniland—over 1,500 persons per square kilometre—are also the sites of the largest oil wells. Ogoniland's customary productive base was provided by fishing and agricultural pursuits until the discovery of petroleum, including the huge Bomu field, immediately prior to Independence. Part of an enormously complex regional ethnic mosaic, the Ogoni were drawn into internecine conflicts within the delta region, largely as a consequence of the slave trade and its aftermath, in the period prior to the arrival of colonial forces at Kono in 1901. The Ogoni resisted the British until 1908 (Naanen 1995) but thereafter were left to stagnate as part of the Opopo Division within Calabar Province. As Ogoniland was gradually incorporated during the 1930s, the clamour for a separate political division grew at the hands of the first pan-Ogoni organization, the Ogoni Central Union, which bore fruit with the establishment of the Ogoni Native Authority in 1947. In 1951, however, the authority was forcibly integrated into the Eastern Region. Experiencing tremendous neglect and discrimination, integration raised longstanding fears among the Ogoni of Ibo domination.[21] Politically marginalized and economically neglected, the delta minorities feared the growing secessionist rhetoric of the Ibo and consequently led an ill-fated secession of their own in February 1966. Ogoni antipathy to what they saw as a sort of internal colonialism at the hands of the Ibo led to their support of the federal forces during the civil war. While a Rivers State was established in 1967—which compensated in some measure for enormous Ogoni losses during the war—the new state recapitulated in microcosm the larger 'national question'. The

[21] As constitutional preparations were made for the transition to home rule, non-Igbo minorities throughout the Eastern Region appealed to the colonial government for a separate Rivers State. Ogoni representatives lobbied the Willink Commission in 1958 to avert the threat of exclusion within an Ibo-dominated regional government, which had assumed self-governing status in 1957, but minority claims were ignored (Okilo 1980; Okpu 1977).

new Rivers State was multi-ethnic but presided over by the locally
dominant Ijaw, for whom the minorities felt little but contempt.[22]

During the first oil boom of the 1970s, Ogoniland's fifty-six wells
accounted for almost 15 per cent of Nigerian oil production[23] and
in the past three decades an estimated $ 30 billion in petroleum
revenues have flowed from this Lilliputian territory. It was, as local
opinion had it, 'Nigeria's Kuwait'. Yet according to a government
commission, Oloibiri, where the first oil was pumped in 1958, has
no single kilometre of all-season road and remains 'one of the most
backward areas in the country' (cited in Furro 1992: 282; see also
Okonta and Douglas 2001). Rivers State saw its federal allocation
fall dramatically in absolute and relative terms. At the height of the
oil boom, 60 per cent of oil production came from Rivers State but it
received only 5 per cent of the statutory allocation (roughly half of
that received by Kano, Northeastern States and the Ibo heartland,
East Central State). Between 1970 and 1980 it received in revenues
one-fiftieth of the value of the oil it produced. Few Ogoni households
have electricity, there is one doctor per 100,000 people, child mortality
rates are the highest in the nation, unemployment is 85 per cent, 80
per cent of the population is illiterate and close to half of Ogoni youth
have left the region in search of work. Life expectancy is barely 50
years, substantially below the national average. If Ogoniland failed
to see the material benefits from oil, what it *did* experience was an
ecological disaster—what the European Parliament has called 'an
environmental nightmare'. The heart of the ecological harms stems
from oil spills—either from the pipelines which criss-cross Ogoniland
(often passing directly through villages) or from blowouts at the
wellheads—and gas flaring. As regards the latter, a staggering 76 per
cent of natural gas in the oil-producing areas is flared (compared
to 0.6 per cent in the US). As a visiting environmentalist noted in
1993 in the delta, 'some children have never known a dark night

[22] The Ogoni and other minorities petitioned in 1974 for the creation of a new
Port Harcourt State within the Rivers State boundary (Naanen 1995: 63).

[23] According to the Nigerian government estimates, Ogoniland produces
about two per cent of Nigerian oil output and is the fifth largest oil-producing
community in Rivers State. Shell maintains that total Ogoni oil output is valued
at $ 5.2 billion before costs.

even though they have no electricity'.[24] Burning 24 hours per day at temperatures of 13–14,000 degrees Celsius, Nigerian natural gas produces 35 million tons of CO_2 and 12 million tons of methane, more than the rest of the world (making Nigeria probably the biggest single cause of global warming). The oil spillage record is even worse. There are roughly 300 spills per year in the delta and in the 1970s alone the spillage was four times than the much-publicized Exxon Valdez spill in Alaska. In one year alone, almost 700,000 barrels were soiled according to a government commission. Ogoniland itself suffered 111 spills between 1985 and 1994 (Hammer 1996). Figures provided by the NNPC document 2,676 spills between 1976 and 1990, 59 per cent of which occurred in Rivers State (Ikein 1990: 171), 38 per cent of which were due to equipment malfunction.[25] Between 1982 and 1992 Shell alone accounted for 1.6 million gallons of spilled oil, 37 per cent of the company's spills worldwide. The consequences of flaring, spillage and waste for Ogoni fisheries and farming have been devastating. Two independent studies completed in 1997 reveal total petroleum hydrocarbons in Ogoni streams at 360 and 680 times the European Community permissible levels (Rainforest Action Network 1997; Human Rights Watch 1999).

The hanging of Ken Saro-Wiwa and the 'Ogoni Nine' in November 1995—accused of murdering four prominent Ogoni leaders—and the subsequent arrest of nineteen others on treason charges, represented the summit of a process of mass mobilization and radical militancy which had commenced in 1989. MOSOP necessarily built upon previous cultural and political organizations like the Ogoni Klub and Kagote (both elite organizations), and most especially the Ogoni politician Naaku Paul Birabi who established, in 1950, the Ogoni State Representatives Association to promote Ogoni interests in the new eastern Region Government. The civil war hardened the sense of

[24] *Village Voice*, 21 November 1995, p. 21.

[25] The oil companies claim that sabotage accounts for a large proportion (60 per cent) of the spills, since communities gain from corporate compensation. Shell claims that 77 of 111 spills in Ogoniland between 1985 and 1994 were due to sabotage (Hammer 1996). According to the government commission, however, sabotage accounts for 30 per cent of the incidents but only 3 per cent of the quantity spilled. Furthermore, all oil-producing communities claim that compensation from the companies for spills has been almost non-existent.

external dominance among Ogonis. A 'supreme cultural organization' called Kagote, which consisted largely of traditional rulers and high-ranking functionaries, was established at the war's end. Kagote in turn gave birth in 1990 to MOSOP. A new strategic phase began in 1989 with a programme of mass action and passive resistance on the one hand and a renewed effort to focus on the environmental consequences of oil (and Shell's role in particular) and on group rights within the federal structure on the other. Animating the entire struggle was, in Leton's words, the 'genocide being committed in the dying years of the twentieth century by multinational companies under the supervision of the Government' (cited in Naanen 1995: 66). A watershed moment in MOSOP's history was the drafting in 1990 of an Ogoni Bill of Rights (Saro-Wiwa 1992). Documenting a history of neglect and local misery, the Ogoni Bill took head on the question of Nigerian federalism and minority rights. Calling for participation in the affairs of the republic as 'a distinct and separate entity', the Bill outlined a plan for autonomy and self-determination in which there would be guaranteed 'political control of Ogoni affairs by Ogoni people...the right to control and use a fair proportion of Ogoni economic resources... [and] adequate representation as of right in all Nigerian national institutions' (Saro-Wiwa 1990: 11). In short, the Bill of Rights addressed the question of the *unit* to which revenues should be allocated—and derivatively the rights of minorities (Human Rights Watch 1999; Okonta 2002). At the heart of Saro-Wiwa's vision was an Ogoni state.

In spite of the remarkable history of MOSOP between 1990 and 1996, its ability to represent itself as a unified pan-Ogoni organization remained an open question. There is no pan-Ogoni myth of origin (characteristic of some delta minorities), and a number of the Ogoni subgroups (clans) engender stronger local loyalties than any affiliation to Ogoni 'nationalism'. The Gokana clan, for example, was the most populous and well educated and its elites wielded disproportionate influence in Ogoni. Conversely, the Eleme clan-head did not even sign the Ogoni Bill of Rights and Eleme's leading historian has argued that they are not, in fact, Ogoni. In 1994, Eleme leaders proposed the creation of Nchia state which comprised non-Ogonis from Bonny, Andoni, Opobo and Etche, thereby turning their backs on Saro-Wiwa's goal (Okonta 2003). Furthermore, the MOSOP leaders were actively opposed by elements of the traditional clan leadership, by prominent leaders and civil servants in state government, and by some critics who felt Saro-Wiwa was out to gain 'cheap popularity' (Osaghae 1995: 334). Some Ogoni notables (Edward Kobani, Dr. Leton) aspired to participate in conventional politics by running for the two major parties rather than assisting in the birth of a nation. MOSOP, moreover, was a political movement of the elite led by the elite; it was not a mass movement, and youth and women were not represented on its first Steering Committee. Gradually, the youth wing of MOSOP, which Saro-Wiwa had used, emerged as militant but the leadership was often incapable of controlling it. MOSOP, in short, was wracked by tensions. There were, as Okonta says, 'cracks in the pot' (2003: 12).

Saro-Wiwa built upon over fifty years of Ogoni organizing and upon three decades of resentment against the oil companies, to provide a mass base and a youth-driven radicalism—and an international visibility—capable of challenging state power. Yet at its core, the indigenous subject—and the indigenous space—was contentious and problematic. Ike Okonta (2002) has brilliantly shown, how in the Ogoni case, indigeneity unravelled into fragments of class, clan, generation, and gender. These tensions came to the fore after Saro-Wiwa's death and MOSOP declined as rapidly as it had ascended.

What sort of articulation of indigenous identity and political subjectivity did Saro-Wiwa pose? What sort of governable space did Ogoniland represent? It was clearly one in which territory and oil were the building blocks upon which ethnic differences and indigenous rights were constructed. And yet it was an unstable and contradictory sort of articulation. First, there was no simple sense of 'Ogoniness', no unproblematic unity, and no singular form of political subject (despite Saro-Wiwa's claim that 98 per cent of Ogonis supported him). MOSOP itself had at least five somewhat independent internal strands embracing youth, women, traditional rulers, teachers, and churches. It represented a fractious and increasingly divided 'we', as the splits and conflicts between Saro-Wiwa and other elite Ogoni confirmed (NFG 1996).[26] Second, Saro-Wiwa constantly invoked Ogoni culture

[26] Saro-Wiwa was often chastised by Gokana (he himself was Bane) since most of the Ogoni oil was in fact located below Gokana soil. In other words, on

and tradition yet he also argued that war and internecine conflict had virtually destroyed the fabric of Ogoni society by 1900 (Saro-Wiwa 1992: 14). His own utopia then rested on the re-creation of Ogoni culture and suffered like all *ur*-histories from a quasi-mythic invocation of the past. Third, ethnicity was the central problem of postcolonial Nigeria—the corruption of ethnic majorities—and for Saro-Wiwa its panacea (the multiplication of ethnic minority power). To invoke the history of exclusion and the need for ethnic minority inclusion as the basis for federalism, led Saro-Wiwa to ignore the histories and geographies of conflict and struggle among and between ethnic minorities. Saro-Wiwa's brilliance, then, was to make MOSOP a green, indigenous movement (with international backing and visibility) and to take the movement to the poor and the young to secure a powerful identity, in the face of elite opposition (and his own marginal position in the 1980s). Saro-Wiwa's crowning glory was Ogoni National Day on 4 January 1993 when he presided over the birth of the Ogoni flag, the Ogoni anthem and the National Youth Council of the Ogoni People.

Paradoxically, the MOSOP surfaced as a foundational indigenous movement even though Ogoni's significance as an oil-producing region was diminishing. By the late 1990s, MOSOP had fallen apart as a movement and inter-group struggles deprived it of much of its previous momentum and visibility. But it gave birth to what one might call indigenous movements among oil-producing communities. The same forces have spawned a raft of self-determination indigenous movements among the Ijaw, Isoko, Urhobo, Itsekiri, Ogbia among others (Obi 2001). MOSOP itself fell apart precisely as these other movements gained power. Since the return to civilian rule in 1999, there has been a rash of such minority movements across the delta calling for 'resource control', autonomy, and a national sovereign conference to rewrite the Nigerian constitution. At the same time the Niger Delta has become ever more engulfed in civil strife: militant occupations of oil flow stations, pipeline sabotage, intra-urban ethnic violence, and the near-anarchy of state security operating in tandem with company security forces. The shock troops of many of these

---

occasion, the key territorial unit became the clan or clan territory rather than a sense of pan-Ogoni territory.

indigenous movements are youth and women, and the multiplication of ethnic youth movements is one of the most important political developments in contemporary Nigeria. And it is here that the politics of oil-producing communities meet up with the politics of oil-producing indigenous groups.

What does the Ogoni case reveal, then, as a governable space? Particular 'populations' have been constructed as indigenous. As I explain ahead, this construction emerged from the nationalist struggle as customary rights were added to a discourse of citizenship. But the process received enormous energy as indigeneity as a political category garnered international support in the last part of the twentieth century, a resource that Saro-Wiwa deployed brilliantly (Bob 2002). The emergence of a national debate in Nigeria over resource control in the late 1990s is precisely a product of indigenous claims making on the state, a process by which ethnic identifications must be discursively and politically produced. The Ogoni case shows that there is no pre-given ethnic identity, but complex and unstable genealogies of identification that have emerged in the last century (see Li 1996). The indigene has to be made—interpellated—around a strong sense of territory and tradition but in the context of cultural, economic and political heterogeneity. This was achieved through an imbrication of things and people—oil and ethnicity—and it has been generative of a profusion of indigenous movements. Indigeneity has, in this sense, unleashed the huge political energies of ethnic minorities who recapitulate in some respects the postcolonial history of 'spoils politics' in Nigeria. The effect of this multi-ethnic mobilization was the production of political and civic organizations and new forms of governable space, a veritable jigsaw of militant particularisms. The Kaiama Declaration in 1999 indicates that there is a pan-ethnic solidarity movement in the works, but its contours are at present limited (see Okonta and Douglas 2001; Environmental Rights Action 2000). As the Ogoni case shows, much of this visibility and identification turned on the invention and reinvention of tradition and local knowledge, with an eye to the Nigerian constitution and international politics (Nelson 1999). This is a case of the multiplication of governable spaces which stand in some tension or even contradiction with each other—they account for the explosion of inter-ethnic tensions in the delta—and within the national space of Nigeria, to which I now turn.

The Space of Nationalism

One of the striking aspects of the governable spaces of indigeneity as they emerge in the delta is that they become vehicles for political claims, typically articulated as the need for a local government or, in some cases, a state. Indigeneity necessarily raises the question of a third governable space, that of the nation state, an entity that pre-existed oil and came to fruition in 1960 at Independence. Oil in this sense became part of the nation-building process—the creation of an 'oil nation'. Nature and nationalism become inextricably linked. But how did petro-capitalism—understood as a state-led, and thoroughly globalized, development strategy—stand in relation to the creation of the governable space called modern Nigeria?

As Mahmood Mamdani (1996, 2000) has observed, colonial rule and decentralized despotism were synonymous. The Native Authorities consolidated local class power in the name of tradition (ethnicity) and sustained a racialized view of civic rights. The Nationalist movement had two wings, a radical and a mainstream. Both wished to deracialize civic rights but the latter won out and reproduced the dual legacy of colonialism. They provided civic rights for all Nigerians, but a bonus 'customary rights' for indigenous people. The country had to decide which ethnic groups were indigenous and which were not a basis for political representation, a process that became constitutionally mandated in Nigeria. Federal institutions are quota-driven for each state but only those indigenous to the state may apply for a quota. As Mamdani (1998: 7) puts it: 'The effective elements of the federation are neither territorial units called states nor ethnic groups but ethnic groups with their own states.... Given this federal character every ethnic group compelled to seek its own home its NA, its own state. With each new political entity the non-indigenes continues to grow.' Once the law enshrines cultural identity as the basis for political identity, it necessarily converts ethnicity into a political force. As a consequence, in Nigeria, clashes in the postcolonial period were ethnic, and such ethnic clashes, which dominated the political landscape in the last three decades, are always at root about customary rights to land and, derivatively, to a local government or to a state that can empower those on the ground as ethnically indigenous.

Into this mix enters oil, which is to say a valuable, centralized (state-owned) resource. It is a *national* resource on which citizenship claims can be constructed. As much as the state uses oil to build a nation and to develop, so communities use oil wealth to activate community claims on what is seen popularly as unimaginable wealth—black gold. The governable space of Nigeria is as a consequence re-territorialized through ethnic claims making (Adebayo 1993; Suberu 2001). The result is that access to oil revenues amplifies what I call sub-national political institution making; politics becomes then a massive state-making machine. This partly explains how, between 1966 and the present, the number of local governments has grown from fifty to almost 1,000, and the number of states from three to thirty-six! Nigeria as a modern nation state has become a machine for the production of ever more local political institutions. The logic is ineluctable and terrifying.

What sort of national governable space emerges from such multiplication in which, incidentally, the political entities called states or LGAs become vehicles for massive corruption and fraud—or the disposal of oil revenues? The answer is that it works against precisely the creation of an imagined community of the sort that Benedict Anderson (1998) saw as synonymous with nationalism. Nation building, whatever its style of imaging, rests in its modern form on a sort of calculation, integration, and state and bureaucratic rationality which the logic of rent seeking, petro-corruption, ethnic spoils politics, and state multiplication works to systematically undermine. Lauren Berlant has said that every nation—and hence every governable national space—requires a 'National Symbolic'; a national fantasy which 'designates how national culture becomes local through images, narratives and movements which circulate in the personal and collective unconsciousness' (1991: 61). My point is that the Nigerian National Symbolic grew weaker and more attenuated as a result of the political economy of oil. There was no sense of the national fantasy at the local level; it was simply a big pocket of oil monies to be raided in the name of indigeneity. At Independence, Obafemi Awolowo, the great western Nigerian politician, said that Nigeria was not a nation but a 'mere geographical expression'. Forty years later this is still true.

What we have in other words is not nation building—understood in the sense of a governable space—but perhaps its reverse: the 'unimagining' or deconstruction of a particular sense of national community. Nicos Poulantzas (1978) said that national or modern unity requires a historicity of a territory and a territorialization of a history. Oil capitalism (and its attendant governmentality) in Nigeria has achieved neither of these requirements. The 'fictional' governable space called Nigeria was always something of a public secret. Forty years of postcolonial rule has made this secret more public as ethnic segregation has continued unabated and undermined the very idea of the production of governable subjects. The double-movement of petro-capitalism within the frame of a modern nation state has eviscerated the governable space of the nation; it has compromised it and worked against a sense of a governable subject. The same, incidentally, might be said of the impact of oil on the Muslim communities of Nigeria (Watts 1998: 2000). Oil and identity—people and things—have produced an unimagined community on which the question of Nigeria's future hangs.

BLOOD AND OIL

The entire history of petroleum is, as Daniel Yergin (1991) details in his encyclopaedic Whig account of the industry *The Prize*, replete with criminality, violence and the worst of frontier capitalism. Graft, autocratic thuggery, and the most grotesque exercise of imperial power are its hallmarks. As the US armoured divisions roll up the Iraqi oil corridor around Basra, this point hardly needs further empirical confirmation. And it is to be expected in an age of unprecedented denationalization and market liberalization—to say nothing of the horrific rise of the gas-guzzling Sports Utility Vehicle in the US—the mad scramble to locate the next petrolic El Dorado continues unabated. Eastern Russia looks ever more like a slice of Mafiosi sovereignty. Petro-violence is rarely off the front pages of the press. The Caspian basin reaching from the borders of Afghanistan to the Russian Caucasus is a repository of enormous petro-wealth; Turkmenistan, Kazakhstan, Azerbaijan, Georgia and the southern Russian provinces (Ossetia, Dagestan, Chechnya) have however become, in the wake of the collapse of the Soviet Union, a 'zone of civil conflict and war'.[27] The oil companies jockey for position in an atmosphere of frontier vigilantism and what the Azerbaijani president calls 'armed conflict, aggressive separatism and nationalism'.

Based on the Nigerian case, I have suggested that petro-capitalism operates through a particular sort of oil complex (a configuration of firm, state and community). The complex is strongly territorial, operating through local oil concessions. The presence and activities of the oil companies as part of the oil complex constitute a challenge to forms of community authority, inter-ethnic relations, and local state institutions principally through the property and land disputes that are engendered, and via forms of popular mobilization and agitation to gain access to (i) company rents and compensation revenues, and (ii) the petro-revenues of the Nigerian state largely through the creation of regional and/or local state institutions. The complex generates differing sorts of governable spaces in which contrasting identities and forms of rule come into play; in some cases youth and generational forces are key, in some cases gender, in others the clan or the kingdom or the ethnic minority (or indigenous peoples), in some cases local chiefly or governmental authorities, and in others the forces of the local state. A striking aspect of contemporary development in Nigeria is the *simultaneous* production of differing forms of rule and governable space—different politics of scale (Smith 1992)—all products of similar forces and yet which work against, and often stand in direct contradiction to, one another. I have focussed on youth, the indigene or ethnic minority, and the nation. These idioms are inseparable from oil, but their forms of identification and the robustness of their spaces are often incompatible. Standing at the centre of each governable space is a contradiction: at the oil community, the overthrowing of gerontocratic authority but its substitution by a sort of violent Mafia youthful rule. At the level of the ethnic community is the tension between civic nationalism and a sort of exclusivist militant particularism. And at the level of the nation, one sees the contradiction between oil-based state centralization and state fragmentation, or multiplication, as oil becomes a sort of generalized equivalent put to the service of massive corruption. I have tried to root these contradictions in the double-movement of petro-capitalism

[27] *San Francisco Chronicle,* 11 August 1998: A8.

which is generative of an authoritarian governmentality constituted
by the three forms of governable space that I have described. Such
is the heart of the so-called crisis of the postcolonial state in Africa.
It is in this sense that I invoke the idea of 'economies of violence' to
characterize governmentality in contemporary Nigeria.

7

Natural Resources and Capitalist Frontiers*

ANNA LOWENHAUPT TSING

A frontier is an edge of space and time: a zone of not yet—not yet mapped, not yet regulated. It is a zone of un-mapping even in its planning, a frontier is imagined as unplanned. Frontiers aren't just discovered at the edge; they are projects in making geographical and temporal experience. Their wildness is made of visions and vines and violence; it is both material and imaginative. Frontiers move back and forth in time energizing old fantasies, even as they embody their impossibilities. On the resource frontier, the small and the great collaborate and collide in a climate of chaos and violence. They wrest landscape elements from previous livelihoods and ecologies to turn them into wild resources, available for the industries of the world.

* Most of the material in this chapter was published in Tsing (2005). A slightly different version of the chapter also appears in the volume *Histories of the Future*, edited by Susan Harding and Daniel Rosenberg. I am grateful to the editors for their permission to publish it in the rather different context of a discussion of natural resources. Meanwhile, I am also grateful to both cultural theory and natural resource readers for their excellent suggestions: From the 'History of the Future' seminar, Susan Harding, Daniel Rosenberg, Stephen Best, Liisa Malkki, Joseph Masco, Vicente Rafael, and Kathleen Stewart; from the workshop on natural resources, Amita Baviskar, Itty Abraham, and the assembled members of the workshop. I gave an earlier version of this paper for the Boas-Benedict annual symposium plenary address at Columbia University in April 1997. Kathryn Chetkovich, Paulla Ebron, and Lisa Rofel have been particularly helpful in the rewriting process.

Most descriptions of resource frontiers take the existence of resources for granted. Most descriptions label and count the resources and tell us who owns what. The landscape itself appears inert: ready to be dismembered and packaged for export. In contrast, the challenge I've set myself is to make the landscape a lively actor. Landscapes are simultaneously natural and social, and they actively shift and turn in the interplay of human and non-human practices. Frontier landscapes are particularly active: hills are flooding away, streams are stuck in mud, vines swarm over fresh stumps, and ants and humans are on the move. On the frontier, nature goes wild.

The place I describe is a mountainous, forested strip of southeast Kalimantan. My companions in travelling and learning this landscape are the Meratus Dayaks, old inhabitants of the area, whose livelihood has been based on shifting cultivation and forest foraging (Tsing 1993). For the Meratus, the frontier has come as a shock and a disruption; it is with their help that I experience the trauma of transformation. There are other perspectives: for some, such as migrants and miners, the frontier is an opening full of promise. They come in expectation of resources, and so they can ignore how these resources are traumatically produced. I leave their stories for other chronicles, of which there are many.

In the mid-1990s, the political regime in Indonesia was called the New Order. The New Order was a centralized and repressive political machine that depended heavily on the power of its military, particularly to control the countryside. In the 1970s and 1980s, the regime flourished through a rhetoric of state-led development. In the 1990s, however, privatization became a regime watchword; in practice, the new policies further concentrated economic power in the hands of the president's family and close cronies. In Kalimantan, state policy privileged corporate control of natural resources; huge tracts were assigned to logging companies, mining companies, and pulp-and-paper as well as oil palm plantation companies. The military played an important role in transferring these tracts from previous residents to their corporate owners; military men also took their own interest in resources. It seems fair to say that the military played a central role in creating the 'wildness' of the frontier. This seminal period, which has gone on to shape the wildness of the early twenty-first century, is the moment I describe.

AN ABANDONED LOGGING ROAD

An abandoned logging road has got to be one of the most desolate places on earth. By definition, it doesn't go anywhere. If you are walking there, it is either because you are lost or you are trespassing, or both. The wet clay builds clods on your boots, if you have any, sapping your strength, and if you don't have any boots, the sun and the hot mud are merciless. Whole hillsides shift beside you, sliding into the stagnant pools where the mosquitoes breed. Abandoned roads soon lose their shape, forcing you in and out of eroded canyons and over muddy trickles where bridges once stood but are now choked by loose soil, vines crawling on disinterred roots and trunks sliding, askew. Yet, ironically, the forest as a site of truth and beauty seems clearer from the logging road than anywhere else, since it is the road that slices open the neat cross-section in which underbrush, canopy, and high emergent trees are so carefully structured.

In 1994, I walked on a lot of abandoned logging roads in the eastern sector of South Kalimantan, Indonesia, between the Meratus Mountains and the coastal plains now covered with transmigration villages—Block A, Block B, Block C—and giant, miles-square plantations of oil palm, rubber, and acacia for the pulp and paper trade. The region was transformed from when I had last seen it in the 1980s. Then, despite the logging, I had thought the forest might survive; local villagers were asserting customary resource rights and transmigration here was just a gleam in one engineer's eye, and he wasn't in charge. Now, even beyond the newly planted industrial tree plantations lay miles of scrub and vines. These were landslides of slippery red and yellow clay, with silted-up excuses for water. The logging roads had eroded into tracks for motorcycles, water buffalo, and the still-streaming mass of immigrant and local blood and sweat that the government calls 'wild': wild loggers, wild miners, and bands of roving entrepreneurs and thieves. I had seen resource booms before: When the prices for rattan shot up in the 1980s, for example, people went crazy cutting rattan until all the rattan had been cut to the ground. But this was something different. Something easy to call degradation was riding through the land. It was the kind of scene that informs so many powerful theories of resource management: The human presence was leaving the landscape all but bare. This, they

say, is ordinary behaviour on the resource frontier where everything
is plentiful and wild. It's human nature, they say, and the nature
of resources.

In the violent clarity of the abandoned logging road, questions
come to mind that might seem simple or even idiotic elsewhere.
How does nature at the frontier become a set of resources? How are
landscapes made empty and wild so that anyone can come to use and
claim them? How do ordinary people get involved in destroying their
environments, even their own home places?

This is a business that gets inside our daily habits and our dreams.
Two complementary nightmares come into being; the frontier emerges
in the intertwined attraction and disgust of their engagement. Consider
in comparison the urban frontiers of southern California. Orange
County is full of planned communities, industrial tree plantations of
neatly spaced condominiums, row on row on row, which give way only
to identical roads and shopping malls. There are truly no directions, no
place marks, only faceless serenity, and time on hold. Orange County
is one kind of nightmare. Its flip side is South Central Los Angeles, the
mere thought of which drives masses of whites and Asian Americans
behind the Orange Curtain. Time is not on hold in that bastion of
short lives. Yet these two nightmares play with each other. Just as the
fear of hell drives the marketing schemes of paradise, so too does the
desire of paradise fuel the schemes of hell. Both rise and fall on the
spectacular performances of savvy entrepreneurs.

The same is true in Kalimantan. The giant monocrop plantations
are the flip side of the wild resource frontier: On one side, endless
rows of silent symmetry and order, biopower applied to trees; on the
other side, wild loggers, miners, and villagers in the raucous, sped-
up time of looting. Each calls the other into existence. Each solves
the problems put in motion by the other. Each requires the same
entrepreneurial spirit. In that spirit, gold nuggets, swifts' nests, incense
woods, ironwood posts, great logs destined to be plywood, and whole
plantations of future pulp are conjured. Here I find the first answer
to my impertinent questions. Resources are made by 'resourcefulness'
in both plantation and wild frontier. The activity of the frontier is to
make human subjects as well as natural objects.

The frontier, indeed, had come to Kalimantan. It had not always
been there. Dutch plantation schemes mainly bypassed Kalimantan

in the colonial period, allowing colonial authorities to treat their natives as subjects of kingdoms and cultures. Kalimantan's Dayaks, to them patently uncivilized, were still seen as having law and territorial boundaries, not a wilderness that needed to be filled up. In its first years the postcolonial nation maintained Kalimantan's villages, fields and forests. Commercial logging only got underway in the 1970s. Administrative expansion and resettlement followed, with the goal of homogenizing the nation. In the 1980s, conflicts broke out between village people and commercial loggers. Massive fires and waves of immigration disrupted emergent localisms. Through the 1980s, however, it was possible to see rural Kalimantan as a landscape of villages, small cultivations, and traditional agro-forestry, with discrete patches of estate agriculture and large-scale logging and mining here and there.

The late 1980s and 1990s witnessed a national wave of entrepreneurship. Spurred on by economic 'liberalization' with its international sponsors, and a consolidating regional capitalism, entrepreneurs shot up at every level from conglomerates to peasant tour guides. In this great surge of resourcefulness Kalimantan became a frontier.

The frontier, then, is not a natural or indigenous category. It is a travelling theory, a blatantly foreign form requiring translation. It arrived with many layers of previous associations. 'Indonesian Miners Revive Gold Rush Spirit of 49ers', proclaimed a headline in the Los Angeles Times.[1] Indonesian frontiers were shaped to the model of other wild times and places. Nor was 1849 California the only moment of frontier-making available to be reworked and revived. There is the dark Latin American frontier: a place of violence, conflicting cultures, and an unforgiving nature driving once-civilized men to barbarism, as Domingo Sarmiento, soon to be president of Argentina, argued in 1845 (Sarmiento 1998). This savage vision of the frontier has continued to percolate through later frontier optimism. There is the nation-making frontier, as famously articulated by Frederick Jackson Turner in his 1893 address, 'The Significance of the Frontier in American History' (Turner 1994). Wild, empty spaces are said to

[1] Nick Williams Jr., 'Boom Time Along "Rim of Fire": Indonesian Miners Revive Gold Rush Spirit of 49ers', Los Angeles Times 108, sec. 1 (12 December 1988).

have inspired white men to national democracy and freedom in the United States. Amazing for its erasures, the power of this formulation is suggested by the fact that US historians remained in its thrall for nearly a hundred years. Finally, in the 1960s, frontier chroniclers dared to mention that there were Native Americans, Asians, Hispanics, and women in these empty spaces, and they may not have benefited from that nation-making freedom quite so much as Anglo-American men. Finally, in the 1980s, environmental historians dared mention that someone despoiled the land, forests and rivers.[2] But the proud frontier story of the making of 'America' will probably be around a long time, particularly because it was remade in an internationally colonizing form after World War II in the concept of the techno-frontier, the endless frontier made possible by industrial technology. The closing of national borders, dense settlement and resource scarcity need no longer lead to frontier nostalgia; the techno-frontier is always open and expanding. In the guise of development, the dream of the techno-frontier hit Indonesian centres hard in the late 1960s. By the 1990s, it had dragged its older frontier cousins, those entangled stories of the wild, to the rural peripheries.

Frontiers are notoriously unstable, and it is fitting that Kalimantan landscapes should have a role in forging new frontier conceptions. The frontier arrived in Kalimantan *after* environmentalism had already become established, not just among activists, but also among government bureaucrats and corporate public relations agents. No one could be surprised this time to find that frontier making is destructive of forests and indigenous cultures. Susanna Hecht and Alexander Cockburn write that in the Amazon, heroic development plans unexpectedly turned to smoke, mud and violence: 'The generals had unleashed forces beyond their control, and now the Amazon faced its apocalypse' (1989: 141). But in New Order Kalimantan, the Amazon apocalypse was already known. Plans were set in motion to save the environment in the process of destroying it. Tree plantations were introduced to restore deforested and degraded land. Only then was the landscape deforested and degraded to make way for the restorative tree plantations. Giant mining conglomerates were licensed to save

---

[2] For an introduction to these literatures, see Limerick (1987) and Worster (1992).

the land from the pollution and depreciations of wild miners, yet legal and illegal prospectors were inseparable. 'They go where we go', a Canadian engineer explained, 'and sometimes we follow them'.[3] The national timber king, also the czar of plywood and the crown prince of mines, hosted the 10K 'Run for the Rainforest' and produced a glossy coffee-table book of disappearing species. This is the salvage frontier, where making, saving and destroying resources are utterly mixed up, where zones of conservation, production and resource sacrifice overlap almost fully, and canonical time frames of nature's study, use and preservation are reversed, conflated and confused.

By this point it should be clear that by frontier I don't mean a place or even a process but an imaginative project capable of moulding both places and processes. Turner describes the frontier as 'the meeting point between savagery and civilization' (1994: 32). It is a site of transformations; 'the wilderness masters the colonist . . . .Little by little he masters the wilderness . . .' (ibid.: 33). It is a space of desire: it calls; it appears to create its own demands; once glimpsed, one cannot but explore and exploit it. Frontiers have their own technologies of space and time: their emptiness is expansive, spreading across the land; they draw the quick, erratic temporality of rumour, speculation, and cycles of boom and bust, encouraging ever-intensifying forms of resourcefulness. On the Kalimantan salvage frontier, frontier intensification and proliferation lurch forward in a hall of mirrors, becoming showy parodies of themselves. Time moves so quickly that results precede their causes, and the devastation expected behind the line of frontier expansion suddenly appears, as it seems, ahead of its advance.

The Kalimantan frontier is not the enactment of a principle of commodification or conquest. The commodification of forest products is centuries old in this area, and while the new frontier draws on the earlier trade, it is not a logical intensification of this earlier trade. The frontier is not a philosophy but rather a series of historically non-linear leaps and skirmishes that pile together to create their own intensification and proliferation. The most helpful scholarship,

[3] Nick Williams Jr., 'Boom Time Along "Rim of Fire": Indonesian Miners Revive Gold Rush Spirit of 49ers', *Los Angeles Times* 108, sec. 1, p. 1 (12 December 1988).

then, is not to be found in abstract treatises but rather in historical descriptions and ethnographies. Thus, accounts of the US West tell us how the rush to grab one landscape element can jump off into another, as when gold prospectors made property claims on stream water. Legal precedents unexpectedly link one region and another. Aesthetic models are carried to new homes, as colonial conservation inspired the national parks movement (Worster 1985).

As these kinds of moves are repeated, they gain a cultural productiveness even in their quirky unpredictability. Thus, Marianne Schmink and Charles Wood (1992) describe frontiers in Amazonia as a series of ironic twists. Planned communities lead to unplanned settlement; resource nationalization leads to private control; land titling leads to forgery; military protection leads to generalized violence. Such twists are more than irony: they predict and perform their own reversals, forming productive confusions and becoming models for other frontiers. In Kalimantan, related paradoxes produce frontier degradation and salvage. The frontier is made in the shifting terrain between legality and illegality, public and private ownership, brutal rape and passionate charisma, ethnic collaboration and hostility, violence and law, restoration and extermination.

Legal, Illegal

Shifting cultivation is illegal in Indonesia, despite the fact that it is the major subsistence technology for many rural people in Kalimantan, including the Meratus Dayaks. Perhaps that is why, as I hiked down the Meratus Mountains into the eastern coastal plains with Meratus friends, the lines of legality were not clear to me, and I was hardly aware that the immigrant loggers I passed were out of bounds, wild men. As soon as we hit the old logging roads we found them, singly or in groups of three or four, each with a small chainsaw or a water buffalo to haul out the logs. Their living places were bed-sized bamboo platforms along the road with only a sheet of plastic hung over to keep out the rain; they seemed to have no possessions but a coffee pot and a can of mackerel, the poor man's sardines. We stopped to drink sticky thick coffee, loaded with sugar, and to talk of the pleasures and dangers of the forest world they knew. They chanted the prices of wood, the names of logs. They spooked themselves, and us, with tales of stolen chainsaws and armed men on the roads. They were always planning to leave in a few days, when the earnings looked good, and before fiercer men arrived. Even as quick-moving transients, they gave us a human face for the frontier.

My friends thought the men worked for Inhutani, a government forest company, and while this turned out to be technically wrong, they were right that the lines between public, private and criminal enterprise were unclear. These loggers have both legitimacy and access. They sell their logs to the properly concessioned logging companies or to small construction firms. Where environmental regulations keep the companies off mountain slopes or village claims push them back, that's where the wild loggers go. They fill out logging economies of scale, and their earnings are the only prosperity that logging is likely to bring to the province. Their chainsaws come to them through networks of renting and profit sharing that cross local, ethnic and religious lines. They form the slender end of channels of capital reaching from rich Chinese entrepreneurs, conglomerates, and—at that time—the family of the president, flowing in ever narrowing channels out into the forest. Usually, the police and the army do not bother them, although the police and the army can be unpredictable. Many pay fees to official Meratus village heads to give them permission to cut in village forests, and while villagers complain that village heads keep it all for themselves, this privatization is common, even proper, for government village subsidies.

And yet, both despite and because of all this respectability, these lonely loggers carried and spread the wildness of the frontier. Even in sitting with them, chatting with them, we partook of that wildness. They encouraged our fears of armed men; 'Oh, no one will attack you', they joked, 'because they will assume you are carrying a lot of guns'. And who can tell the difference between a logger and an armed thief? Each time we came upon another man, another logger /thief, we stopped, hoping to domesticate him with our chatter. Perhaps he wouldn't attack us; perhaps he would alert us to the presence of other logger/thieves. Soon our nerves were jangling from all those cups of coffee, and by then we had formed a silent pack, each huddling in his or her own unspoken fear.

They modelled frontier behaviour for us, teaching us the value of wood until my Meratus companions began looking at familiar forest trees with eyes like cash registers. 'Oh, that one could bring me a million rupiah', Ma Salam sighed, interrupting our conversation about environmentalism. In writing their names or initials on the logs they cut, the wild loggers had introduced the new practice in this area of writing one's name on trees—to claim the tree to hold it or sell it to a logger with a chainsaw before someone else did. The proliferation of naming brought new identities for trees and men, wrapping both in fearless assertion and violence, for, people said, armed men came by and cut the name off the tree, or cut the tree above the mark, and wrote their own names on the logs. If you confront them with five men, my friends said, they would come at you with ten or twenty. Sell quickly and move on to write your name again.

Who were these men, so human and yet so transiently identified? They came from everywhere and spoke the common language of trade and calculation based on the hope of a quick windfall. They were called *penyingso*, 'chainsaw men', or *pembaluk*, 'square log men', after the shape of their logs. No one knew them as wild, but they were men without ordinary culture. Appendages to their equipment and their products, they had names but no houses, families, meals, work schedule, or ordinary time. And in this stripped-down human form, they communicated across cultures, arranging ethnic collaborations. They offered a hot human connection to still the chills of fear. This thrilling connection was an anaesthetic, blocking out the damaged world in which they operated—a world already left behind by bigger frontier makers, the soil sloughing off the hills, trees falling, waters muddied. Looking in and through that damaged world, can't you see the resources waiting to be claimed?

It is difficult to find the words to discuss this kind of transethnic, translocal collaboration and the regional resource dynamics it sets in motion. Resource economists and bureaucrats recognize no localisms; to them, the world is a frontier. There is no point in asking how frontiers come to be; they are nature itself. To counter that perspective, anthropologists, rural sociologists, and geographers have drawn attention to non-frontier-like (or even anti-frontier) environmental social forms, such as common property, community management and indigenous knowledge. They have returned attention to the cultural specificity of capitalism and state bureaucracy.[4] This important and quite wonderful work has come to dominate local and regional analyses of environment and society in Kalimantan; scholars point to the long-term social making of the rainforest, to a community 'ethic of access' that sustains forest commodities, and to the bizarre stereotypes of government planners.[5] My own work has developed within this dialogue.

Yet, in contrasting community conventions with state and corporate schemes, there is little room for discussing the call of the wild, with its region-wide collaborations for aggressive resource grabbing and the seemingly-unstoppable spread of the frontier. One might call this 'the tragedy of the tragedy of the commons', that is, the tragic result of state and corporate policies that assume and enforce open-access conventions as the flip side and precondition of private property.[6] By refusing to recognize alternative forms of access, these policies will alternatives to disappearance. But this is a tragedy that cannot be well described with the vocabulary of management, property and access rules. From the perspective of the abandoned logging roads, the divide between community and state-corporate standards feels nostalgic: too little, too late. The logging road and its illegal-legal loggers from everywhere call me towards more dangerous country.

One look back: Grand schemes never fully colonize the territories upon which they are imposed. If the frontier is an environmental project, not a place, it can never fill the landscape. Away from the logging road, there are trees, fields, and villages, and not everyone is so caught up in frontier schemes. The frontier could move on, and

[4] For an introduction to this literature, see Bryant and Bailey (1997) and Peet and Watts (1996).

[5] See, for example, Dove (1999); Li (1999a); Peluso (1996) In the last few years, Kalimantan scholars have turned much more intensively to problems of ethnic violence and resource conflict. See, for example, Peluso and Harwell (2001).

[6] I am referring to the much-discussed thesis called 'the tragedy of the commons' (Hardin 1969), which argued that common property—in contrast to private property—is invariably degraded by its users. Many commentators have showed that this thesis is wrong, despite the fact that it has considerable authority among policy makers (see, for example, McKay and Acheson 1987). Indeed, as I suggest here, the thesis itself as applied in policy can be destructive to the environment.

something else could happen in its place. The forest might regener-
ate. Although . . . those industrial tree plantations are truly huge,
and through them the frontier claims powerful national and international players.

THE PUBLIC PRIVATE

Riding from the provincial capital up the east coast and towards the
mountains in an airless, overcrowded van with the music so loud it
closes down my senses, there is more than enough anaesthetic; yet the
difference between legal resource concessions and the wild is perfectly
visible here. The road runs for miles through land without underbrush
or animal life but only neatly planted tree stock, row on row on row.
The transmigration villages recently placed here to provide the labour
force for these future trees are similarly orderly, blank, and anonymous;
in striking contrast to everywhere else I've been in Indonesia, the
passengers get on and off at these nameless stops without looking at
us or speaking. Sometimes we stop in noisy frontier towns, full of gold
merchants, truckers and hungry, aggressive men. But soon enough
we are back among the silent army of young trees. This is the kind of
discipline that boosted Indonesia—for a while—among the so-called
Asian dragons. Under the name of political stability, discipline made
economic indicators soar.[7]

Appearances are important here. No weeds, no trash timber.
Indeed, it is unclear to what extent appearances were not the New
Order economy's most important product. Oil palm, the darling of
the export-crop set, was sponsored by foreign and domestic plantation
subsidies (Hill 1996: 124); perhaps the companies will have moved on
before the oil is pressed. The national reforestation programme, the
answer to environmentalists' concerns for the rainforest, financed the
pulp plantations. New international agreements offered plantation
timber as the solution to rainforest destruction; timber companies put
in plantations, sponsored by the government, to earn the right to cut
down more forest, useful for future plantations. Meanwhile, the young
trees await future pulp factories. And as they wait, what will befall

---

[7] Consider the relationship between mass murder and 'banking output'
suggested by Figure 9.1 in Hill (1996: 180), which shows the soaring line of
growth exactly on the years of the army-sponsored massacre of 1968–9.

them? Many of the acacias are cloned from the same parent stock, making them highly vulnerable to disease (Brookfield et al. 1995: 105). They are also affected by a rot that causes hollow boles, an apt image for an economy of appearances.

There were government corporations here, and there were private ones, but most fell awkwardly across this distinction. In 1994, the oil palms were said to belong to the wife of then-president Suharto, Mrs Tien Suharto, who died in 1996 but before her death was widely parodied as Mrs Tien (Ten) Percent, after her voracious interest in the economy. The loggers told villagers who complained about the invasion of village forests to 'go ask Mrs Tien'. The president's family served both a material and a mythical role in the plantation economy. The capital they controlled was both public and private. And it was the confusion of these categories that allowed frontier investments to flourish. For whom were these resources discovered and developed: the national interest, the army, the president, the foreign corporations, or, perhaps, all of the above?

Even the staunchest of neoclassical economists admit that it was difficult to distinguish among domestic, foreign and government ownership in New Order Indonesia, given the mix of investors, the central importance of patronage, and the back and forth slippage between military and private enterprise. The confusion proliferated at every level. Foreign was domestic: foreign aid formed a major portion of domestic revenue, and foreign firms worked through domestic partners. Public was private: the explicit goal of the government was to sponsor entrepreneurship at every level. Even peasant subsidies in the 1990s were individual entrepreneurship loans. Licenses and concessions were both public and private. Civil servants were paid a low base salary and expected to gain the rest of their living from perks and benefits of their discretionary authority.

You could call this corruption, or you could call it, as one North American corporate executive, gracefully submitting to government demands for a share of his company's enterprise, dubbed it, 'Indonesia's political, economic, and social environment'.[8] One must also consider

[8] The quotation is from David Walsh, the president of the ill-fated gold mining company Bre-X, as reported by Borsuk (1997: B3A). For more on this company and its arrangements with the Indonesian government as well as its actions on the Kalimantan frontier, see Tsing (2000).

these public-private arrangements in relation to the worldwide post-Cold-War infatuation with the market. Soon after the collapse of the Soviet Union in 1989, every nation-state redoubled its endorsement of the market, or at least the appearance of the market, and New Order Indonesia was exemplary. The bureaucracy was the market; its goal was to promote entrepreneurship. The military was the market; generals and common soldiers, at different levels, had the muscle to make the best deals. Environmental management was the market, offering another chance to claim resources and improve free trade. In this context, the fluidity between public and private was a fertile space for the capital, the deals, the plans, and the appearance of the economy itself. The president's family and friends were exemplars of what every citizen was supposed to be doing; and their capital flowed out through trans-regional networks in small deals that complemented the large ones. Furthermore, this was a dynamic that supposedly sped up modernization and development, the stated goal of the state. Secrets passed through personalistic ties encouraged speculation in which investments preceded contracts; for those tracking money and resources, an impatient anticipation emerged, speeding up the experience of time. A boom-time excitement was stimulated by the fluidity of deals, trickling down and then streaming between official coffers, foreign firms, and those-in-the-know. Rumours spread the excitement, and the wild men flocked to the frontier following or anticipating news of gold strikes and quick timber harvests, before the plantations rolled in. In this productive space, quick, erratic, anticipatory frontier time intensifies and spreads, ricocheting back and forth between centres and peripheries, and getting ahead of itself in death-defying leaps. Here, alternative appearance-based scams—disciplined or wild—are born, and the only promise that must surely be kept is of fabulous, unearned wealth.

Roads that Empty the Territory

Between the tree plantations and the mountains are networks of more- and less-maintained logging roads, with their heavy cargoes of legal logs by day and illegal logs by night. For bosses and managers, the roads shrink and simplify the territory, making it quicker to get from here to there. For almost everyone else, the logging roads expand landscape emptiness, separating off- and on-road sites and creating obstacles between once-connected forest places even as they speed the trip to town. The roads are also conduits for migrants, fugitives, and thieves, who expand both danger and wildness for everyone who lives or visits there.

Natural treasures themselves become fugitive in this landscape of movement and flight, just as once, people said, a man stumbled over a nugget of gold as big as a rice mortar and marked the place, oh so carefully to come back later with help—but when he did, nothing was there. Masculine magic and charisma is required, for even safe in one's possession, treasures disappear. Thus every man on the road with a splinter of gaharu incense wood or a palm full of immature swifts' nests, unwraps it from its plastic bag, shows it like a secret talisman, wraps it, stows it carefully in his pocket, chants the price, pulls it out again to rewrap it, trying thereby to stabilize its presence on his person. And how much more flighty are the incense trees and swifts themselves.

Take the swifts, for example. The saliva nests they build in limestone caves are the key ingredient of Chinese bird's nest soup and fetch startling prices even locally: a million and a half rupiah for a kilo of the white clean ones and 800,000 for the debris-filled black.[9] In this area, they have long been associated with fugitive luck and danger. In the 1980s, people told me that the only way to find birds' nests was to bring a freshly sacrificed human head to the spirits who could reveal them. Now, with armed men on the roads, the birds' erratic flight has intensified beyond the reach of headhunters, as have attempts to hold them in place. Where military men have found productive caves, they have posted guards and signs: This is the property of the army. And so the Meratus, who consider themselves rightful traditional owners, hurry to guard remaining caves, building their homes and clearing swiddens in the dark glens directly in front of the caves, never leaving them. Still, they are out-manoeuvred by the men on the roads, who come around with guns and flashlights and demand entry, peeling off the birds' nests long before they are fully built and indeed ensuring that the birds will not return. Quick harvesting leads

---

[9] These are prices from the mid-1990s, before the currency devaluation of 1997. At the time, one US dollar was worth a little over 2,000 rupiah.

to quicker harvesting, and nests the size of nail clippings are removed, depriving the birds of any place to raise their young. In this fugitive landscape, armed men are the best part of the law, and parodies of property appear. One Meratus man who built his house in front of a cave to guard it showed me the letter written by the most recent gang to have come by to rob the cave, which warned off future gangs on the principle of this group's precedence. My host got nothing, as did the swifts, who could only fly to other fugitive locations.

Men arm themselves with old war stories, and invulnerability magic from the 1958 rebellion has been revived, with its metaphors of penises as weapons and semen as spent bullets. As much as I tried to steer around the concerns of a simple ecofeminism, it was difficult not to conclude that an emergent masculinity fuelled this regionally spreading dynamic, with its ability to unite men across lines of local culture and religion in a competitively intensive virility. Men arouse each other on the roads with stories of women who will do anything ('and then', he said, 'she tore off her bra'). They work themselves and each other into a constant state of masculine anxiety, forever talking about deals and opportunities and prices in the sped-up time of the chase. They forget day-cycles, life cycles, seasons. They call to, and challenge each other to, greater efforts.

Hiking the logging roads in the hot sun, I find it difficult to refuse a ride from the men in the truck. But crammed into the cab with the crew behind a windshield covered with stickers of busty naked ladies and my male Meratus friends stuck in the back with the water buffalo, fear hits me like an avalanche. Within 30 seconds, they are feeling my arms and legs and breasts, and I must concentrate on how to get them to let me off at the next crossroads, where I heave a sigh of relief that I made it out, again, this time. 'Yes', says a wizened Meratus friend, 'they grab your breasts even if you are a wrinkled old woman, they must have no eyes, and every woman longs and must learn to jump out of the truck.' But a younger friend replies to my stories with bravado: 'Why didn't you do it? Weren't they handsome enough?' I had heard similar bravado from young men when soldiers cowed a peer: 'If they had come at me, I would have shown them something!' And indeed, one's only choices are to hide or to play. Women can be resourceful too, and prostitution brings new resources to the frontier. But this is a world made by an intensive, peculiar, exaggerated masculinity.

This is a masculinity that spreads and saturates itself with images and metaphors, amulets, stickers of naked women, stories based on the confusion between rape and wild sex. Its moving force is perhaps best seen in the imagistic effects of the 'water machine', the high-pressure hydraulic pump, small enough for one man to carry and connect to any local stream, but whose power in the spray emerging from the taut blue plastic piping can gouge a hole four feet deep into the land and thus expose the gravel underneath the clay, gravel mixed with which, perchance, small flakes or nuggets of gold can be found. What charismatic force! And what possibilities it unveils.

The water machine, introduced in this area around 1990, is the key technology of small-scale or 'wild' gold mining. It's much too expensive for an ordinary Meratus man, but networks of renting and share splitting, with borrowed funds and imagined profits split among more and more make it possible for many ambitious men to join a mining group, or more aggressively yet, to bring the machine and a team upstream towards home. Nor are Meratus the only players. The miners, like the loggers, come from everywhere, building makeshift settlements along the logging roads with names like 'Kilometre 105 and a half'. At their excavations, they erect camps of bamboo platforms hung with plastic sheets; they have coffee pots, sugar, and mackerel cans. But I know some of these people; they are Meratus farmer-foragers. I know they are perfectly capable of stopping anywhere in the forest and, in half an hour, building a cosy, rain-tight shelter of bamboo, palm leaves or bark. I know, in other circumstances, they would carry rice; they would hunt and fish and gather wild fruits and vegetables and make a tasty meal. But here, surrounded by familiar forest, they observe the proprieties of rain-soaked plastic sheets and nutrition of coffee and rancid fish. It feels like nothing so much as 'culture' in its most coercive, simplistic form: a way of life that draws us in, ready or not, sensible or not.

Among the huddled mining shelters, men and women disagree. Women join the profit-sharing groups, panning the gravel with men until their own jealous menfolk arrive, sending them back to the village. The men attack the land with new vigour, sharing the washing with other women, and women sneak back to join the gold parties of strangers.

But what is the result of all this passion? Despite obsessive attention
to secrets and signs, much of the gravel exposed yields no metal at all;
and when it does, the gold flakes are quickly spent in the extortionate
prices of coffee, sugar and cigarettes. No one I heard of had made
much money; meanwhile, water machines broke and huge debts were
accrued. Most strikingly, the land lay pockmarked and deeply eroded
beyond recovery. Those trees that remained clung tottering by the
tips of their roots, their bases airily exposed. Broken streams formed
muddy pools; even grass was banished. 'They have ruined the land for
many generations', said the old people. But perhaps it doesn't matter
if the industrial tree plantations and their transmigrant labour force
are coming anyway. Their mission is to make and restore degraded
lands; why not get started?

Frontier Citizenship

Frontier men and resources, I have argued, are made in dynamics
of intensification and proliferation. Confusions between legal and
illegal, public and private, disciplined and wild are productive in
sponsoring the emergence of men driven to profit, that is, entrepreneurs,
as well as the natural objects conjured in their resourceful drives.
These men and objects are contagious, recharging the landscape
with wildness and virility. The frontier, then, appears to roll with its
own momentum.

The frontier is a globally travelling project, but it requires localization to come to life. I've tangled with this restless localization by
moving back and forth between the intense physicality of the frontier
landscape, its guiding models, and its unplanned insights. Let me re-
site it one more time in the hesitant emergence of frontier politics.

The frontier has been associated with distinctive political models of
citizenship and culture. Most famously, frontier conditions are said to
have made a freewheeling white male democracy in the New World.
There is an ongoing populist appeal here, not just in nostalgia for the
US West, but more recently in respect for the independent miners of
Brazil, who found their representatives and fought for their rights.
Frontier fears of apocalypse have also stimulated models of protection:
extractive reserves, indigenous reserves, nature reserves; each, at its
best, produces an alliance among small collectors, native peoples and

forest advocates. Neither of these models made an easy entry into the
cultural politics of Indonesia's New Order. In New Order models for
the countryside, ethnic groups gained respect for cultural difference
only with political submission: a custom to keep farmers in their place.
Yet frontier dynamics can unseat the obedience of custom to create
a wider, wilder citizenship. Drawing men from everywhere, frontier
culture can mobilize them both for and against each other.

A rhetoric of democracy is possible in official acts of protection
of frontier culture, as when a governor of South Kalimantan once
defended illegal logging as the livelihood of the people. Of course,
this is a particular kind of democracy, in which women and indigenous
residents—and, more firmly still, nature—are excluded. Then there
is the question of race and ethnic violence, even genocide. This is
the way frontier democracy has been made from below, at least
historically. Thus far I have stressed transethnic collaboration, but
this history alerts me to the lines and limits it also creates. Indeed,
ethnic violence has come to fill out the Kalimantan frontier. In the mid
1990s, Dayaks mobilized in violent clashes with Madurese migrants
in West Kalimantan. The year 2001 brought an eerily self-conscious
echo in even more dramatic violence in Central Kalimantan; for a
few days Dayak-Madurese clashes dominated international news. In
the distorted lens of international journalism, one might imagine the
scene as the return of the US Wild West—in its Hollywood version—
with the Dayaks as bloodthirsty savages scalping and encroaching,
but civilized settlers. This is a ridiculous parody; the clashes have
their own political and cultural histories (Peluso and Harwell 2001).
Yet the emerging frontier is a place for the historical repetition of re-
imagined savagery. Sometimes the army stages it; sometimes young
men find themselves in its wild tropes. One's only choices are to hide
or to play.

The reserve model has also attracted global attention. It arises
in places where environmentalists are panicked by the possibility of
total destruction; it argues that *something* must be saved. The most
promising feature of this model is the mobilization it has inspired,
which brings the possibility of citizenship claims to those who never
had them before: small collectors, tribes, trees. In Brazil, a moment of
alliance between rubber tappers and Indians offered conservationists
a strategy to save the forests. Yet, in Indonesia, the alliance between

frontiersmen and indigenous residents has only recruited the latter to the frontier. This has not been an alliance that saves forests.

Conservationists, in turn, have taken their pleas to corporations and the state, and these, indeed, have found some use for reserves. Resource companies support nature reserves because they cordon off a small area in exchange for permission to destroy the remaining countryside. Given the collusion between legal and illegal, disciplined and wild, and the new frontiersmen who come to complement development, corporate giants can rest assured they will get those reserves back, once appropriately degraded from below. Then too, in an age of natural simulation, it is never quite clear what is being preserved, what is degraded, and what is restored. The zones overlap and tease each other, and Indonesia now has national parks zoned as logging concessions. It is hard to know what one is seeing. Environmental activists say tree nurseries of hard-to-grow indigenous species are really cutback natural forest, with young trees disguised as nursery seedlings. This, after all, is the salvage frontier. Meanwhile, maps contradict each other. A nature reserve sketched on one map is a production forest on another map, and a village territory on a third. A community forest designation is assigned to a treeless plain on which only dry stumps left by loggers recall living trees. The worst social coercions of conservation politics have been avoided in the areas I know best by not conserving anything at all.

In the late 1990s, the frontier began to spin out of control even from the perspective of capitalist investors and migrant entrepreneurs. In 1997, great fires broke out across Kalimantan, many of them set by the plantation companies who hoped to use this cheap method to clear their land. Since drought had been predicted due to the El Niño Southern Oscillation, the Ministry of Forests had warned the companies not to burn. But why consider regulation or prudence on the frontier? The fires spread beyond all expectation, destroying settlements and forests and forming a dangerous haze across Southeast Asia. Then the financial crisis that had begun in Thailand spread to Indonesia and wiped out the promises of the New Order economic boom. Kalimantan villagers were most hurt by the crisis in the 'wildest' frontier areas, where subsistence agro-forestry had already been threatened or ruined by corporate and immigrant expropriations as well as destruction of the forest landscape. Meanwhile, in West Kalimantan, ethnic violence between indigenous Dayaks and immigrant Madurese flamed into a war. In 1998, demonstrations in Jakarta, together with international pressure, toppled the government. In the ensuing moment of political freedom, community groups, entrepreneurs and gangsters seized corporate resource sites. Mines were occupied. Logging camps were destroyed. The wildness sponsored by the New Order had veered out of control.

With the passing of the New Order, great possibilities opened up. Finally, there was hope for an Indonesian democracy. Students and activists in Jakarta were jubilant. In Kalimantan, non-governmental organizations (NGOs) and activist alliances took a newly assertive role in advocating for the rights of rural communities. Yet the frontier sponsored by the New Order only proliferated, taking off in new leaps and bounds. The resources were surely there; who could ignore them? Decentralization of resource rights, begun in 2000, pitted government officials at different levels against each other, such that the provincial governor and the regency assembly might fight continually over what forms of resource exploitation should be allowed—and who would get the proceeds. Meanwhile, regional groups within the military—no longer the tool of the central government—provoked ethnic violence and disorder. In 2001, the Dayaks and the Madurese became bloodily embroiled in Central Kalimantan. Still, hope rested on the possibility of new kinds of politics—as long as international powers allowed it. The US government decision in 2002 to re-arm the Indonesian military for domestic surveillance in the 'war against terrorism' was a painful reminder of the international sponsorship of frontier violence. The frontier is no neighbourhood storm. It gathers force from afar, entangling multiple local-to-global scales.

Back in California, I remember the frontier hero John Wayne—a man who wasn't even a Wild West cowboy but instead an actor who made his living *pretending* to be a Wild West cowboy. He never served in the military, but a congressional medal honoured him as the embodiment of American military heroism (Slotkin 1992: 243). Orange County has dedicated its airport to him, attracting visitors to the frontier—where adventure still leads to wealth, and a man with guns can stand tall. The frontier, like a film, can be played and replayed. That's resourcefulness on the salvage frontier.

8

Cultural Theory, Climate Change, and Clumsiness

MICHAEL THOMPSON

'They will never agree', said the nineteenth-century wit, the Reverend Sidney Smith, when he saw two women shouting at each other from houses on opposite sides of an Edinburgh street, 'they are arguing from different premises'. Cultural theorists (for example, Adams 1995: 50 and Douglas and Wildavsky 1982: 174) like to use this story as a way of getting to grips with the disputes that characterize environmental policy. The different premises, in these disputes, concern human and physical nature, and cultural theory maps them in terms of a fourfold typology of forms of social solidarity (see Figure 1). Two of these solidarities—individualism and hierarchy—have long been familiar to social scientists; they are usually referred to as markets and hierarchies (see, for example, Williamson 1975 and Lindblom 1977). The theory's novelty lies in its addition of the other two solidarities and in its making explicit the different premises—the different social constructions of nature, physical and human—that sustain these four fundamental arrangements for the promotion of social transactions.

Hierarchies institute status differences (asymmetrical transactions) and, by requiring forms of behaviour appropriate to those of differing rank and station (accountability), set all sorts of limits on competition. Markets—the transactional arrangements that accompany individualism—do the diametrical opposite; they institute equality of opportunity (symmetrical transactions) and promote competition (no accountability, as in 'If I don't do it someone else will'). The other two permutations: symmetrical transactions with accountability (labelled *egalitarianism* in the cultural theory scheme), and asymmetrical transactions without accountability (labelled *fatalism* in the cultural theory scheme) tend to be ignored by social science in general and by policy science in particular. This, for instance, was evidently the case with the enormous Brent Spar oil storage structure, the deep ocean disposal of which was proposed by the market actor—Shell—and approved by the hierarchical actor—the British government's regulatory agency. Had there been only markets and hierarchies the Brent Spar would now be mouldering in its watery grave, but of course it isn't! Another actor—Greenpeace—from a third form of solidarity (egalitarianism) forced its way in, at the eleventh hour, by audaciously, and very publicly, landing a helicopter on the structure as it was being towed out into the Atlantic. The disposal plans were abruptly abandoned by Shell (motorists, particularly in Germany, having stopped buying its petrol) and the British government was left with egg all over its face (John Major, the prime minister at the time, called Shell's senior management 'wimps'). Shell then entered into lengthy negotiations with Greenpeace, and the Brent Spar has now been cut up into cylindrical sections to help form a ferry terminal in Norway. Those British citizens who managed to remain ignorant of the whole affair (and they were many), or who found themselves totally convinced by whoever they happened to have last seen arguing their case on television, were evidently bound into none of these 'active' solidarities—individualism, hierarchy or egalitarianism—and constituted a fourth and rather 'inactive' solidarity—fatalism—assuring one another either that 'ignorance is bliss' or that 'nothing we could do would make any difference anyway'.

So cultural theory, by doubling-up from two solidarities to four, is able to make sense—predictive sense—of something that must always remain beyond the explanatory reach—a perennial source of surprise—of those who have equipped themselves with conventional social science wisdom. That, I would argue, is why this theory merits our attention.

THE FOUR SOLIDARITIES

- For upholders of the *individualist* solidarity, nature is benign and resilient—able to recover from any exploitation (hence the iconic myth of nature: a ball that, no matter how profoundly disturbed,

Asymmetrical Transactions

FATALISM	HIERARCHY

Nature: Capricious

Nature: Perverse/ Tolerant

Man: Fickle and Untrustworthy

Man: Deeply flawed but redeemable by firm, nurturing and long-lived institutions

Unfettered Competition (Unaccountability)

Fettered Competition (Accountability)

INDIVIDUALISM

EGALITARIANISM

Nature: Benign

Nature: Ephemeral

Man: Everywhere self-seeking

Man: Caring and sharing

Symmetrical Transactions

Figure 8.1: The Four Forms of Social Solidarity and their Associated Premises (or Myths of Nature)

always returns to stability)—and man is inherently self-seeking and atomistic. Trial and error, in self-organizing ego-focused networks (markets), is the way to go, with Adam Smith's invisible hand ensuring that people only do well when others also benefit. Individualists, in consequence, trust others until they give them reason not to and then retaliate in kind (the winning 'tit for tat' strategy in the iterated Prisoner's Dilemma game [Rapoport 1985]). They see it as only fair that (as in the joint stock company) those who put most in get most out. Managing institutions that work 'with the grain of the market' (getting rid of environmentally harmful subsidies, for instance) are what are needed.

- Nature, for those who bind themselves into the *egalitarian* solidarity, is almost the exact opposite (hence the ball on the up-turned basin)—fragile, intricately interconnected and ephemeral—and man is essentially caring and sharing (until corrupted by coercive and inegalitarian institutions: markets and hierarchies). We must all tread lightly on the earth, and it is not enough that people start off equal; they must end up equal as well—equality of result. Trust and levelling go hand-in-hand, and institutions that distribute unequally are distrusted. Voluntary simplicity is the only solution to our environmental problems, with the 'precautionary principle' being strictly enforced on those who are tempted not to share the simple life.

- The world, in the *hierarchical* solidarity, is controllable. Nature is stable until pushed beyond discoverable limits (hence the two humps), and man is malleable: deeply flawed but redeemable by firm, long-lasting and trustworthy institutions. Fair distribution is by rank and station or, in the modern context, by need (with the level of need being determined by an expert and dispassionate authority). Environmental management requires certified experts (to determine the precise locations of nature's limits) and statutory regulation (to ensure that all economic activity is then kept within those limits).

- *Fatalist* actors (or perhaps we should say non-actors, since their voice is seldom heard in policy debates; if it was they wouldn't be fatalistic!) find neither rhyme nor reason in nature, and know that man is fickle and untrustworthy. Fairness, in consequence, is not to be found in this life, and there is no possibility of effecting change for the better. 'Defect first'—the winning strategy in the one-off Prisoner's Dilemma—makes sense here, given the unreliability of communication and the permanent absence of prior acts of good faith. With no way of ever getting in sync with nature (push the ball this way or that and the feedback is everywhere the same), or of building trust with others, the fatalist's world (unlike those of the other three solidarities) is one in which learning is impossible. 'Why bother?' therefore, is the rational management response.

These solidarities, in varying strengths and patterns of pair-wise alliance, are clearly discernible almost anywhere you care to look: in debates over water engineering in South Asia (Gyawali 2001); in international fora where delegates struggle to do something about climate change (Thompson et al. 1998; Verweij 2001); in the different ways international regimes cope with trans-boundary risks such as water pollution (Verweij 2000) and municipalities go about the business of transport planning (Hendriks 1994); in the various ways households set about making ends meet (Dake and Thompson 1999); in the different diagnoses of the pensions crises in countries with ageing populations (Ney 1997); and in the different panaceas that are variously championed and rejected by theorists of public administration (Hood 1998), to mention but a few.

  In all these examples we find that each solidarity, in creating a context that is shaped by its distinctive premises, generates a storyline that inevitably contradicts those that are generated by the other solidarities. Yet, since each distils certain elements of experience and wisdom that are missed by the others, and since each provides a clear expression of the way in which a significant portion of the populace feels we should live with one another and with nature, it is important that they all be taken some sort of account of in the policy process. That, in essence, is the case for *clumsiness*, and I can now expand it with the help of a worked example: climate change.

THE CONTESTED TERRAIN OF CLIMATE CHANGE[1]

The global climate change debate, of course, is still going on, but an analysis of that debate in the mid-1990s provides us with a convenient

[1] This section is based on Ney and Thompson (2000).

point of entry: three *policy stories* (three, because the fatalist solidarity has no voice; if it had it would not be fatalistic). Each policy story provides a setting (the basic assumptions), a villain (the policy problem), heroes (policy protagonists), and, of course, a moral (the policy solution). Depending on the socio-institutional context of the particular policy actor, each story emphasises different aspects of the climate change issue. What is more, each story defines itself in contradistinction to the other policy stories.

Profligacy: An Egalitarian Story

This story begins by pointing to the profligate consumption and production patterns of the North as the fundamental cause of global climate change. Rich industrialized countries, so the argument goes, are recklessly pillaging the world's resources with little regard to the well being of either the planet or the peoples of its poorer regions. Global climate change is more than an issue that is amenable to quick technical fixes; it is a fundamentally moral and ethical issue. The setting for this story is a world in which everything is intricately connected to everything else: Nature Ephemeral (see Figure 1). Whether this concerns human society or the natural world, this story urges us to think of Planet Earth as a single living entity. Environmental degradation, then, is also an attack on human well being. Humans, so the argument goes, have, until now, successfully deluded themselves that they can live apart from the natural environment. In reality, however, there is no place for humans outside nature and thus no particular reason for considering humans as superior to nature. In short, this story is set in an eco-centric world.

The villain, in the profligacy story, is the fundamentally inequitable structure of advanced industrial society. In particular, the profit motive and the obsession with economic growth—the driving forces of global capitalism—have not only brought us to the brink of ecological disaster; they have also distorted our understanding of both the natural and the social world. Global commerce and the advertising industry lead us to desire environmentally unsustainable products (bottled water, fast cars, or high protein foods, for example) while our real human needs (living in harmony with nature and with each other: the egalitarian's social construction of human nature) go unfulfilled. What is more, advanced capitalism distributes the spoils of global commerce highly inequitably. This is true within countries (the increasing gap between the rich classes and the poor classes) and among countries (the increasing gap between the affluent countries of the North and the destitute countries of the South). In short, prevailing structural inequalities have led to increasingly unsustainable patterns of consumption and production.

Since everything is connected to everything else, this story continues, we cannot properly understand environmental degradation unless we see it as a symptom of this wider social malaise. The way humans pollute, degrade and destroy the natural world is merely a very visible indicator for the way they treat each other and particularly the weaker members of society. The logic that allows us to fell thousands of square kilometres of rainforests, to dump toxins in waterways, or pollute the air is precisely the same logic that produces racism, misogyny and xenophobia. Tackling one problem inevitably implies tackling all the others.

The heroes of the profligacy story are those organizations and individuals who have managed to see through the chimera of progress in advanced industrial society. They are those groups and persons that understand that the fate of humans is inextricably linked to the fate of Planet Earth. The heroes understand that, in order to halt environmental degradation, we have to address the fundamental global inequities. In short, the heroes of the profligacy policy argument are those organizations of protest such as, most prominently, Greenpeace or Friends of the Earth. These organizations, I need hardly point out, are strongly biased towards the egalitarian social solidarity.[2]

---

[2] Earth First!, however, is probably a better example now, since both Greenpeace and Friends of the Earth have in recent years gone some distance along the egalitarian-to-hierarchist road: a road that Max Weber dubbed the *routinization of charisma*. Indeed, they are now so far along that road that Earth First! is able to define itself in contradistinction to them: 'To avoid co-option, we feel it is necessary to avoid the corporate organizational structure so readily embraced by many environmental groups. Earth First! is a movement, not an organization. Our structure is non-hierarchical. We have no highly-paid 'professional staff' or formal leadership' [http//:www.earthfirstjournal.org/efj/primer/index.html (26 July 2002)].

What, then, is the moral of the profligacy story? Its proponents point to a number of solutions. In terms of immediate policy, the profligacy tale urges us to adopt the precautionary principle in all cases: unless policy actors can prove that a particular activity is innocuous to the environment, they should refrain from it. The underlying idea here is that the environment is precariously balanced on the brink of a precipice. The story further calls for drastic cuts in carbon dioxide emissions; since the industrialized North produces most of these emissions, the onus is on advanced capitalist states to take action. Of course, this policy argument calls for a total and complete ban on chlorofluorocarbons.

Yet none of these measures, the story continues, is likely to be fruitful on its own. In order to really tackle the problem of global climate change, those in the affluent North will have to fundamentally reform their political institutions and their unsustainable lifestyles. Rather than professionalized bureaucracies and huge centralized administrations, the advocates of the profligacy story suggest we decentralize decision-making down to the grass roots level. Rather than continuing to produce ever-increasing amounts of waste, we should aim at conserving the fragile natural resources we have: we should, in a word, move from the idea of a waste society to the concept of a *conserve* society. Only then can we meet real human needs. What are real human needs? Simple, they are the needs of Planet Earth.

Population: A Hierarchist Story

This policy argument tells a story of uncontrolled population growth in the poorer regions of the world. Rapidly increasing population in the South, this story argues, is placing local and global eco-systems under pressures that are fast becoming dangerously uncontrollable: more people mean more resource consumption which inevitably leads to environmental degradation. The setting of the population policy

---

All this helps to make clear that Cultural Theory is emphatically a dynamic theory, with its typology identifying the timeless components in the ever-changing positions that are the destinations and points of departure for all that endless movement. Cultural theorists, therefore, are in full agreement with Guiseppe di Lampedusa (author of *The Leopard*) when he writes 'If things are to stay the same then there's going to have to be some changes'.

story differs slightly, but significantly, from the settings in the other two diagnoses. Like the protagonists of the profligacy story, the population policy argument maintains that global climate change is a moral issue. Human beings, due to their singular position in the natural world, are the custodians of Planet Earth; since civilization and technological progress have allowed us to understand the natural world more than other species, we have a moral obligation to apply this knowledge wisely. Unlike the profligacy story, the population tale assumes that humans have a special status outside natural processes. The population story, like that of the proponents of the pricing argument (see next story), contends that human actions are rational. However, unlike the pricing argument, the population story tells us the sum of individual rational actions can lead to irrational and detrimental outcomes. The population story, then, is set in a world that needs rational management in order to become sustainable. Yet, while the motive of rational management is an ethical duty to preserve the planet, the means of management are technical. Economic growth, and the socio-economic system that underpins that growth, are necessary components in any global climate change policy response. However, economic growth in itself is no solution: it must be tempered, directed, and balanced by the careful application of knowledge and judgement.

The villain in the population tale is uncontrolled population growth. Since each individual has a fixed set of basic human needs (such as food, shelter, security, etc.) and these needs are then standardized at every level of socio-economic development (the hierarchist's social construction of human nature), population increase, other things being equal, must lead to an increase in the aggregate demand for resources. Humans, the story insists, satisfy their basic human needs by consuming resources. It follows that population growth must lead to an increase in resource consumption: more people will produce more carbon dioxide to satisfy their basic needs (though this can be mitigated, in the longer term, by carefully planned and managed changes in technology: away from fossil fuels and towards renewables or nuclear—fission and eventually fusion). Given the limited nature of most resources, population growth must invariably lead to over-consumption and degradation of natural resources.

The heroes of the population story are those institutions with both the organizational capacities (that is, the technical knowledge) and the 'right' sense of moral responsibility. In short, the global climate change issue should be left to experts situated in large-scale, well-organized administrations (the IPCC—the Intergovernmental Panel on Climate Change—for instance). In terms of our typology of ways of organizing, the population story emerges from hierarchically structured institutions.

The moral of the population story is to rationally control population growth. In particular, this means the introduction of family planning and education in the countries most likely to suffer from rapid population growth. Here, the onus for action is quite clearly on the countries of the South. Rapid population growth has eroded societal management capacities; if we are to tackle the global climate change issue we must first establish the proper organizational preconditions.

Prices: An Individualist Story

This story locates the causes of global climate change in the relative prices of natural resources. Historically, prices have poorly reflected the underlying economic scarcities; the result, plain for all to see, is a relative over-consumption of natural resources.

The setting of the prices tale is the world of markets and economic growth. Unlike the profligacy story, the prices diagnosis sees no reason to muddy the conceptual waters with extraneous considerations of social equality. Yes, it says, global climate change is an important issue, but it is an issue that is amenable to precise analytical treatment. It is, in short, a technical issue to which we can apply a technical discourse. Economic growth, far from being a problem, is the sole source of salvation from environmental degradation. Environmental protection, the proponents of this policy argument contend, is a very costly business. In order, then, to be able to foot the huge bill for adjusting to a more sustainable economy, societies will have to command sufficient funds. These funds, in turn, will not materialize from thin air: only economic growth can provide the necessary resources to tackle the expensive task of greening the economy.

In sum, the prices tale takes place in a world determined by the Invisible Hand. Here, people know and can precisely rank their preferences (the individualist's social construction of human nature). In the prices story, individual pursuit of rational self-interest (economic utility) leads, as if by magic (though economists such as Hayek prefer to call it 'self-organization'), to the optimal allocation of resources. If market forces are allowed to operate as they should then resource prices will accurately reflect underlying scarcities; the price mechanism then keeps environment-degrading consumption in check. However, if someone (usually the misguided policy maker) meddles with market forces, prices cannot reflect real scarcities; this gives rise to incentives for rational economic actors to over- or under-consume a particular resource.

The villain in the prices story is misguided economic policy. Barriers to international trade, subsidies to inefficient national industries, as well as price and wage floors, introduce distortions to the self-regulatory powers of·the market. These distortions have historically led markets to place a monetary value on natural resources that belies the true market value. The result, the protagonists of this policy argument maintain, has been wholesale over-consumption and degradation of the natural world. The heroes of the prices story are those institutions that understand the economics of resource consumption. In the global climate change debate, these institutions comprise players such as the Global Climate Coalition and trans-national energy companies.[3] In terms of the cultural theory typology, the heroes of this story are those institutions that are strongly permeated by the individualist solidarity (*The Economist*, for instance, and think tanks such as Britain's Institute of Economic Affairs and the US's Competitive Enterprise Institute).

The moral of the prices story is as simple as its prognosis: in order to successfully face the challenge of global climate change we have to 'get the prices right'. Unlike the profligacy story, the prices tale sees no necessity to restructure existing institutions. If it is the distortions of global, national and regional market mechanisms that undervalue natural resources then any climate change policy that fails to remove these distortions is 'fundamentally flawed'. Policy responses must work 'with the market'. Here, concrete policy proposals consist of both general measures, such as the liberalization of global trade, as well

---

[3] These players call themselves contrarians, because they do not accept the problem definition by which the global climate change debate is at present framed. In consequence, they tend to find themselves excluded from that debate. For an analysis of 'hegemonic discourses' such as this, and their inevitable transformations, see Box 4.3, Vol. I of Rayner and Malone (1998: 292–3).

as more specific measures, such as carbon taxes or tradable emission permits (with a strong preference for the latter, taxes being seen as more likely to distort the market).

Consequently, it is only by teasing out these sorts of policy arguments, and their diverse adherents, that we can understand the social constructions of needs and resources: how they are generated, how they are reproduced and transformed, and how they shape the policy process. This understanding has some important implications.

- The three stories tell plausible but conflicting tales of climate change. All three tales use reason and logic to argue their points. None of the tales is 'wrong', in the sense of being implausible or incredible. Yet, at the same time, none of the stories is completely 'right'; each argument focuses on those aspects of climate change for which there is a suitable solution cast within the terms of a particular form of organization.
- These three policy discourses are not reducible to one another. No one of the policy arguments is a close substitute for the others. Nor are any of the stories' proponents ever likely to agree on the fundamental causes of and solutions to the global climate change issue. And, since these stories implicitly convey a normative argument, namely that of the good life (either in egalitarian enclaves, in hierarchies, or in markets), they are curiously immune to enlightenment by 'scientific' facts; we cannot, in any scientific sense, prove or falsify policy stories.[4]
- These stories also define what sort of evidence counts as a legitimate fact and what type of knowledge is credible. The profligacy story discounts economic theory as the obfuscation of social inequalities and dismisses rational management as the reification of social relations. The tale of prices views holistic eco-centrism as amateur

[4] Some qualification is needed here. Policy arguments that require water to flow uphill, say, or the sun to go round the earth, or motion to be perpetual (what a great way to mitigate the greenhouse effect!), are unlikely to be persuasive because the scientific facts they seek to overturn lie outside the 'challengeable pale' (the English Pale was a small area around Dublin, beyond which the writ of English law did not run). For some indication of how that pale (which, of course, is far from fixed) can be mapped and coped with, see Thompson et al. (1986) and Adams and Thompson (2002).

pop-science and pours scorn on the naïve belief in benign control. Last, the population story rejects laissez-faire economic theory as dangerously unrealistic and questions the scientific foundations of more holistic approaches.

This leaves us with a dynamic, plural and argumentative system of policy-definition and policy framing that policy makers can ignore only at their cost, for two reasons. First, each policy story, as we have seen, thematizes a pertinent aspect of the climate change debate; very few would argue that Northern consumption habits, population growth or distorted prices have no impact on global climate change at all. However, as we have seen, each story places a different emphasis on each aspect. Any global climate change policy, then, based on only one or two of these stories, will merely provide a response to a specific aspect of the global climate change problem. It will, in short, provide a partially effective response. Second, and more significantly, each of the stories represents a political voice in the policy process. Ignoring any of these voices means excluding them from policy making. Within democratic polities, this inevitably leads to a loss of legitimacy. What is more, in democracies, dissenting voices will eventually force their way into the policy process (as we have seen for instance, with the Brent Spar and, more recently, with the World Trade Organization in Seattle and Prague and the G8 riots in Genoa). Neither the cost of acrimonious and vicious political conflict, nor the loss of public trust experienced by those who (perhaps inadvertently, perhaps not) suppress dissenting voices, are particularly attractive. The former often leads to policy deadlock; the latter may well result in a legitimacy crisis in the polity as a whole.

So these three policy stories have important implications, not just for global climate change policy making, but (and this is where the range of applications I mentioned earlier comes back into the picture) for policy, and for risk management, generally.

- *Endemic Conflict*: In a policy process where politics matters (that is, in any policy process) there will always be at least three divergent but plausible stories that frame the issue, define the problem, and suggest solutions. Thus conflict in policy-making processes is endemic, inevitable, and desirable, rather than pathological, curable or deviant. Any policy process that does not take this into account does so at the risk of losing political legitimacy.

- *Plural Policy Responses*: We have seen that each story tells a plausible, but selective, story. Any policy response modelled solely in terms of just one or two of these tales will be, at best, partial and, at worst, irrelevant.

- *Quality of Communication*: Since policy making is inherently conflictual, and since effective policy responses depend on the participation of all three voices, policy outcomes crucially depend on the quality of the communication within the debate. A policy debate that can harness the inherent communicative and argumentative conflict between different storytellers will profit most from the potentially constructive interaction between different proponents. Conversely, a policy debate in which all three positions are sharply polarized will probably lead to policy deadlock. This is a structural argument that concerns the implicit and explicit 'rules' that govern policy deliberation in a polity. If the 'rules of the game' permit or even force policy actors to take seriously different types of stories, then what Sabatier and Jenkins-Smith (1993) call 'policy-oriented learning' can take place. If this is not the case, then the policy debate will be an unconstructive dialogue of the deaf.

Summarizing all of the above, we have at one extreme an unresponsive monologue and at the other a shouting match amongst the totally deaf. Between these extremes we occasionally find a vibrant multivocality in which each voice puts its view as persuasively as possible, sensitive to the knowledge that others are likely to disagree, and acknowledging a responsibility to listen to what the others are saying. This is the condition—clumsiness—we must strive for if we value democracy or, as is the case with many regulatory agencies, we are mandated to develop and implement policy on behalf of a democracy. Getting there and staying there is, of course, not easy.

At the monologue end of the spectrum the policy process is seductively elegant and reassuringly free (it would seem) from the defiling intrusion of politics. Here we find the mind-set characterized by single-metric rationality. At the other extreme we wallow in the incoherence of complete relativism. The cultural theory typology presented here suggests that between these extremes there is the possibility of constructive dialogue. It will often be a noisy, discordant, contradictory dialogue, but this is the clumsy beast that democratic policy makers and regulators must seek to harness and ride.

MAKING OURSELVES CLUMSY

The term 'clumsy institution' was coined by Michael Schapiro (1988) as a way of escaping from the idea that, when we are faced with contradictory definitions of problem and solution, we must choose one and reject the rest. Clumsy institutions, we can say, now that we have the cultural theory typology, are those institutional arrangements in which none of the voices—the hierarchist's calling for 'wise guidance and careful stewardship', the individualist's urging us to 'get the prices right', the egalitarian's insisting that we need 'a whole new relationship with nature', and the fatalist's asking 'why bother?'—is excluded, and in which the contestation is harnessed to constructive, if noisy, argumentation.

Clumsiness emerges as preferable to elegance (optimizing around just one of the definitions of the problem and, in the process, silencing the other voices) once we realize that what looks like irreconcilable contradiction is, in fact, *essential contestation*. Moreover, since each voice usually argues that its solution will strengthen democracy, whilst those being urged by the others will weaken it, democracy too becomes an essentially contested concept: a concept which, following Gallie (1955), can never be pinned down in a single way but can be clarified only through regular argument; that is, through discourse.

Each solidarity, therefore, has its own social construction of democracy: its 'model'(Hendriks and Zourides 1999) or 'image' (Jensen 1999). Clumsiness, in consequence, has normative implications that link policy, technology and democracy in ways that mainstream political science has disregarded (see, for instance, Ney and Thompson 2000, and Tranvik et al. 2001).[5] If we haven't got all the models of democracy—clearly voiced and engaged with one another in the

---

[5] Though I have not dwelt explicitly on technology in this essay, it is of course central to the whole business of climate change. It is our technologies that have put the greenhouse gases into the atmosphere, it is our technologies that have enabled us to detect that increase, and it is changes in our technologies—from fossil fuel-based to renewables—that will help us remedy the situation.

public sphere—then, so the normative argument goes, we haven't *got* democracy!

- *Hierarchists*, siding with Plato and his philosopher-king, subscribe to the *guardian* model, in which it is only right that those with superior insight and virtue should do their trustee-like duty and make all the decisions. Democracy should be indirect, majoritarian and representative, with the political class being given primacy over public affairs on the basis of popular elections every few years.
- *Individualists* see self-determination as crucial and dislike both paternalism and majoritarianism (which, they point out, can result in even quite large minorities being prevented from 'carrying out their plans'). Theirs is a *protective* model and, siding with Locke, they see government's *raison d'être* as 'the protection of life, liberty and estate'.
- *Egalitarians* are more with Rousseau, rejecting deference and seeing self-interest as something to be reined in, not amplified. They plump for the *participatory* model, in which the equal right to self-development is what matters, and this means that choice should be by broad and direct participation, ideally in a small-scale, face-to-face way and at a single level: the grass roots.
- *Fatalists*, too, have their distinctive, and characteristically unenthusiastic, model: a *non-model*, really. Despite the other solidarities' fine words about public goods, private goods and common-pool goods, fatalists know that these are all really club goods, from which they have been excluded. Hence struggling to define who the decision-maker should be is a waste of effort. It does not matter who you vote for, fatalists assure one another, the government always gets in.[6]

---

[6] The interlocking of the social constructions of public, private, common-pool and club goods with the social constructions of democracy (and, for good measure, of information, technology and information technology) is explained in Thompson (2000), along with the acknowledgement that the former is shamelessly borrowed from Verweij (1999) and the latter from Hendriks and Zourides (1999).

9

Who's in Charge?
Reflections on the Worldwide Displacement of Democratic Judgement by Expert Assessments

STEVE RAYNER

EMERGENCE OF THE AGE OF ASSESSMENT

Some four decades ago, Jacques Ellul (1964) published a classic work of science studies that warned of the dangers of technocracy displacing democracy in modern society. His concern was not the isolated alarmism of a mid-twentieth century European intellectual. His alert came on the heels of a warning by one of the century's hardest-headed American realists, Dwight D. Eisenhower, who, upon his retirement as US President, issued his famous caution to beware of the growing power of the military-industrial complex and what it might portend for democracy.

Subsequent decades have demonstrated the prescience of these very different mid-twentieth century minds. Although its prime locus may have shifted in some countries from government to the private sector, technocracy is not only alive and well but through the development and control of new technologies, it has colonized almost every aspect of human existence. We are now faced with the introduction of radical new technologies that touch on the very nature of life and what it means to be human. The pace of such change has been truly unprecedented. The first controlled genetic experiment was conducted only in 1972. The first successful human in-vitro fertilization was performed in 1978. Leading neuroscientists seriously propose that the day is not far off when we will be able to combine neuroscience, nanotechnology and information technology to radically reconfigure the scope and reach of action that can be achieved by the human brain.

Technological innovations have been accompanied by a dramatic increase in the scope and reach of technical expertise in the lives of citizens. In the US, for example, the late 1960s saw the development of important efforts to tame the unruly negative effects of modern industrial society. The National Environmental Policy Act (NEPA), which was signed into law by Richard M. Nixon in 1969, exemplifies a whole raft of environmental and technological legislation that, in seeking to control industrial excesses, created new and unprecedented types of technical analysis and review, including a model for environmental assessment that has been emulated around the world (Rayner 1993). To assist it in the evaluation of technology and its role in society, the US Congress adopted the techniques of technology assessment and established the Office of Technology Assessment, which was abolished by the Republican-dominated Congress in the mid 1990s.

NEPA's mandating of environmental impact assessment, the establishment of the Environmental Protection Agency and the Clean Air and Clean Water Acts, have almost certainly contributed to a better world than the one we would have inherited without them. However, along with these benefits, the legislative initiatives launched in the 1960s and 1970s have also spawned whole new industries and government organizations based on developing and applying formal techniques of environmental and technological assessment.

In the four decades since Ellul's warning that technocracy was depoliticizing society, governments on both sides of the Atlantic have made increased use of benefit-cost analysis to justify a wide range of public policy decisions. In fields where science promises useful input to decision making, there has been an increased reliance on a variety of techniques, such as probabilistic risk analysis, pollution dispersion models, urban planning models, traffic-flow models, dose-response curves, and so on. International negotiations on trans-boundary environmental issues, such as climate change, rely heavily on models of emissions, atmospheric chemistry and dynamics, and climate impacts.

Growth in the reliance on such assessment techniques has been accompanied by an expansion of expertise to design, operate and in-

terpret such tools. Contradicting Franklin Delano Roosevelt's epithet
that the twentieth century was the 'Century of the Common Man',
Perkin (1989) has dubbed it the 'Century of the Professional Expert'.
Jasanoff (1990) has described the growing reliance of regulatory agencies on scientific and technical advisors and advisory bodies as the
emergence of a formidable 'Fifth Branch' of the US government.

In the US, the requirement for 'science-based policy' is enshrined
in legislation. In this case, science usually means 'give me a number'
(Porter 1995). In Britain, the government champions an 'evidence-
based policy'. Again, 'evidence' is usually equated with a numerical
threshold, such as a pollutant concentration in air, water, soil, or
foodstuffs that can be invoked to trigger action or justify inaction.
Politicians demand technical information on which to base decisions.
They also benefit from the ability to deflect responsibility onto
technical failures when those decisions do not turn out for the best.
Bad decisions can be blamed on inadequate science. This was clearly
the pattern in Britain with respect to the government's mishandling
of the transmission of the cattle brain disease, Bovine Spongiform
Encephalitis (BSE), to human beings, which lead to worldwide bans
on British beef exports in the 1990s, or in the more recent outbreak
of Foot and Mouth Disease (FMD) that resulted in the decimation of
British herds.

THE INTERNATIONALIZATION OF ASSESSMENT

The Age of Assessment is not a phenomenon confined to the wealthy
industrial countries. A common vehicle for their extension into the
less-industrialized world has been the operation of international
development aid programmes, particularly those of the World Bank.
In many parts of the developing world, technical needs assessments,
benefit-cost analyses, and environmental impact analyses, usually
performed by consultants from the donor countries, are likely to play
a bigger role in shaping people's lives than the operation of their local
and national institutions of, hopefully democratic, governance.

Science and technology are essential aspects of international
economic, social and political development. The concentration of
scientific and technical expertise in the advanced industrial nations,
such as the UK, tends to disadvantage less-industrialized countries

in their relationships with the industrialized world. I have seen first-hand how limited technical capacity restricts the participation of less-industrialized countries in bodies such as the Intergovernmental Panel on Climate Change (IPCC), which prepares scientific assessments that inform the policy choices of national governments around the world.

Issues of technology transfer and the promulgation of developmentally appropriate technologies often echo, on an international scale, the kinds of debates that we associate with controversial scientific and technical innovations and practices at home, and often pit experts against experts and against wider interests in society. In some cases, however, the alliances and allegiances that dominate the development discourse challenge conventional assumptions about the role of various stakeholders in domestic debates. For example, international environmental negotiations often pit Northern scientists, governments and NGOs, acting in the name of a global sustainable development agenda that is heavily informed by the earth sciences, against Southern governments and citizen organizations, whose concept of sustainable development is focused on more local needs and local knowledge. Opposition to the World Trade Organization (WTO) is at least partially rooted in resistance to global cultural homogenization, which is propelled by the universalization of scientific and technological assessment that usually trumps local knowledge and concerns, as much as it is driven by financial forces. Thus, in both the North and the South, science, rather than society, shapes the agendas for science-in-society debates.

Electoral Decline in the Age of Assessment

The growth in governmental reliance on expert techniques and formal decision-making technologies in all walks of public life has been accompanied, over the same period, by a disconcerting decline in electoral participation in many industrialized countries, especially Britain and the United States (Dalton and Wattenberg 2000). This decline is puzzling to the dominant model of political participation in political science—the civic voluntarism model—which predicts that voter turnouts will increase as educational opportunities expand and incomes rise (Parry et al. 1992; Verba et al. 1995). Is it possible that the concatenation of rising demand for evidence- and science-based policy and the displacement of moral judgement from the public sphere could have something to do with the decline of electoral participation? Whereas most citizens feel that they are competent to judge whose moral or aesthetic values appeal to them, they are less confident in their competence to second-guess technical expertise.

Where once citizens voted on the basis of their assessments of candidates' values, such judgements have become marginal in importance and much harder to make. Technocracy is clearly an important aspect of the drift to the centre in both US and UK politics. On the one hand, the dominance of technique appears to reduce the scope for political differentiation, which comes to be seen as deviation from a technically defined reality. At the same time, if the decision is to be based on purely 'technical' criteria, what difference does it make who is in charge? Such reasoning suggests that it is not worthwhile participating in electoral democracy. 'It doesn't matter who you vote for, the government always gets in!' Where once statesmen based decisions on some idea of the good, politicians and businessmen now look to technical experts to inform decisions.

PUBLIC CONSULTATION AND PARTICIPATION

Social scientists have responded to the triumph of technique and attendant electoral decline by advocating and designing increasingly sophisticated techniques of their own to re-establish a role for non-experts in scientific, environmental and technological decision making. In the US at least, the inspiration for these efforts can be located in the same legislation that nourished the growth of technical assessment. NEPA not only requires that government agencies consider the environmental consequences of any contemplated action, it requires public consultation, known as scoping, to assist the assessors in determining the range of issues to be included. NEPA also requires that the findings of the technical analysis be subject to public comment, to which the proposing agency must respond, before such a report is accepted. These requirements represent a landmark in the evolution of public consultation and eventually public participation in technological decision making in the US. Another source was the right of the public interest groups to act as interveners in the nuclear power plant licensing process through the 1970s and 1980s. In Britain, the practice of instituting public inquiries, for example the 1977 Windscale Inquiry into the THORP nuclear reprocessing facility proposal (Wynne 1982), provided some of the inspiration for designing new methods of public engagement in debate and decision making.

The ideal of involving different perspectives and values of interest groups has been a central theme of technology assessment almost since its beginnings (Carroll 1971: 647–53; Coates 1975: 67–9; Paschen et al. 1975) although through most of the first decade it was more of a principle than a practice. The Technology Assessment Bureau of the German Parliament established the practice of stakeholder evaluation of controlled confrontation of expertise and counter-expertise. However, this remained a highly mediated technique.

Environmental decision making has also been a source of inspiration for the greater engagement of non-experts in scientific assessment. In contemplating the issues in global environmental change, O' Riordan and Rayner (1991) called for the extension of conventional science into 'vernacular' science in which participants from many walks of life would bring their particular expertise to bear on emerging problems. Similar calls emanated from other quarters. Kai Lee (1993), examining the problem of balancing salmon habitat and power production in the US Pacific Northwest, provided a more expanded vision of 'civic' science. Various experiments in public consultation and participation in scientific, environmental and technological decision making were already underway in Europe and North America, including citizen juries, consensus conferences (especially in Norway on biomedical issues), citizen advisory bodies (such as the US Department of Energy's Site Specific Advisory Boards or SSABs), planning cells, regulatory negotiation, participatory integrated assessment and so forth (for example, Irwin 1995; Renn et al. 1995; van Asselt 2000). Each of these techniques was informed by social science theory or practice.

All of these techniques attempt to equip groups of citizens to make informed decisions about issues involving complex science or technology. The best of them also seek to enable scientists and policy makers to better understand the origins of citizen concerns. Some particularly interesting innovations have confronted citizens with technical expertise embodied in computer models that enable individuals and focus groups to specify and compare alternative environment and development scenarios (for example, Darier et al. 1998; Robinson 1998). The assumptions underlying all of these approaches to public participation are that it leads to better decisions through transparency and that expertise can and should be harnessed through the exercise of the popular will of citizens.

MOTIVATIONS FOR PUBLIC PARTICIPATION AND MODELS OF THE CITIZEN

The motivations of various actors for encouraging public participation in assessment processes are varied. However, each seems to embody a particular ideal of the citizen. Governments and natural scientists with a stake in the technology or project being assessed seem to view public participation as the source of a social licence to operate. For these actors, public participation is essentially an extension of science communication as informed by the so-called deficit model of science communication. This suggests that public concern about, or opposition to, scientific, environmental or technological development is primarily driven by lack of information or understanding about science. Although this view is now explicitly rejected in the rhetoric of most government agencies and firms, it remains firmly entrenched in their practice.

Critics of the deficit model have rightly pointed to the shortcomings of the standardized view of the citizen that is implicit in the deficit approach (for example, Leach and Scoones 2002; Wynne 2002). This is the citizen of liberal thought who:

- Is the individual beneficiary of rights granted by the state.
- Seeks to manage a portfolio of rank-ordered preferences.
- Focuses on safety as the core value of public life.
- Must rely on expert help to interpret uncertainty.

Public participation within this framework most often consists of mechanisms for offering individuals the opportunity to select from among a limited array of options or services, but not playing a significant role in setting policy agendas (Gaventa and Cornwall 2002).

However, it seems that the same reflexive critics are often rather unreflexive about the standardized model of the citizen that is embodied in the alternative models of citizen-science relationships that they embrace in explaining their own engagement in public participation exercises. Social scientists and NGOs tend to explain their motives for supporting public participation in terms of extending democratic control. The standardized citizen of the public participation paradigm:

• Is socially embedded in a community.
• Is locally knowledgeable and intuitively reflexive about society and nature .
• Focuses on common good as the core value of public life.
• Relies on inclusionary deliberation to reveal truth.

Deliberative democracy is the key to this alternative vision of the citizen. However, its key assumptions about ideal free speech (Habermas 1984) may mask the realities of indifference, politics and power that characterize real communities.

The industry also has its standardized model of the citizen as consumer, which lies at the heart of its approach to public participation, principally as an information collection exercise to inform management and marketing decisions. Ironically, the view of citizen as consumer may seem plausibly rational to citizens alienated from the electoral process as described above. Indeed, it seems to many of us that our consumption decisions are likely to have a greater impact in shaping our lives than our ballots. Thus, popular choices about governance seem to be increasingly made in the marketplace rather than in the legislature. In Sagoff's (1990) terms, the consumer is displacing the citizen in political importance. Shopping is becoming the new voting.

More compelling than any of these single standardizations of the citizen is the notion that people have multiple, overlapping identities that they are able to mobilize and diverse reference groups to which they refer for legitimation and support. Citizenship is thus redefined, in effect, as engagement through emergent social solidarities, which, as Ellison (1997) emphasizes, are likely to be 'increasingly messy and unstable'. These forms of engagement, involving new processes of

social and political interaction may be directed towards more diverse
sets of actors and institutions than notions of citizenship that are
derived entirely from the state or even the singular community (Leach
and Scoones 2002).

A perspective on citizenship as emergent solidarity suggests a view
of democracy that emphasizes the capacity of citizens to actively
participate and engage in the discourses that affect their lives
(Pateman 1970). Locating the concept of citizen and consumer in
emergent solidarities differentiates *democratic governance* in which
citizens themselves determine the institutional forms and shape the
terms of the debate from mere *participatory management*, which permits
rational debate only within received expert framings. The theory of
democratic governance also stresses that citizenship is a dynamic
learning process that creates and enhances citizenship capabilities
(Sirianni and Friedland 2000: 23).

However, little of this kind of thinking about citizenship seems
to inform official or even social science thinking around issues of
science and technology. Much of the debate about participation and
deliberation in technology assessment and science policy has relied
upon rather traditional notions of stable, not to say static conceptions
of the public, community, the state, knowledge, and interests that
do not challenge dominant managerial perspectives. Whatever the
motivations for supporting participatory exercises in science and
technological decision making, the most common explicit justifications
offered in support of the widespread employment of formal assessment
techniques are that they promote efficiency and transparency.

The Efficiency Rationale

As an explicit value to guide decision making, the concept of
efficiency was almost unknown in commerce or government prior to
the eighteenth century. It arose alongside the practice of commercial
accounting for the stocks and flows of goods. The extension of this
practice to government was the emergence of statistics—literally,
measurement of the state. It was but a short step from the idea that
one could calculate

what would contribute to the greatest happiness of the greatest number into
the imperative to pursue that goal. The solution that provides the greatest

happiness of the greatest number must also be an efficient solution, since any departure from efficiency, also by definition, reduces the amount of good available for distribution (Rayner and Malone 1998: 60).

Thus was born the ethical doctrine of utilitarianism. 'A bias towards efficiency is inherent in the methods of policy analysis and utilitarianism has been the ideological position most forthrightly incorporating this standard as a central value' (Heineman et al. 1990: 38). However, efficiency is not merely a technical issue or an indication of rational behaviour within utilitarianism, but is also an intrinsically moral imperative. Perhaps that is why neoclassical economists seem to be personally offended by inefficient solutions.

The utility principle domesticates moral diversity for decision-making authorities by offering the capability to measure and monitor stocks and flows of societal good, the proxy for good being wealth in some form. The same process systematically attenuates decision makers' awareness of alternative ethical considerations. The imperative to provide for societal good at the highest level of aggregation provides no guidance for securing the happiness of minorities and individuals, even those individuals in the happy majority. 'The guiding criterion for policy is the greatest good for society, quantitatively defined. But contemporary utilitarians, primarily economists and theorists of public choice, like Bentham, still have no principle for distributing this social goods according to manifest principles of equity' (Heineman et al. 1990: 40).

Increasing insight into the diversity of motives, values and preferences of individuals actually tends to frustrate utilitarian social accountancy, which depends on blending out such distinctions in the process of aggregation.

Most utilitarians assume, like the politics of interest, that the sole legitimate basis of social good is what individuals happen to value. And they view the process of social choice as an aggregative one, in which individual preferences are added to one another in arriving at decisions on the substance of social welfare (Heineman et al. 1990: 71).

It is hardly surprising, therefore, that insights into individual and social diversity are not merely considered irrelevant to utilitarian decision making, but actually have to be excluded from it in order to preserve the rationality and legitimacy of the utility principle. Yet scientific, environmental and technological decisions are not oriented by a unique consistent value system. Even a single individual may be influenced by several value systems that contradict each other (Jaeger et al. 1998). These conditions exacerbate Arrow's (1951) classical result demonstrating the impossibility of a general procedure for aggregating given individual preferences in a democratic fashion (see Sen 1995 for a more recent discussion). Yet half a century on, the smearing out of diverse values continues unabated within the technical assessment paradigm.

Ironically, just as technical criteria have increased in prominence for public policy decisions, the past half-century has been one of increased recognition of cultural diversity, much of it driven and justified by references to the postmodern movement in social science. At its best, this recognition has taken the form of greater appreciation of variety among value systems and the need to understand the diverse sources of concern that people have about public policy decisions. However, a darker side of the recognition of diversity has emerged with the idea that because values are so diverse, the only way to make sound policy is to exclude explicit consideration of diverse values from policy debates altogether. It supports the idea that policy can only be based on technical criteria that are somehow believed to be objective and independent of all value systems. This drives valid differences in values underground. Debate is conducted in the idiom of independent science, even when the issues at stake are not really scientific at all. For example, the view that it is simply wrong or a violation of the divine pattern of creation to engage in genetic manipulation receives no standing in courts, legislatures or the WTO. Someone of that conviction is forced to frame his or her arguments in terms of the potential for tangible harm.

THE TRANSPARENCY RATIONALE

Transparency is the other plank of justification for the ubiquitous adoption of formal assessment techniques. Interestingly, whereas critics who invoke other values such as individual equality or natural rights often contest the technocratic utilitarian value of efficiency, the principle of transparency seems to have been almost universally embraced.

A classic defence of benefit-cost analysis is that it is surely better to make the various dimensions in decision making explicit so that they can be reviewed for completeness (Are all of the appropriate issues taken into consideration?) and are subject to scrutiny than it is to take decisions based on implicit, partial or intuitive understandings. Surely no one would argue against the idea that consequential decisions should be made on a thorough examination of all of the relevant evidence that is available. The difficulties arise where there is disagreement about what is relevant and what counts as evidence. These difficulties are compounded by the reduction of incommensurable values to a single metric that permits the bottom-line benefit-cost ratio to be determined (Self 1975). The problem is further exacerbated when the original values of some of the non-marketable items in the calculation have to be inferred by surrogate techniques, such as willingness to pay or contingent valuation.

Benefit-cost analysis represents the aggregation of incommensurables in monetary terms. Another form of such aggregation takes the form of risk assessment, in which a diverse range of technical and social considerations are reduced to the common metric of 'risk', usually expressed as the probability of mortality. Like efficiency, risk is a modern invention of Western thought that serves the Benthamite calculation of aggregate social welfare. In earlier times and in non-Western traditions today, danger is specific, embedded in particular objects or activities, and quite different from the abstract universalizable concept of risk. Now, in the West, the discourse of governance is reduced to a discourse of science. The discourse of science is reduced to risk. Thus, the whole business of governance is reduced to a discourse of risk management. Nowhere is this alarming pattern more evident than in the November 2002 report of the UK Prime Minister's Strategy Unit entitled *Risk: Improving Government's Capability to Handle Risk and Uncertainty*, which alarmingly equates the business of governance with risk management.

Social scientists have argued that as an ordinary language category, the concept of risk continues to embody people's expectations for factors such as trust in risk managers and regulators, arrangements for liability distribution and compensation in the event of accidents, and whether people believe that they have been given an opportunity to give or withhold consent to risk. I refer to these as the TLC factors, referring both to the issues of trust, liability and consent, and the duty to exercise tender loving care of our fellow humans and the environment. They are essentially issues of judgement rather than calculation. Since they may not be amenable to mathematical quantification, they are likely to be ignored or even ruled out of order in professional assessments of technological, environmental or human health assessments (Rayner 1984, 1987; Rayner and Cantor 1987).

Technical analysis reduces risk to purely quantitative factors determinable by calculation. But, societal disagreements about risk cannot be resolved by recourse to expert assessments of potential damage. They must be addressed through political processes as ethical or even aesthetic disagreements. The key to understanding public controversies about risk (particularly about low-probability, high-consequence events) is not a calculation of the statistical probability of death or 'How safe is safe enough?' The real question often is, 'How fair is safe enough?' In other words, are people satisfied that the process of decision making has been just and wonder if the distribution of benefits and costs accord with their ideas of distributive justice.

Both benefit-cost analyses and risk assessments are often highly technical in their execution. Thus, they tend to be incomprehensible to people lacking the appropriate technical background. They may not be transparent to other technical experts, even in the same field. Critics claim that they remain firmly opaque to ordinary citizens. In addition to the technical transparency of assessment techniques themselves, there is the issue of their use in decision making. Even if we assume the adequacy of economic and technical assessments, we should still ask the empirical question whether they are really the basis for policy decisions? Ironically, extensive studies of knowledge utilization (mostly conducted in the US) suggest that technical analysis mostly provides cover for the implicit exercise of judgement (Rayner and Malone 1998). Whereas policy makers demand analysis with a strong 'bottom line', that bottom line seldom, if ever, finds its way into legislation or regulation. Policy makers mostly treat technical analyses as background information. Where numbers are explicitly used, the existence of competing assessments allows decision makers to select the analysis that most closely conforms to their pre-existing preference. So while the triumph of technique promises objectivity and transparency, it seems just as likely to be a means to buffer decisions from public scrutiny.

The problems of public participation are not confined to issues of motivation and inspiration justification for participatory exercises, there are also issues arising from the conduct of the exercises themselves. This essay will specifically discuss three of these—evaluation, representation and agenda setting.

EVALUATION

Evaluation of the performance of public participation remains problematic. It is almost exclusively self-evaluation performed by the organizers of the consultation or engagement activity or sympathetic evaluation by social scientists known to be committed to the principle and techniques being employed. Most evaluation is of single projects. There is very little systematic or comparative evaluation across multiple sites and different techniques. The focus of evaluation is almost exclusively process-based, for example, looking at how closely the activity corresponded to Habermas' (1984) 'ideal free speech' or how the participants behaved or said they felt about each other. There have been almost no credible outcome-based evaluations that have established that a public participation technique has led to a technically or socially sound outcome that otherwise would not have been reached.

Clients have expressed satisfaction with these activities. For example, the US Department of Energy (DOE) claims that the SSABs established to assist in environmental remediation at its former nuclear weapons sites have saved millions of dollars in clean-up costs. However, the reality is that DOE has never performed a systematic outcome-based evaluation. It has no way of knowing if experts alone would have saved as much or even more money if left to themselves. Of course, this illustrates the general problem facing outcome evaluation: it is incredibly difficult to establish a causal link between the process and its outcomes and to establish what the counterfactual situation would have been in the absence of the advisory board.

Another problematic aspect of participatory approaches is their evaluation from the standpoint of the participants. O'Neill (2001) suggests that members of citizen juries go on to heightened levels of civic engagement. More common are reports of anger on the part of citizens who invested time and energy into deliberative processes that subsequently had little or no effect on the policies or decisions that they were invited to consider. Part of the problem here is the constitutional difficulty that legislatures may have in binding themselves to decisions made by less representative bodies. The fact is that the efficacy of public participation remains largely a matter of faith and political commitment.

REPRESENTATION

One of the most persistent criticisms of participatory techniques relates to the problem of representativeness, both in terms of validity of the sample of the public that is drawn upon and in the sense of its legitimacy to shape decisions for those who were not included directly, in the process. It is not always easy to distinguish claims about these two meanings of representativeness. For example, Carson and Martin (2002) claim that sample bias can be overcome by random selection of participants. However, a close examination of their methodology reveals that their citizen juries were far from fully random. The pool from which they were drawn was self-selected from an initial random mailing and the actual juries were then selected to conform to a predetermined socio-demographic profile of the population in question. While this method may be considered to have produced panels that were representative in a sampling sense, the authors also claim legitimacy for them in that they performed well by process criteria. However, these juries were also heavily mediated by the researchers, which suggests that their conformance to deliberative norms of ideal free speech may have little to do with their representativeness.

Other studies that have compared the influence of recruitment on deliberative performance suggest very different relationships. In 1998, I participated in an evaluation of the SSABs at the DOE's former nuclear weapons production sites. We distinguished three modes of recruitment:

- Opportunistic
- Random representation of predetermined socio-demographic categories (closest to the approach of Carson and Martin)
- Nomination of delegates by a cross-section of civic organizations

Measured by process criteria (how well the boards functioned as deliberative bodies) the boards nominated by civic organizations performed best. Opportunistically recruited boards performed worst. The socio-demographically representative boards fell in the middle of the range. The ability of SSAB members to hold individual members accountable through back channels among the network of a community's civic organizations appeared to be a significant factor in ensuring constructive conduct. However, such accountability was only operational among the participating organizations. Issues of legitimacy arise from the fact that other organizations may not have been represented.

The other side of the question of 'who is included?' in participatory exercises is their potential for exclusion. Agarwal (2001) working with forestry initiatives in India and Nepal vividly describes how seemingly participatory institutions can systematically exclude significant sections of the affected population, especially women. Ultimately, the issue of representativeness folds back into the conception of citizenship that one embraces. The perspective that views citizenship in terms of emergent solidarity clearly requires that any forum which is intended to serve as a surrogate microcosm of the wider society must be capable of reproducing or otherwise capturing the emergent properties of that society, which suggests that neither randomness nor categorical representation will do.

AGENDA FRAMING

Almost inevitably, where new techniques of public participation are implemented in a political culture of science- and evidence-based expertise, they are forced to permit science to set the stage. Technical perspectives often frame the debate as hard-edged, binding constraints on decisions, while social and cultural perspectives enter the stage as malleable perceptions and preferences, to be corrected by promoting public understanding of science. For example, the current controversy in the UK over commercialization of genetically modified crops represents a marked contrast with the uncontroversial acceptance of such crops in the US. There is no difference between US and European technological competence when it comes to genetic engineering. The differences are cultural (Levidow 2001).

American farms are huge food factories that have very little to do with American ideas of nature, which Americans tend to associate with pristine wilderness, untouched by human intervention. In contrast, European ideas of nature are rooted in what the British call the countryside or continental Europeans call the 'culture landscape'. Genetic crop modification in Europe is not merely an industrial innovation, but an alteration of the lived-in environment, thus a potential threat to both nature and culture. However, it seems unlikely that the British government's decision on commercialization of genetically modified crops will be shaped by these kinds of argument. It seems much more likely that, once the process of consultation has been concluded, the government will make and justify its decision by reference to probabilistic risk assessments of physical harm.

The framing of ethical and aesthetic issues as scientific ones is characteristic of this and other public debates, such as those over BSE and FMD. Ironically, while social scientists seek to facilitate public expressions of concern by participants in such debates, their own voices are often marginalized by the official and media definition of the issues as 'scientific'. The advice sought by government and the voices sought by the media are most usually those of natural or physical scientists, preferably venerable Fellows of the British Royal Society or the US National Academy of Sciences. Social scientists are more rarely consulted and quoted on issues of substance, although their advice may be sought about issues of process. This situation reflects the more general instrumental or 'handmaiden' conception that both scientists and politicians have of social science. This view casts social scientists in the role of marketers or public communicators of the knowledge and expertise that resides with natural scientists and which forms the basis of their claims to authority. Social scientists may be perpetuating this role insofar as we continue to evaluate participatory mechanisms according to process criteria and generally shrink from providing evaluations of outcomes.

CONCLUSION

Over the past two decades, my initial enthusiasm for innovative techniques of public engagement has been tempered by a more general concern for the increasing reliance of public and private decision makers on expert techniques of all kinds. Are consultative and participatory decision processes, devised by social scientists, a true path to increased democracy or just another layer of technocracy? Is it possible that rather than digging us out of the technocratic hole we are really just digging ourselves in deeper? Are we seeking to compensate for the triumph of technique by devising new techniques, this time social science techniques of consultation? As social scientists, we need to ask whether such initiatives move us closer towards or further still from the participation of an informed citizenry in key decision making.

It seems that the discourse of participation is essentially a managerial discourse, perhaps, even more narrowly, a crisis-management discourse masquerading as a theory of democracy. It leaves the concept of 'risk' intact and presents citizens with a largely predetermined range of remedial or damage-mitigating options from which to select. It is consensus seeking with respect to both knowledge and values and, as such, it is depoliticizing. Its adequacy is evaluated overwhelmingly in terms of process rather than outcome.

To create a governance discourse, one might begin by contrasting the concepts and practices of participation with a term that seems to have fallen out of favour in the last thirty years: 'mobilization'. A discourse of mobilization around science in society suggests a very different approach. It begins with social issues of identity and emergent solidarity rather than technocratic ideas of risk. It seeks to destabilize taken-for-granted knowledge. Since it is explicitly values-based, it is inevitably conflictual. Rather than addressing science, technology and environment from the standpoint of remediation it seeks to address them from a standpoint of anticipation and authentic social choice. Its adequacy is evaluated in terms of outcome as much as process.

Within a governance discourse, I am still (just about) inclined to believe that new processes of public discourse, informed by social science, have significant potential to inform and supplement (but not substitute for) decision making in representative democracies.

However, under current arrangements, it is very difficult, perhaps impossible, for such techniques to break free of the political and cultural constraints that reduce complex moral and aesthetic issues to scientific framings. The solution to the problem of democratic participation is not so much dependent upon the democratization of expertise, but on what Giddens (1999) has called 'the democratization of democracy'. I remain sceptical that the first can be achieved in the absence of the second. Meanwhile, we can expect to see electoral participation continue to fall and consumption to carry on rising, to unprecedented levels.

10

Situating Resource Struggles*
Concepts for Empirical Analysis

TANIA MURRAY LI

In Indonesia, since the fall of Suharto in 1998, resource conflicts have generally been classified into two types: 'vertical' conflicts that pit rural people against the state or state-sponsored corporations, and 'horizontal' conflicts that pit one social, ethnic or religious group against another. This classification is problematic on many counts. Vertical conflict invokes a model of 'virtuous peasants' versus 'vicious states' (Bernstein 1990) that neglects to specify the diversity of 'peasant' interests, and positions peasants as pure subjects resisting power from the outside. It does not account for the diversity of state projects, many of which are not intentionally vicious but aim to bring about some kind of 'development' or improvement. The concept of horizontal conflict takes differences between social groups as given, rather than inquiring into the processes through which identities are constructed and oppositions formed. State policies and programmes often play a role in creating conflicts between groups, usually as a by-product of projects that had 'improving' goals: vertical relations are implicated in horizontal conflicts in ways the binary classification obscures.

* The research reported here was sponsored by the Canadian Social Science and Humanities Research Council. Time for analysis and writing was supported by the Programme on Global Security and Sustainability of the John D. and Catherine T. MacArthur Foundation (2001–03). A fuller account of the conceptual repertoire deployed in this essay, the farmers' occupation of the park, and the conjuncture at which it occurred can be found in Li (2007).

The concept of 'stakeholder' appears to offer a way into the complexities of resource conflicts, but it too has its limitations. It takes the positions that people hold and the projects they pursue as given, and abstracts them from the practices in which they engage, and the processes in which they are embedded. This essay proposes a framework that makes projects, processes, and practices and positions the focus of analysis. It then applies this framework to the analysis of a resource conflict in the uplands of Central Sulawesi, Indonesia, in which farmers have occupied the corner of a national park.[1]

SITUATING RESOURCE STRUGGLES: GOVERNMENTALITY, SOVEREIGNTY, AND POLITICS

Conflicts over natural resources are situated rather obviously within the logic of capitalism, as various parties struggle to control the means of production. They are situated within the logic of sovereignty, or rule by command, where the landlord-state (Coronil 1997) assumes the right to use, allocate and profit from resources, and exercises coercive control to that end. But they are also situated within the field of power Foucault labelled governmental, in which experts in and out of the state machinery attempt to enhance the quality of the population, rearranging landscapes, livelihoods and identities according to techno-scientific criteria (Foucault 1991; Gordon 1991). The bounding of territory into zones designated for farming or conservation, the resettlement of populations from one place to another, and efforts to 'develop' rural livelihoods are interventions of a governmental kind.

As Foucault recognized, governmental rationality does not displace but rather co-exists with the logic of sovereignty. In Indonesia as

[1] My sources on this conflict include fieldwork, media reports and the voluminous, intense debate carried out over Internet news groups and mailing lists. For accounts of the origins of the park, conditions in the border villages, the trajectory of the farmer occupation, and key positions in this dispute, see FPM (2001); Laban (2002); Sangaji (2001); Schweithelm et al. (1992); WALHI (2001a, 2001b, 2001c); ANZDEC (1997). Also see H. Laudjeng, 'Jangan Cemarkan TAP MPR/IX/2001', dated 9 May 2002 at fktnll@yahoogroups. com and e-mail from Aliansi Tolelembunga (*tolelembunga@plasa.com*), dated 26 July 2001.

elsewhere, the state-as-sovereign allocates land and other natural resources as gifts to the regime's favoured clients. The inter-weaving of the logics of profit seeking, sovereignty and governmental rationality creates a complex field of power. State patronage is key to gaining access to resources for private profit, and governmental projects described as improvement are always tainted with the suspicion that they are masks for elite gain.

Governmental rationality is antipolitical: it seeks to displace the political process of debating, and struggling over the question of how to live by applying techno-scientific rationales and managerial procedures. Yet in practice, governmental interventions politicize (Moore 1998): at myriad, particular sites where governmental projects collide with layered formations of landscape, livelihood and identity, a space opens up for people to challenge the truths in the name of which they are governed. Practices of patronage also politicize, still more so when they contradict the claim to rationality and improvement. So too do the tensions and pressures set up by processes of capital accumulation and displacement which are refractory to the apparatus of planning. The identifications around which people mobilize are correspondingly complex, situated, contingent and relational, as people form communities or connect to ideologies (be it nature-loving, indigenism, 'development' or radical Islam) that help them make sense of their situation (Li 2000).

Projects

Drawing from the conceptual scheme outlined above, projects can be classified into three kinds. First, there are *governmental projects*, which seek to rearrange landscapes, livelihoods and identities according to technical criteria and the logic of improvement. Besides state agencies, many so-called NGOs are engaged in projects to 'conduct the conduct' of others, contributing to broad assemblages of knowledge and power. Second, there are *economic projects* aimed at gaining control over resources for private gain. These range from the efforts of farmers to secure access to resources for current and future livelihoods, to appropriations aimed at capital accumulation on a large scale. In both cases, but especially the latter, access often routes through the authority and coercion of the state apparatus. Third, there are *political projects*, intended to contest governmental interventions or resource appropriation, questioning the hegemony of these overlapping fields of power. Political projects also have varied proponents, including rural producers rich and poor, activists and intellectuals, and dissident members of the ruling apparatus. They are manifested in words and actions, including debates over custom, the practice of cutting or planting trees, and mass rallies among others.

Positions

In keeping with the dynamic nature of the projects outlined above, it is useful to consider people as taking or being assigned positions, rather than fixed identities. Identities, as Stuart Hall argues, 'come from somewhere, have histories. But far from being eternally fixed in some essentialized past, they are subject to the continuous "play" of history, culture and power' (Hall 1990: 225). They are 'unstable points of identification or suture.... Not an essence but a *positioning*' (ibid.: 226). History is crucial since, as I indicated earlier, there are no subject positions outside the reach of power, only positions within its 'continuous play'. Positively asserted on the one hand, positions are also limited and pre-figured by the 'places of recognition' which others provide (Li 2001). The formation of alliances and the making of connections depend crucially upon assuming or filling positions assigned. Note too that the term position usefully signals the spatial dimension of identification: people occupying particular kinds of landscape are expected to behave in 'appropriate' ways, and their actions are evaluated accordingly.

Practices

Practices follow from projects and positions, making them concrete. They need to be examined ethnographically. Governmental projects, for example, are associated with practices of research, planning, the implementation of specified procedures, evaluation and so on. But they are also associated with the practice that I have elsewhere described as compromise: the tacit agreement to look the other way when rules are broken, the failure to gather information that contradicts the premises upon which an intervention is planned, the construction of data to demonstrate unerring 'success' (Li 1999b). These are observable practices crucial to the longevity if not the performance of projects, and although they are external to the formal plan they too have significant effects. Economic projects come associated with practices that can be read in multiple ways: is a person who cuts down a tree making a garden, degrading the environment, or stealing timber revenues from the forest department? Political projects also unfold through practices that become routinized and recognized. In Indonesia, activists seeking to challenge relations of rule engage in policy critique, legal drafting, advocacy, facilitation, and 'accompanying' rural people engaged in direct conflict. The political practices of rural people include making links with activist supporters, staging demonstrations, seeking media coverage, writing letters and statements to officials, occupying land, blockading roads, burning buildings, and more.

Processes

The term process, finally, highlights the unplanned effects of numerous, uncoordinated projects and practices as they unfold across time and space. The most notable process is, of course, the uneven accumulation of capital and resources that we gloss with the name capitalism. The price of commodities on international markets, the demand for land or labour, the influence of the media on patterns of consumption and desire, a family illness that stimulates a land sale and eventual impoverishment: these are processes that emerge independently of projects, although they intersect with them in particular ways. They form the complex terrain with which governmental rationality is always engaged, as it seeks to reorder and improve

men in their relations, their links, their imbrication with those other things which are wealth, resources, means of subsistence, the territory with all its specific qualities, climate, irrigation, fertility, etc.; men in their relations to ... customs, habits, ways of acting and thinking, etc.; lastly, men in their relation to ... accidents and misfortunes such as famine, epidemics, death, etc. (Foucault 1991: 93).

In Foucault's formulation, governmental rationality is not a project of total control or social engineering. It recognizes that society—like the economy—is hugely complex and largely self-regulating. The 'art' of government lies precisely in devising ways to intervene 'with economy'—working upon and through existing social and economic processes, setting the conditions so that people will be inclined to behave 'as they ought'. In relation to capitalism in particular, governmental rationality has sought not to halt the process of accumulation and displacement, but to counterbalance its more negative effects through ongoing management and adjustment, so that idle populations are set to work, revolutions averted, and resources optimally deployed. Such interventions have come to be understood as the responsibility of the state as 'trustee' (Cowen and Shenton 1996: x) and are currently shared among numerous agencies assembled into national and transnational 'development regimes' (Ludden 1992).

Occupying a National Park in Central Sulawesi

Guided by this framework, I will try to explain how and why conflict emerged over a national park in Sulawesi, and explore its particular forms and significance. The need to trace relevant links across time and space will produce a narrative that is not linear, although it is loosely organized around the categories outlined above. Beginning with a description of contradictory projects, a later examination of practices and processes will draw the reader towards a deeper understanding of positions and the 'continuous play' of culture, history and power in resource conflicts.

Projects

In June 2001, 1,030 households occupied the corner of Lore Lindu National Park, and began to cut trees. They claimed to be landless, and argued that their intention was to establish a new farming settlement. Each household would clear two hectares for that purpose. Their project was thus primarily economic. It had, however, a political edge, because they argued their entitlement to land based on a critique of a governmental programme designed for their 'improvement'.

Three decades earlier, they had been defined by state agencies as 'backward and isolated communities' (*masyarakat terasing*), because they practised shifting cultivation in hilly terrain inaccessible to everyday state monitoring and control. Positioned as subjects in need of state-sponsored supervision and 'development', they had been removed from their hamlets and resettled in three villages in a valley area supposedly suited to 'modern' wet rice agriculture and accessible to education, health, transportation and other facilities. In practice, however, they had not been given the two hectare land allotment promised to each family, and even the land assigned was not of good quality: it was prone to flood, and could not be irrigated.

To meet their livelihood needs, they had planted coffee under the forest canopy behind the resettlement site, an arrangement that had worked well until the forest was designated as part of Lore Lindu National Park. Thereafter, the park authorities permitted them to harvest the coffee they had planted within the new park boundaries, but not to clean or extend the coffee groves, which were expected to die out, gradually extinguishing the farmers' claims. Farmers were also forbidden from collecting rattan and other forest products they had used for subsistence purposes and to supplement their incomes. Exclusion from the park was thus a second point of contention, and the occupation of parkland for farming can be read as a political critique of a conservation agenda pursued at their expense.

The action of the farmer group was supported by several NGOs based in the provincial capital, Palu. They highlighted both the livelihood needs of the farmers, and the political significance of the occupation as a protest against governmental policies of imposed resettlement and conservation. They argued for a more democratic approach in which the 'target group' would have the opportunity to debate and negotiate both the purpose and the terms of any programmes designed to transform or 'improve' their lives. At a minimum, park borders and land use zoning should be established through a participatory process that takes into account existing claims and uses, as well as anticipated livelihood needs. They challenged the entire park-based conservation model, which they labelled 'eco-fascist'. It was, they said, an inappropriate import that had also devastated livelihoods in its original site, Yellowstone (Sangaji 2001).

The NGOs supporting the farmer occupation had a track record of supporting communities in conflict with the park, including several located within the park borders that had been threatened with compulsory resettlement. Their arguments had emphasized the communities' claims as indigenous people whose relationship with the land and forest was governed by ecologically benign, customary resource management systems. These claims were supported by a set of maps and documents that carefully delineated the traditional wisdom of the 'indigenous' groups, and their deep knowledge of, and attachment to, their landscape. Faced with the combination of organized protest by villagers rejecting resettlement, and documented proof of their conservation-compatible practices and commitments, the park manager declared these communities 'an inseparable component of the park management system', with the right to continue to live and farm in their customary ways (Sangaji 2001). In so doing, he had gained national attention as an 'eco-populist', a state official who could work with communities and NGOs and forge new democratic practices for conservation suited to the post-Suharto era of *reformasi*.

The land occupation in question, however, posed the park manager with a new dilemma: the farmer group did not fit into the 'indigenous' slot. They had no ancestral claims to the land they had occupied, nor could they supply evidence of eco-friendly traditions. The park manager could not simply extend to them the recognition he had extended to the three 'indigenous' cases. These were ordinary farmers, not very special people with deep knowledge of a unique ancestral landscape.[2] Thus there were, in his view, no grounds for recognition (cited in WALHI 2001a). For the supporting NGOs, on the other hand, the farmer occupation presented an opportunity to expand their political project from indigenous rights advocacy to advocacy on behalf of all poor people whose resource rights had been abrogated by the state. The park manager, they said, should not discriminate: whether or not they qualified as 'indigenous', all sixty villages surrounding the park had problems with the way the park was established and contested its boundaries. The conservation model needed a radical overhaul, not just a concession to accommodate a few, apparently unique villages. The farmer group had an additional claim because they had been doubly victimized by governmental programmes: resettled on inadequate land, and then excluded from

---

[2] I have examined the dilemmas of indigenous positioning in Li (2001, 2002a).

the adjacent forests on the grounds of conservation (Sangaji 2001; WALHI 2001a).

Opposition to the farmer occupation came from two main sources. First, there was the state apparatus, including the provincial governor, the district regents, and the park authority, each concerned to assert their authority. The occupation posed a direct challenge to their right to determine who should live where, and how resources should be used and distributed. The park manager, concerned to retain his 'eco-populist' credentials, argued that the occupied land was a key catchment area for the surrounding valleys including the Palu valley, notoriously dry. Concern for the people required, in this case, consideration of the impact of deforestation upon the livelihood and well being of the population on a larger scale.

The governor and regents agreed that the farmers needed land, and proposed to find an alternative resettlement site. They threatened to call in police and military forces to expel the farmer group should they refuse to move to the new site. Official responses thus sought to defend and confirm the role of the state as sovereign power and technical administrator, granting the gift of land, and managing population and territory for purposes of security and improvement. Continued occupation exposed the incapacity of the 'landlord-state' to assert its sovereignty or fulfil its managerial responsibilities.

The second group challenging the occupation was assembled around the banner of conservation. It included a US-based, international conservation organization with an office in Palu dedicated to protecting the national park, and other NGOs working directly with them or affiliated through a coalition called the Partnership Forum for Lore Lindu (FKTNLL). This group had been alarmed by the park manager's recognition of the three 'indigenous' communities whose territories were wholly or partially inside the park boundaries. They feared that, bowing to pressure from the communities and the 'radical' NGOs, the park manager was losing control over the park: other groups would claim the same entitlements. His populist inclination had already extended beyond those three cases to another concession affecting all sixty-seven border villages. Modifying the previous rule that limited border communities to harvesting their coffee located within the park, he granted them permission to clean around the coffee plants. This concession created an unanticipated transformation of the landscape as people removed the forest canopy covering their old coffee groves, replaced dead stock, and intercropped their coffee with the new boom crop, cocoa. A few scattered coffee bushes in the undergrowth became the justification for clearing the land between them. Border villages had, in the view of the Forum, taken advantage of the park manager's populist inclinations to increase the extent and intensity of 'agricultural encroachment'. For the Forum, the farmer occupation was further evidence that farmer designs on the park had to be stopped if conservation was to have a future. The sight of fallen trees on both sides of the road in the occupation zone was dramatic provocation: a statement that conservation had lost, and farmers had won. This scene was captured on video by one of the protagonists, and circulated through the activist network in Java.

The NGOs supporting the occupation regarded the FKTNLL with suspicion: its members were opportunists, concerned mainly to profit from donor support for conservation. Significant donor funds had been dedicated to improving farming techniques and devising alternative income sources for farmers in the park border zone. Projects included a $32 million effort funded by a loan from the Asian Development Bank, intended to divert farmers' attention from the park and compensate them for lost incomes. But, argued the pro-farmer NGOs, these donor efforts had been utterly ineffective: experiments with butterfly breeding, honey extraction, fish ponds or ecotourism, and the handout of fertilizers and seedlings to people who had no land, had scarcely made a dent on the livelihoods of tens of thousands of people in the border villages. The tactics of diverting, persuading, 'helping' and educating villagers so that they would understand and appreciate the 'importance of conservation' failed to address the fundamental issues of land rights and democratic process in defining conservation zones or objectives.

The FKTNLL found an ally in a rights-oriented NGO, centrally concerned with indigeneity. This NGO argued that the farmer occupation not only threatened the conservation and catchment function of a forest that should be protected, but had also trespassed on the territory of the indigenous group associated with that land. In contesting the boundaries of the park, the farmer group had neglected to ask the permission of the true indigenous owners whose claims long preceded the establishment of the park. Like the park authorities, the farmer group was accused of making a unilateral land grab. The farmer group had added insult to injury by seeking to legitimate their occupation with a ritualized feast, to which their NGO supporters and the media were invited. By this act they had attempted to assimilate their cause to that of indigenous people, calling upon their ancestors for blessings, and creating a media show. But neither they nor their ancestors had any claim to this land. Moreover, they had not provided any data to support their claim that they were indeed landless 'victims' of the resettlement scheme.[3]

Conflicting perspectives created a bitter divide within the NGO movement in Palu and beyond. The NGOs now divided into pro-farmer versus pro-conservation-and-indigenous rights factions had previously seen these as inseparable struggles, and had worked on campaigns together. The pro-farmer NGOs had envisaged the occupation as a protest against the state apparatus and the park: a 'vertical' conflict. They did not anticipate that it would cause, or be interpreted, as a 'horizontal' conflict between one impoverished group—landless farmers—and another, claiming the indigenous slot. They did not deny the indigenous claim, but they did question the timing and spatial logic of the 'indigenous' protest against the occupation. They argued that the indigenous group should focus on contesting the park's appropriation of land directly bordering their own villages, rather than contesting a farmer occupation on the fringe of their domain, some 20 kilometres away. In turn, the NGO promoting the indigenous case accused the pro-occupation faction of bad faith and opportunism: supporting conservation and indigenism strategically, as vehicles for political activism, rather than for their intrinsic significance. Farmers who need land should take it from officials and corporations, not from indigenous people, a group already severely marginalized.

The divide extended to the networks of the Palu NGOs in Jakarta, Bogor and Bandung, the centres for national advocacy.[4] It threatened alliances that had drawn together broad constituencies by downplaying

---

[3] See H. Laudjeng, 'Jangan Cemarkan TAP MPR/IX/2001', dated 9 May 2002 at fktnll@yahoogroups.com.

[4] See A. Nababan, 'Respon Untuk Cermatan Kasus Dongi Dongi', dated 24 August 2001 at adat@yahoogroups.com.

tensions between contending platforms. To simplify, one group clusters around conservation and indigeneity, arguing that indigenous people have environmentally sound practices and internationally recognized rights of a special kind. Their hope is that indigenous groups to whom the right to manage their lives and resources have been restored will later negotiate with other 'local people' and migrants in a spirit of generosity and mutual respect. The other group is clustered around the concept of land reform, and highlights the problem of landlessness caused by unjust appropriations by state agencies or state-backed corporations. It includes indigenous people as one among many groups whose resource rights were trampled during thirty years of Suharto's New Order rule. This group also hopes for peaceful settlements between indigenous and migrant groups, but they place fair access to land higher on the list of priorities. Emphasizing the areas of overlap, these two political agendas are often pursued in tandem, and many individuals and organizations would barely distinguish between them. The occupation of Sulawesi's park, however, fractured the 'wish-laden middle ground' (Conklin and Graham 1995) in which conservation, indigenous rights and economic justice can all be achieved simultaneously.

Practices

To further understand the dimensions of this conflict and how it unfolded, I now explore some of the practices that accompanied the various projects outlined above. Some of these practices were explicitly enunciated as part of a formal plan. Many of them are better understood as a kind of habitus, taken-for-granted modes of acting in the world. Some practices, notably those of the farmer group, were self-conscious, intended not only to accomplish economic goals but also to symbolize and communicate a particular positioning.

I have already noted that the farmer group organized a ritual land-blessing celebrated with a feast, which included the sacrifice of four heads of cattle. They put up banners stating 'Give us Land, Peace in the National Park' (*Beri Kami Lahan, Taman Nasional Aman*). At one stage they were reported to have put up roadblocks to vet passing vehicles.[5] They held several demonstrations in Palu before and after

[5] See D. Sargeant, 'Update: Birding Logistics in the National Parks of Northern Sulawesi', dated 21 August 2001 at the Indonesia Worldtwitch website.

the land occupation, petitioning for the recognition of their right to land. On site, their labour process was also intended to communicate. They claimed to be organized into groups to work collectively on clearing blocks of land that would then be distributed among the families, two hectares per household. They stated their intention to formulate their own rules, enforced by strict sanctions derived from, and legitimated by, the customary practices of the three constituent ethno-linguistic groups. These would include a sanction on anyone who sold timber for profit, or sold land. Cut timber would be used only for building houses and public buildings such as places of worship. Declaring these restrictions was crucial to establishing the legitimacy of the occupation as a movement driven by the need for land to farm, and not by an opportunistic search for quick profit. At one of their demonstrations in Palu, they brought bundles of freshly harvested corn and cassava to the parliament building, emphasizing the link between land and livelihood. Thus they tapped into the symbolic fields associated not only with the life of a farmer but with traditions many Indonesians view as 'indigenous': a commitment to collective action, mutual well being, democratically-agreed and community-enforced discipline, and an orientation to subsistence and sustainable resource management.

The practices of the state agencies were remarkable mainly for their omissions. Crucially, it should be noted that although they threatened to violently evict the farmer group, so far they have not carried out this threat. In previous years, when smaller groups had attempted to occupy the same site, they had indeed been evicted by the park patrol backed by the police and the military, with the participation of the FKTNLL. On this occasion, however, the occupation was well organized and on a much larger scale, and the group very quickly began to change the landscape by clearing land, building huts, and planting corn and cocoa. When the threat of violent expulsion seemed imminent, demonstrations, media coverage, and the support of various organizations for the farmers' position expressed through public statements and letters made it very clear to the authorities that harshness (*kekerasan*) would make the state apparatus look very bad. Practices that were normal in the Suharto era were now being severely scrutinized within the province and beyond. The art of ruling through the exercise of governmental rationality does not

eliminate the exercise of the sovereign's right to rule by force, as
Foucault appreciated, but resort to force indicates that the art has not
been mastered—precisely the conundrum confronting the provincial
apparatus in this instance.

The solution, the provincial officials proposed, was to find an
alternative resettlement site that was acceptable to the farmer group.
But this they were unable to deliver. Their failure exposes some of the
core contradictions in the resettlement programme, and exposes the
weakness of the state's claim to have either the technical or operational
capacity to rearrange populations and environments, still less to
improve them. According to the farmer group and their supporters
who had inspected the proposed sites, they were inaccessible: they
could be reached only on foot, one of them requiring more than a
day's walk and the fording of eighteen rivers, some of them deep.
The irony was intense: it was the inaccessibility of their ancestral,
hillside hamlets that had caused these farmers to be resettled into the
valley in the first place. Further, the land in the proposed sites was
already densely settled and farmed: placing newcomers there would
cause 'horizontal conflicts'. Moreover, the land was steeply sloped,
and farming it would cause environmental damage. It could not
produce secure and sustainable livelihoods. Thus the official solution
to the farmer occupation was deeply flawed, and flawed precisely on
the 'official' techno-scientific grounds usually arrayed to justify state
initiatives to reorder landscapes and move people around.

Corrupt practices connected with official resettlement schemes
were also exposed. A significant portion of the land in the original
resettlement site (175 of 600 hectares) had been appropriated by
a former provincial governor. Other officials connected with the
resettlement scheme had taken land for themselves, or sold it off
to outside buyers. In this province and beyond, there are numerous
examples of resettlement projects carried out in the name of the poor
being used by officials for private gain. With this history, the farmer
group would be foolish to give up the land it had occupied to put
its future back in the hands of the resettlement programme. The
usual compromise through which a certain amount of corruption is
tolerated so long as the target group also obtains some benefits would
no longer suffice. The corrupt practices associated with resettlement
were no longer just a public secret: they were openly being called.

Having been misled by promises of security and improvement once before, the farmer group insisted that the alternative site had to be at least as accessible, fertile and promising as the site they had occupied, and the two hectares allocation free of competing claims, or they would not move.

The practices of the NGOs supporting the farmer group also merit scrutiny. Indeed, they were thoroughly scrutinized by the FKTNLL. The Forum accused the pro-farmer NGOs of creating the farmer group, and provoking them to break the law in order to gain attention, demonstrate their heroic support for popular justice, and advance an irresponsible, anti-conservation agenda. In this critique they echoed the official line. During the Suharto era and since, NGOs were often accused of manipulating gullible, uneducated masses for their own purposes, provoking and exaggerating conflicts for media effect. In addition, critics from within and outside the ruling apparatus often hint that NGOs who present themselves as being on the side of the people are actually pursuing economic gain. In the case of this land occupation, it was suggested that the farmer group and their supporters were in league with timber barons seeking to rob the park for profit.

The pro-farmer faction responded that had they merely supported and 'accompanied' (*mendamping*) the farmer group in a struggle the farmers themselves both led and initiated. The practice of *bendampingan* (offering assistance and solidarity) is part of the habitus, the routine behaviour and positioning of Indonesia's NGO movement. It locates NGOs not as the vanguard of the people, but as their associates, ready to offer help as needed. This might be help on technical matters such as agro-forestry or mapping community lands, or help in organizing community meetings, mass demonstrations, or negotiations with state authorities.

The line between accompanying, educating and leading is obviously a fuzzy one. Some of the critics of the role of the pro-farmer NGOs in this conflict seemed to accept that an NGO should indeed be an educator, leading and guiding rural people, 'conducting' their conduct in a governmental fashion, but argued that the goal should be to teach them respect for the law and conservation. When it became clear that some members of the farmer group were indeed selling timber for profit, one critic stated that the NGOs had failed as guides and tutors of their dependent subjects, their *masyarakat binaan*.[6] The term *warga binaan* (literally, subjects of guidance) is used by the Department of Social Affairs to refer to the waifs, strays, prostitutes, and 'isolated and estranged' people (masyarakat terasing) under its paternalistic care and tutelage. Recall that the farmer group had themselves once been warga binaan of the Department of Social Affairs. The suggestion was that they are still backward, still misbehaving, and the NGOs that have set themselves up as tutor and guide have failed to do their jobs. The agency, indeed the adulthood, of the farmer group, their capacity to analyse their own situation, to further their interests, and to understand that much of what passed for conservation or 'improvement' was inept and unjust, was thereby denied.

Proof that timber from the occupation zone was indeed being sold for profit was, needless to say, a major embarrassment for the NGOs that supported the farmer group, a betrayal of the political and economic goals of the occupation. It is not clear how many farmers were involved in this practice, but the leader of the farmer group—the one who had made all the brave statements about customary sanctions and livelihood priorities—was implicated. There could be many explanations for why this practice emerged. For critics of the occupation, timber stealing had been the motivation all along. A defender of the occupation might argue that the farmers were only human and some, indeed, had made mistakes. Besides, they were not the only ones involved in illegal logging: state officials at various levels were also implicated.

Stepping back, it is possible to see the practice of timber selling in a different perspective. If the land had not been classified as a national park, and the farmers had not promised to use the timber only for their own needs and refuse the cash offered to them by the timber merchants daily prowling the site, the practice of selling the timber would not have occasioned any comment. Indeed, selling timber is part of the normal procedure of land clearing for cultivation on the forest frontier. Owners of chainsaws negotiate with a farmer to cut the timber on the intended farm plot. The farmer's land is cleared 'free of charge' and he or she receives half to a third of the timber for

---

[6] Anon, 'WALHI Sulteng Perlu Memberikan Pemahaman FPM Dongi Dongi', *Nuansa Pos*, 8 November 2002.

personal use, or the equivalent in cash. The cash helps the farmer survive until the first food crop, usually corn, can be harvested. The timber is used for building a dwelling. Establishing a new farm plot and timber harvesting are symbiotic practices. But in this particular 'war of positions', the farmers had to present themselves as pure subjects, exempt from the need or temptation of ready cash. One could also argue that the continued uncertainty about the future of the occupation made it entirely sensible to sell off timber during the open season, and not invest too much in building houses or planting cocoa seedlings that could very well be bulldozed or burned by the army and police.

One more set of practices needs to be highlighted the routine involvement of park, forest department, police and army personnel in logging the park and other protected forests (Laban 2002; Sangaji 2001; WALHI 2001b). This is another public secret. The 'authorities' whose job it is to devise orderly plans for managing population and environment are thoroughly implicated in systematic theft and pillage. If this practice punctures the idea of the governmental state that operates according to techno-scientific rules and plans, it also muddies the state versus people divide. The conduct of illegal logging draws together a complex assemblage of individuals, institutions and ideologies. High-level officials sign the papers to get truckloads of timber through the checkpoints. Staff manning the checkpoints is paid off, but they are also armed, should anyone try to bypass what is effectively a toll booth. The village headman, within whose boundaries the forest falls, must also be complicit, and is sometimes directly involved in recruiting labour. The labour force for logging is drawn from the villages, but is often loyal to a particular labour boss, creating factional splits and rival gangs, sometimes armed. This is another example of how vertical ties—in this case, ties of patronage—can stimulate 'horizontal' conflicts (cf. McCarthy 2000).

The practice of illegal logging looks still more complex when ideological elements are added into the mix. Villagers who believe in protecting their forests for purposes of conservation or the future of their children often protest illegal logging, but cynics easily dismiss them as rival factions concerned only to get their share. 'Empowering' villagers to manage and protect their forests, an important platform of the community-based resource management agenda, and also of the park manager's eco-populism (Laban 2002), amounts to expecting or requiring villagers to confront powerful outsiders, including state officials, and to confront their co-villagers who are directly involved in logging on the front line. Observers also highlight the (ab)use of populist ideologies: when caught, labourers drawn from villages can always claim to be impoverished folk, seeking only some timber to repair their house, or a small patch of land to plant some crops. Poverty is a commodity. From one perspective, it was precisely the commodity on sale by the farmer group in the park occupation. From another perspective, the poverty of the farmers was both the mechanism for the elites to profit from illegal logging, and a convenient cover for their own involvement.

Processes

The projects and practices outlined above are not occurring in a vacuum: they are occurring within a time and space shaped by a set of processes with diverse logics that are, for the most part, refractory to planning. Here I tease out just four distinct processes from the many at work in this conjuncture.

One process, already noted, is the continuous rebalancing of the equation between the exercise of a sovereign's right to violence, and the educative and organizational strategies associated with governmental rationality. Rather than seeing the relationship between sovereignty and governmentality as a unilinear trajectory in which the former is progressively folded into the latter, Achille Mbembe and others argue that the 'arbitrariness and intrinsic unconditionality' and the 'regime of impunity' that were the 'distinctive feature of colonial sovereignty', were inherited intact by postcolonial regimes (Mbembe 2001: 26, 42). In Indonesia, the sovereign's right to kill was all too apparent in the massacres that initiated Suharto's New Order rule and the state violence that continued for the next three decades, resulting in half a million dead (Anderson 1999). Governmental strategies also have a long history in the colony, beginning in the early nineteenth century (Schrauwers 2001). Particular conflicts take their form at the unstable conjuncture between these two modes of rule.

The farmer group did not challenge the right of the state apparatus to govern by, in this case, defining the proper relations between people and forest. What they highlighted was the state's incapacity to bring about the promised improvements. Faced with this challenge, the state apparatus stopped short of exercising the sovereign's right to use brute force. The NGOs supporting the farmers argued that the state's demonstrated incapacity to govern the relations between population and environment according to its own criteria of efficiency, indicated the need to return rights and responsibilities to 'the people'. To their critics, these NGOs have gone too far: trusting the people to govern themselves, they have endorsed popular anarchy and environmental destruction, and undermined the apparatus of planning, regulation, and the rule of law through which security and improvement can be attained not just for some groups, but for the population as a whole.

A second process running through this conjuncture was capitalism. In 1997, as the Asian economic crisis caused the Indonesian currency to plummet, the price of cocoa designated in dollars increased by a factor of 20. The result in Sulawesi, which had begun producing cocoa a decade previously, was to cause a rush among smallholders for access to land on which to plant this brown gold (Li 2002b). Precisely because it recognized the urgency of the demand for land, and the promise of cocoa production to dramatically improve the lot of ordinary smallholders, the park authority could not concede to the farmer occupation. Hot on the tracks of smallholders making livelihood claims would be the land brokers, offering ready cash. Since it became accessible by paved road in the mid 1990s, lots of people, including the provincial elite and state officials at all levels of the hierarchy, had become interested in taking or buying a piece of the park for cocoa.

A further process set in motion by the cocoa boom was smallholder immigration: in some of the villages bordering the park, including the resettlement villages that had been home to the farmer group, up to 50 per cent of the population was comprised of Bugis migrants from south Sulawesi who had arrived in droves in the period 1997–2001. Prospective migrants had rented buses and toured the highlands of Central Sulawesi looking for suitable land, and making deals with land brokers, officials, and individual farmers for its acquisition. Many relatively impoverished farmers, tempted by the quick cash and not yet recognizing the potential of cocoa, had sold up and found themselves landless or land poor, looking on as the migrants began to prosper.

To understand why farmers would sell up their already meagre land resources, it is necessary to locate the process of land accumulation and displacement in the context of the unintended effects of an array of governmental programmes and interventions already layered into this landscape. The farmer group now occupying the park was not the only group that had relocated—so too had almost all the residents in the park border villages. In the period 1910–40, the Dutch had forced many groups out of the hills into the adjacent valleys, and others had scattered from centralized settlements to the forest edge to plant coffee to pay colonial taxes. People moved again during the Japanese occupation and in the first decades after independence when regional rebellions brought violence, famine, forced conscription or religious conversion. As a result of this unsettled regional history, the populations around the park are heterogeneous, and they maintain connections to various ancestral homelands near or far. If they are displaced from their present location, or they sell up, they hope to begin again and prosper somewhere else.

For many people in the border villages, a tenuous sense of belonging to their current village location is compounded by their fragile tenure security. The state apparatus does not recognize customary land claims, and has designated what it claims to be 'state land' for use by corporations, for resettlement sites, and the national park. NGOs have identified seven corporations controlling more than 13,000 hectares in the vicinity of the park, most notoriously Hasfarm, the enterprise of a crony of Suharto (WALHI 2001b). On a smaller scale, and especially in the context of the cocoa boom, village headmen have often sold co-villagers' customary land to incoming migrants. Faced with the risk of arbitrary appropriation, selling land to a migrant or broker offering cash makes sense. In these ways, capitalist processes of uneven accumulation, sovereign appropriations and the effects of governmental initiatives intersect. They shaped what happened, where and how.

Finally, it is worth stating the obvious: that trees once cut down will take a long time to grow again. The process of landscape transformation initiated by the farmer group cannot easily be reversed. The site of the occupation is no longer a biodiverse forest, but *de facto* a farming settlement planted with corn and cocoa. In this state, it evokes the anger of conservationists, and concerns about downstream droughts and floods. Practically speaking, however, the crop cover and eventual cocoa canopy will fill the void more quickly and surely than the eviction of the farmers and a replanting effort that would be continuously sabotaged. Arsonists have already destroyed the park offices, information centre and guesthouses in the adjacent village.[7] At the intersection of processes of landscape change, the realignments of rule and capital accumulation efforts to enforce park boundaries are weak and lacking in legitimacy.

Positions

In the context of the polemics surrounding this case, positions assumed by or attributed to the various parties to this conflict were made quite explicit, described in 'position papers', and widely discussed in the media and activist newsgroups. Unfortunately, but perhaps inevitably, simplified and often binary classificatory schemes came to the fore. State officials, NGOs and villagers positioned themselves or were positioned as pro or anti-conservation, populist or fascist, corrupt or sincere, effective or inept, consistent or opportunist.

The emergence of numerous coalitions, fronts, alliances, and instant NGOs issuing statements and claiming to represent one constituency or another complicated the field, and identification was sometimes difficult. Who are you and whom do you represent was a frequent refrain in the e-mail correspondence. To speak in the name of someone else (*mengatasnamakan*) is a practice that is frequently scrutinized. There was a maverick e-mailer who commented continuously on the ecological damage at the site and the complicity of the farmers and NGOs in illegal logging, but refused when challenged to reveal his or her identity. The controversy within the NGO network was so heated at one stage that there was a moratorium on Internet communications, and also on the practice of *pendampingan*: all the NGOs were to stay away from the occupation site while the farmer group and surrounding villagers worked out their own agreements. Challenged to make its position on the occupation clear, the international conservation NGO argued that its role in relation to the park

[7] Anon, 'Kepala Balai Taman Nasional Lore Lindu: Walhi Dukung Perambahan Hutan', in *Kompas*, 26 October 2002.

was purely technical, and that it had no mandate to become involved in 'politics', a stance immediately critiqued for its implicit *antipolitics* (Ferguson 1994).

The positions attributed to the farmer group were especially complex. Were the members of the farmer group victims of state policies; heroes of democratic politics; model farmers bent on modest, equitable, sustainable, community-based livelihoods; cunning pretenders exploiting the gullibility of their NGO supporters; greedy profit-seeking opportunists; forest destroyers; illegal squatters; criminals; ignorant folk vulnerable to the persuasions of timber merchants; or dependent wards misled by enthusiastic but irresponsible tutors?

Perhaps they were all of the above, in different measure. One resolution to the discrepancy between these various positionings was to make differentiations within the farmer group, to argue that some of its members were indeed landless, hardworking and generally law abiding while others were not. One observer stated that he had been sympathetic to the story of impoverishment, until he noticed that there were motorbikes outside the new houses in the occupation zone. Presumably, however, not everyone had a motorbike. Another critic observed that, a year after the initial occupation, at most 500 households were living and farming at the site, the implication being that the other half had moved on after realizing their land and timber profits.[8] No definitive 'data' about the background or economic situation of the farmer group was collected by the authorities, presumably because wilful ignorance was more amenable to engineering various kinds of compromise than legibility would have been.

Members of the farmer group could not select between the various positions attributed to them: they were limited by the places of recognition provided by others. Yet these positions had consequences: each enabled certain alliances and connections to be made, and foreclosed others. A positioning on the side of conservation seemed to be closed to the farmer group. Although they claimed to care about the environment and promised not to destroy it, the felled trees presented an obvious contradiction, at least from some perspectives. They envisaged a longer time horizon, in which tree cover would be re-established, crops would be biodiverse, and the

[8] Ibid.

area under cultivation limited to two hectares per household. This could be promised, but the outcomes could not be guaranteed even in the short term, still less across the generations. But, argued the farmer groups' supporters, the stability of the park as a conservation area under state management was not guaranteed either. Besides the rampant illegal logging in which officials were complicit, a planned hydroelectric dam, mining concessions and new roads within the park borders threatened to transform the landscape on a dramatic scale. Seen in this context, smallholder activities were ecologically benign (Sangaji 2001; WALHI 2001a).

From the perspective of the park authorities and other critics of the occupation, a positioning as indigenous people also seemed to be closed to the farmer group. Nevertheless, this was a position they attempted to establish through expressive practices such as ritual feasts, statements about collective labour and mutual responsibility, and an oath to stay and die at the site. Substantively, the livelihood practices and customary lore of the farmer group scarcely distinguished them from their 'indigenous' neighbours. The debate that occurred, albeit implicitly, was whether indigeneity is a way of being, and hence portable, or an identity available only to those who happen to have remained in their ancestral place. After all, the farmers in the group were displaced from their ancestral hillside hamlets through no fault of their own. Moreover, the farmer group and the people whose lands they occupied all consider themselves indigenous in relation to the Bugis migrants from south Sulawesi who increasingly monopolize farmland throughout the province. In every village around the park, clusters of households arrived in different migrant waves making original or first (*asli*) and newcomer (*pendatang*) temporally relative terms. No one disputed that the ethno-linguistic group contesting the occupation were the first inhabitants of the area, but there was no consensus on the entitlements that follow. In many versions of customary law, the territorial claims of earlier occupants are thin unless an investment of labour has left an imprint on the landscape. Labour signals rights. Thus, for example, a valuable tree that has been nurtured and marked by its 'owner' is recognized as private property. Land that has been cleared for farming is subject to individual or group ownership rights, even if the forest has long since regrown (Sangaji 2001). At the site of the occupation, the 'indigenous' claimants had made no such investments, but labour *had* been invested by some members of the farmer group. While working as labourers for a timber concession operating at the site a decade earlier, they had planted coffee trees and continued to nurture them, an activity that gave them customary rights.

My purpose in examining the various positions attributed to, claimed by, or disallowed to the protagonists is not to adjudicate or draw conclusions about how diverse objectives—conservation, justice—can best be achieved. It is to emphasize the contingency and mutability of positioning, not as an outcome of unfettered individual 'choice', but as it is configured within the continuous play of culture, history and power. Under a different set of conditions, different connections, alliances and oppositions could have been made, as they will be in future as the conjuncture shifts. Looming on the horizon is the bloody conflict between Muslims and Christians in the town of Poso less than 100 kilometres away, a conflict setting refugees on the move, rearranging populations, and uniting fractious highlanders as a solid Christian block. It is also transforming the landscape, notably the landscape of the park, the favourite spot for contractors building donor-sponsored refugee housing to get cheap timber.[9] Taking advantage of the NGO movement's current disarray, provincial planners are reviving the plan to build a hydro plant within the park, a threat that will again rework the lines of alliance and opposition.

CONCLUSION

To move beyond the limited optic of power and resistant others, virtuous peasants and vicious states, or 'stakeholders' bearing fixed interests, identities and ideologies, this essay focused upon projects, practices, processes, and positions. Its analytical framework proved robust enough to expose the dynamics of a resource conflict in the highlands of Sulawesi, and readers will judge whether it is helpful in untangling the threads of resource conflicts in South Asia and beyond.

---

[9] See Y.K.I YAKIS, 'Semua Kayu Yang Digunakan Oleh Kimpraswil Untuk RTS Poso Illegal', 12 April 2002 at fkkm@yahoogroups.com.

REFERENCES

Abraham, Itty and Willem van Schendel. 2005. *Illicit Flows and Criminal Things: States, Borders, and the Other Side of Globalization*. Bloomington: Indiana University Press.

Adams, J. 1995. *Risk*. London: University College London Press.

Adams, J. and M. Thompson. 2002. 'Taking Account of Societal Concerns about Risk'. Website of the UK's Health and Safety Executive: http://www.hse.gov.uk/research/rrpdf/rr035.pdf.

Adebayo, A. 1993. *Embattled Federalism*. New York: Peter Lang.

Adnan, Shapan. 2004. *Migration, Land Alienation, and Ethnic Conflict: Causes of Poverty in the Chittagong Hill Tracts of Bangladesh*. Dhaka: Research and Advisory Services.

———. 2007. 'Departures from Everyday Resistance and Flexible Strategies of Domination: The Making and Unmaking of a Poor Peasant Mobilization in Bangladesh', *Journal of Agrarian Change*, 7 (2): 183–224.

Agarwal, Bina. 2001. 'Participatory Exclusions, Community Forestry, and Gender: An Analysis for South Asia and a Conceptual Framework', *World Development*, 29 (10): 1623–48.

Agrawal, Arun. 2005. *Environmentality: Technologies of Government and the Making of Subjects*. Durham, NC: Duke University Press.

Agrawal, Arun and K. Sivaramakrishnan (eds). 2000. *Agrarian Environments: Resources, Representations and Rule in India*. Durham, NC: Duke University Press.

Alagoa, M. 2001. *The Report of the Nembe Peace and Reconciliation Committee*. Port Harcourt.

Alam, Md. Shamsul, S. Dara Shamsuddin, Md. Shaderar Rashid, and Md. Delwar Hossain. 1999. 'Sylhet and its Evolving Geographical Environment' in Sharif Uddin Ahmed (ed.), *Sylhet: History and Heritage*. Dhaka: Bangladesh Itihas Samiti.

Ali, Imran. 1987. 'Malign Growth? Agricultural Colonization and the Roots of Backwardness in the Punjab', *Past and Present*. 114 (1): 110–32.

———. 1988. *The Punjab Under Imperialism, 1885–1947*. Princeton: Princeton University Press.

Allami, Abul Fazl. 1927 [1977]. *Ain-i-Akbari*, translated by H. Blochman. Calcutta: Asiatic Society. 3 vols. Reprint, 3rd edition. Delhi: Low Price Publications.

Anderson, David and Richard Grove (eds). 1987. *Conservation in Africa: People, Policies and Practice*. Cambridge: Cambridge University Press.

Anderson, Benedict. 1998. *Imagined Communities*. New York: Verso.

————. 1999. 'Indonesian Nationalism Today and in the Future', *New Left Review*, 235: 3–17.

Anderson, Perry. 2001. 'Scurrying Towards Bethlehem', *New Left Review*. 10: 5–30.

————. 2002. 'Force and Consent', *New Left Review*, 17: 5–30.

Anugwom, E. 2001. 'Federalism, Fiscal Centralism and the Realities of Democratization in Nigeria', Unpublished paper delivered to the Conference on Africa at the Crossroads, UNESCO (www.ethnonet-africa.org/pubs/crossroadsed1.htm).

ANZDEC. 1997. *Environmental Management and Biodiversity Conservation in the Lore Lindu Bioregion*. Palu: Asian Development Bank.

Appadurai, Arjun. 1986. *The Social Life of Things: Commodities in Cultural Perspective*. Cambridge: Cambridge University Press.

Arrow, Kenneth. 1951. *Social Choice and Individual Values*. New York: Wiley.

Ashton, Peter J. 2002. 'Avoiding Conflicts over Africa's Water Resources', *Ambio*, 31 (3): 236–42.

Baechler, Gunther 1999. *Violence through Environmental Discrimination: Causes, Rwanda Arena, and Conflict Model*. Dordrecht: Kluwer.

Baechler, G.A. and K.R. Spillmann (eds).1996. *Kriegsursache Umweltzerstörung. [Environmental Degradation as a Cause of War]*, 3 vols. Zurich: Verlag Ruegger.

Bagchi, Kanana Gopalan. 1944. *The Ganges Delta*. Calcutta: University of Calcutta.

Balla, Balint. 1981. 'Ressourcenknappheit und Soziales Handeln', in Friedrich Rapp (ed.), *Naturverstaendnis und Soziales Handeln*. Munich: Wilhelm Fink.

Bannon, Ian and Paul Collier (eds). 2003. *Natural Resources and Violent Conflict: Options and Actions*. Washington, DC: The World Bank.

Bareh, Hamlet. 1987. 'Khasi-Jaintia State Formation', in Surajit Sinha (ed.), *Tribal Polities and State Systems in Pre-Colonial Eastern and Northeastern India*. Calcutta: K. P. Bagchi.

Barnett, Jon. 2000. 'Destabilizing the Environment-Conflict Thesis', *Review of International Studies*, 26 (2): 271–88.

Baruah, Sanjib. 2006. *Durable Disorder: Understanding the Politics of Northeast India*. New Delhi: Oxford University Press.

Baviskar, Amita.1995. *In the Belly of the River: Tribal Conflicts over Development in the Narmada Valley.* Delhi: Oxford University Press.
———. 2005. 'Red in Tooth and Claw?: Searching for Class in Struggles over Nature', in Raka Ray and Mary Katzenstein (eds), *Social Movements in India: Poverty, Power, and Politics.* Lanham, MD: Rowman and Littlefield.
———. 2007a. 'The Dream Machine: The Model Development Project and the Remaking of the State', in Amita Baviskar (ed.), *Waterscapes: The Cultural Politics of a Natural Resource.* Delhi: Permanent Black.
———. 2007b. *Waterscapes: The Cultural Politics of a Natural Resource.* Delhi: Permanent Black.
Bayly, Christopher A. 2004. *The Birth of the Modern World, 1780–1914: Global Connections and Comparisons.* Malden, MA: Blackwell.
Beinart, William. 2003. *The Rise of Conservation in South Africa: Settlers, Livestock, and the Environment, 1770–1950.* New York: Oxford University Press.
Berlant, Lauren. 1991. *The Anatomy of National Fantasy.* Chicago: University of Chicago Press.
Bernstein, Henry. 1990. 'Taking the Part of Peasants?' in H. Bernstein, B. Crow, M. Mackintosh, and C. Martin (eds), *The Question of Food: Profits Versus People?* New York: Monthly Review Press.
Bhattacharjee, J.B. 1987. 'Dimasa State Formation in Cachar', in Surajit Sinha (ed.), *Tribal Polities and State Systems in Pre-Colonial Eastern and Northeastern India.* Calcutta: K.P. Bagchi.
Bhattacharyya, Suchintya. 1991. *Genesis of Tribal Extremism in Tripura.* Delhi: Gian Publishing House.
Biersack, Aletta and James B. Greenberg (eds). 2006. *Reimagining Political Ecology.* Durham, NC: Duke University Press.
Blok, A. 1974. *The Mafia in a Sicilian Village.* Waveland: Prospect Heights.
Bob, C. 2002. 'Merchants of Morality', *Foreign Policy,* 129: 36–45.
Boot, Max. 2002. *The Savage Wars of Peace: Small Wars and the Rise of American Power.* New York: Basic Books.
Bose, Sugata. 1993. *Peasant Labour and Colonial Capital: Rural Bengal since 1770.* Cambridge: Cambridge University Press.
Borsuk, Richard. 1997. 'Bre-X Minerals Defends Pact With Indonesia', *Wall Street Journal,* 136(41), 2 February, B3A.
Bourdieu, Pierre. 1998. 'The Economy of Symbolic Goods', in *Practical Reason.* Cambridge: Polity Press.
Brara, Rita. 2006. *Shifting Landscapes: The Making and Remaking of Village Commons in India.* New Delhi: Oxford University Press.
Braun, Bruce. 2000. 'Producing Vertical Territory', *Ecumene,* 7(1): 7–46.

Broda-Bahm, Kenneth T. 1999. 'Finding Protection in Definitions: The Quest for Environmental Security', *Argumentation and Advocacy*, 35: 159–70.

Brookfield, Harold Leslie Potter, and Yvonne Byron. 1995. *In Place of the Forest: Environmental and Socioeconomic Transformations in Borneo and the Eastern Malay Peninsula*. New York: United Nations Press.

Brosius, J. Peter. 1999. 'Analyses and Interventions: Anthropological Engagements with Environmentalism', *Current Anthropology*, 40 (3): 277–309.

Bryant, Raymond and Sinead Bailey. 1997. *Third World Political Ecology*. London: Routledge.

Brysk, A. 2000. *From Tribal Village to Global Village*. Stanford, CA: Stanford University Press.

Buckley, Robert Burton. 1908. *Facts, Figures, and Formulae for Irrigation Engineers*. London: E. & F. N. Spon.

Burholt, Vanesa. 2004. 'The Settlement Patterns and Residential Histories of Older Gujaratis, Punjabis and Sylhetis in Birmingham, England', *Ageing and Society*, 24: 383–409.

Canter, Marielle J. and Stephen N. Ndegwa. 2002. 'Environmental Scarcity and Conflict: A Contrary Case from Lake Victoria', *Global Environmental Politics*, 2 (3): 40–62.

Carroll, J. 1971. 'Participatory Technology', *Science*, 171 (3972): 647–53.

Carson, L. and B. Martin. 2002. 'Random Selection of Citizens for Technological Decision Making', *Science and Public Policy*, 29 (2): 105–13.

Cederlof, Gunnel and K. Sivaramakrishnan (eds). 2006. *Ecological Nationalisms: Nature, Livelihoods, and Identities in South Asia*. Seattle: University of Washington Press.

Cesarz, E., S. Morrison and J. Cooke. 2003. 'Alienation and Militancy in the Nigeria Delta', Centre for Strategic and International Studies, Washington DC, Africa Notes #16, May 2003.

Chakrabarti, Dilip K. 2001. *Ancient Bangladesh: A Study of the Archaeological Sources with an Update on Bangladesh Archaeology, 1990–2000*. Dhaka: The University Press Limited.

Chakravarty-Kaul, Minoti. 1996. *Common Lands and Customary Law: Institutional Change in North India over the Last Two Centuries*. Delhi: Oxford University Press.

Chaudhuri, Binay Bhushan. 1993. 'Tribal Society in Transition: Eastern India 1757–1920', in Mushirul Hasan and Narayani Gupta (eds), *India's Colonial Encounter: Essays in Memory of Eric Stokes*. Delhi: Oxford University Press.

Chaudhuri, Dewan Nurul Anward Hussain. 1999. 'Hazrat Shah Jalal (R) and His Life: A Source Study', in Sharif Uddin Ahmed (ed.), *Sylhet: History and Heritage*. Dhaka: Bangladesh Itihas Samiti.

Chaudhuri, Sujit. 1985. *Folklore and History: A Study of Hindu Folk-cults of the Barak Valley of Northeast India*. New Delhi: K. K. Publishers.

————. 2002. 'A "God-sent Opportunity"', *Seminar*, online edition, http://www.india-seminar.com/2002/510/510%20sujit%20chaudhuri.htm

Chaudhuri, Sushil. 1997. 'General Economic Conditions under the Nawabs', in Sirajul Islam (ed.), *History of Bangladesh, 1704—1971*, 2nd edition. Dhaka: Asiatic Society of Bangladesh.

Christian Aid. 2003. *Fuelling Poverty: Oil, War and Corruption*. London: Christian Aid.

CIA. (Central Intelligence Agency). 2000. 'Nigeria: Environmental Stresses and their Impacts over the Next Decade'. CIA DCI Environmental Center.

Coates, J. 1975. 'Why Public Participation is Essential to Technology Assessment', *Public Administration Review*, 35 (1): 67–9.

Collier, Paul. 2000. *The Economic Causes of Civil Conflict and their Implications for Policy*. Washington DC: The World Bank.

Conklin, Beth and Laura Graham. 1995. 'The Shifting Middle Ground: Amazonian Indians and Eco-Politics', *American Anthropologist*, 97 (4): 695–710.

Coronil, Fernando. 1997. *The Magical State: Nature, Money, and Modernity in Venezuela*. Chicago: University of Chicago Press.

Cowen, M.P. and R.W. Shenton. 1996. *Doctrines of Development*. New York: Routledge.

Cronon, William (ed.). 1983. *Changes in the Land: Indians, Colonists, and the Ecology of New England*. New York: Hill and Wang.

————. 1995. *Uncommon Ground: Toward Reinventing Nature*. New York: W. W. Norton and Company.

Dake, K. and M. Thompson. 1999. 'Making Ends Meet, in the Household and on the Planet', *GeoJournal*, 47 (3): 417–24.

Dalby, Simon. 2002. *Environmental Security*. Minneapolis: University of Minnesota Press.

————. 2007a. 'Geopolitical Knowledge: Scale, Method and the Willy Sutton Syndrome', *Geopolitics*, 12 (1): 183–91.

————. 2007b. 'Ecology, Security, and Change in the Anthropocene', *Brown Journal of World Affairs*, 13 (2): 155–64.

Dalton R. and M. Wattenberg. 2000. *Parties without Partisans*. Oxford: Oxford University Press.

Darier, E., C. Jaeger, B. Kasemir, R. Schüle, S. Shackley, and B. Wynne. 1998. *Contributions to Participatory Integrated Assessment*. Darmstadt: ULYSSES WP-98-1.

Dass, Sushanta Krishna. 1980. 'Immigration and Demographic Transformation of Assam, 1891–1981', *Economic and Political Weekly*, 15 (19): 850–9.

Datta, Rajat. 1990. 'Merchants and Peasants: A Study of the Structure of
    Local Trade in Grain in Late Eighteenth Century Bengal', in Sanjay
    Subrahmanyam (ed.), *Merchants, Markets, and the State in Early Modern
    India*. Delhi: Oxford University Press.
————. 2000. *Society, Economy, and the Market: Commercialization in Rural
    Bengal, c.1760–1800*. Delhi: Manohar Publishers.
Davis, Mike. 1999. *Ecology of Fear: Los Angeles and the Imagination of Disaster*.
    New York: Vintage.
————. 2001. *Late Victorian Holocausts: El Nino Famines and the Making of the
    Third World*, London: Verso.
————. 2002. *Dead Cities*. New York: The New Press.
Dean, Mitchell. 1999. *Governmentality: Power and Rule in Modern Society*.
    London: Sage Publications.
Desai, Bharat. 1995. 'Narmada Dam will not Help Save Kutch', *The Telegraph*,
    New Delhi, May 19.
Deudney, Daniel. 1999a. 'Environmental Security: A Critique', in Daniel
    Deudney and Richard Matthew (eds), *Contested Grounds: Security and
    Conflict in the New Environmental Politics*. Albany: State University of
    New York Press.
————. 1999b. 'Bringing Nature Back In: Geopolitical Theory from the
    Greeks to the Global Era', in Daniel Deudney and Richard Matthew
    (eds), *Contested Grounds: Security and Conflict in the New Environmental
    Politics*, Albany: State University of New York Press.
Dewey, Clive. 1991. *The Settlement Literature of the Greater Punjab*. New
    Delhi: Manohar.
Dickinson, H.W. 1936. *James Watt: Craftsman and Engineer*. Cambridge:
    Cambridge University Press.
Diehl, Paul F. and Nils Petter Gleditsch (eds). 2001. *Environmental Conflict*.
    Boulder: Westview.
Diehl, Paul F. and Shannon O'Lear. 2007. 'Not Drawn to Scale: Research on
    Resource and Environmental Conflict', *Geopolitics*, 12 (1): 166–82.
Dimitrov, Radoslav S. 2002. 'Water, Conflict and Security: A Conceptual
    Minefield', *Society and Natural Resources*, 15 (8): 677–91.
Dobkowski, Michael and Isidor Wallimann (eds). 2002. *On the Edge of
    Scarcity: Environment, Resources, Population, Sustainability, and Conflict*.
    Syracuse: Syracuse University Press.
Douglas, Mary and A. Wildavsky. 1982. *Risk and Culture*. Berkeley: University
    of California Press.
Douie, James M. 1972 [1931]. *Punjab Land Administration Manual*.
    Chandigarh: Government of the Punjab.
————. 1985 [1899]. *Punjab Settlement Manual*. Delhi: Daya Publishing
    House.

Dove, Michael. 1992. 'The Dialectical History of "Jungle" in Pakistan: An Examination of the Relationship between Nature and Culture', *Journal of Anthropological Research*. 48 (3): 231–53.

———. 1999. 'Representations of the "Other": The Ethnographic Challenge Posed by Planters' Views of Peasants in Indonesia', in Tania M. Li (ed.), *Transforming the Indonesian Uplands*. London: Harwood Academic Publishers.

Drayton, Richard. 2000. *Nature's Government: Science, Imperial Britain, and the 'Improvement' of the World*. New Haven, CT: Yale University Press.

D'Souza, Rohan. 2006. *Drowned and Dammed: Colonial Capitalism and Flood Control in Eastern India*. New Delhi: Oxford University Press.

Dunn, Ross. 1986. *The Adventures of Ibn Battuta, A Muslim Traveler of the 14th Century*. Berkeley: University of California Press.

DuPuis, Melanie and Peter Vandergeest. 1996. *Creating the Countryside: The Politics of Rural and Environmental Discourse*. Philadelphia: Temple University Press.

Eaton, Richard M. 1993. *The Rise of Islam and the Bengal Frontier, 1204–1760*. Berkeley: University of California Press.

Ellison, N. 1997. 'Towards a New Social Politics: Citizenship and Reflexivity in Late Modernity', *Sociology*, 31 (4): 697–717.

Ellul, J. 1964. *The Technological Society*. New York: Knopf.

Environmental Rights Action. 2000. *The Emperor has No Clothes*. Benin: Environmental Rights Action.

Esty, Daniel C. 1999. 'Pivotal States and the Environment,' in Robert Chase, Emily Hill, and Paul Kennedy (eds), *The Pivotal States: A New Framework for U.S. Policy in the Developing World*, New York: Norton.

Evans, G., J. Goodman, and N. Landsbury (eds). 2002. *Moving Mountains: Communities Confront Mining and Globalization*. London: Zed.

Falkenmark, M., J. Lundqvist and C. Widstrand. 1990. 'Coping with Water Scarcity. Implications of Biomass Strategy for Communities and Policies', *Water Resources Development*, 6 (1): 29–43.

Famine Commission. 1945. *Final Report*. Madras: Government Press. Reprinted Delhi: Usha Press.

Ferguson, James. 1994. *The Anti-Politics Machine: 'Development', Depoliticization, and Bureaucratic Power in Lesotho*. Minneapolis: University of Minnesota Press.

Ferroukhi, Lyes. 1994. *An Ecologically Sound Water Harvesting System under Threat: A Case Study of the Banni Pastoralists' Knowledge in the Grasslands of Kachchh District, Gujarat State, India*. Swedish University of Agricultural Sciences Working Paper 266. Uppsala: International Rural Development Centre.

Firminger, Walter K. (ed). 1917. *The Sylhet District Records*. Shillong: Assam Secretariat Printing Office.

———— (ed). 1969. *The Fifth Report from the Select Committee of the House of Commons on the Affairs of the East India Company* (Dated 28 July, 1812). Calcutta: R. Cambray (Reprint New York: Augustus M. Kelley).

Fisher, William (ed.). 1995. *Towards Sustainable Development?: Struggling over India's Narmada River*. Armonk, NY: M.E. Sharpe.

Fisk, Robert. 2002. 'Water War Looms as Israel Tells Lebanon to Halt River Works', *The Independent*, 26 September.

Flannery, Tim. 2006. *The Weather Makers: How we are Changing the Climate and what it Means for Life on Earth*. Toronto: Harper Collins.

Foucault, Michel. 1991. 'Governmentality', in G. Burchell, C. Gordon and P. Miller (eds), *The Foucault Effect: Studies in Governmentality*. Chicago: University of Chicago Press.

————. 2000. *Power*. New York: The New Press.

Forum Petani Merdeka (FPM), 2001. 'Tidak Benar Kami Melakukan Pembabatan Hutan di TNLL: Kami butuh tanah, bukan kayu seperti yang ditudukan kepada kami': WALHI.

Fuller, C. J. and Veronique Benei (eds). 2000. *The Everyday State and Society in Modern India*. New Delhi: Social Science Press.

Furro, T. 1992. 'Federalism and the Politics of Revenue Allocation in Nigeria', Unpublished Ph.D. Dissertation, Clark Atlanta University.

Gadgil, Madhav and Ramachandra Guha. 1992. *This Fissured Land: An Ecological History of India*. Delhi: Oxford University Press.

————. 1995. *Ecology and Equity: The Use and Abuse of Nature in Contemporary India*. New Delhi: Penguin.

Gain, Philip (ed.). 1995. *Bangladesh: Land, Forest, and Forest People*. Dhaka: Society for Environment and Human Development.

Gallie, W.B. 1955. Essentially Contested Concepts. *Proceedings of the Aristotelian Society*, 56: 167–98.

Gandy, Matthew. 1996. 'Crumbling Land: The Postmodernity Debate and the Analysis of Environmental Problems', *Progress in Human Geography*, 20 (1): 23–40.

Gardner, Katy. 1995. *Global Migrants, Local Lives: Travel and Transformation in Rural Bangladesh*. Oxford: Clarendon Press.

Gary, Ian and Terry Karl. 2003. *Bottom of the Barrel: Africa's Oil Boom and the Poor*. New York: Catholic Relief Services.

Gaventa, John and A. Cornwall. 2000. 'From Users and Choosers to Makers and Shapers: Repositioning Participation in Social Policy', *IDS Bulletin*, 31 (4): 50–62.

Gedicks, Al. 2001. *Resource Rebels: Native Challenges to Mining and Oil Corporations*. Boston: South End.

Giddens, Anthony. 1999. *Runaway World: The 1999 Reith Lectures*. http://
    news.bbc.co.uk/hi/english/static/events/reith_99/default.htm
Giersch, C. Patterson. 2006. *Asian Borderlands: The Transformation of Qing
    China's Yunnan Frontier*. Cambridge: Harvard University Press.
Gilmartin, David. 2006. 'Imperial Rivers: Irrigation and British Visions
    of Empire', in Dane Kennedy and Durba Ghosh (eds), *Decentring
    Empire: Britain, India and the Transcolonial World*. New Delhi: Orient
    Longman.
Gleditsch, Nils Petter (ed.). 1997. *Conflict and the Environment*. Dordrecht:
    Kluwer.
Gleditsch, Nils Petter, Kathryn Furlong, Havard Hegre, Bethany Lacina and
    Taylor Owen. 2006. 'Conflicts over Shared Rivers: Resource Scarcity
    or Fuzzy Boundaries?' *Political Geography*, 25 (1): 361–82.
Gleick, Peter H. 1993. *Water in Crisis: A Guide to the World's Fresh Water
    Resources*. Oxford: Oxford University Press.
Global Witness. 2004. *Breaking the Links between Natural Resources, Conflict
    and Corruption*. Annual Report. Washington DC: Global Witness.
GoB (Government of Bangladesh). 1996. *Bangladesh Population Census, 1991*.
    Community Series. Dhaka: Bangladesh Bureau of Statistics.
GoI (Government of India). 1933. *Census of India, 1931. Vol. I. Pt. II. Imperial
    Tables*. Delhi: Manager of Publications.
————. 1961. *Report on the Population Estimates of India*. Delhi: Government
    of India.
Gold, Ann Grodzins and Bhoju Ram Gujar. 2002. *In the Time of Trees and
    Sorrows: Nature, Power and Memory in Rajasthan*. Durham, NC: Duke
    University Press.
GoP (Government of Pakistan). 1970. *East Pakistan District Gazetteers, Sylhet*.
    Dhaka: Pakistan Government Press.
Gordon, Colin. 1991. 'Governmental Rationality: An Introduction', in G.
    Burchell, C. Gordon, and P. Miller (eds), *The Foucault Effect: Studies in
    Governmentality*. Chicago: University of Chicago Press.
Greenough, Paul and Anna L. Tsing (eds). 2003. *Nature in the Global South:
    Environmental Projects in South and Southeast Asia*. Durham, NC: Duke
    University Press.
Grove, Richard. 1995. *Green Imperialism: Colonial Expansion, Tropical Island
    Edens, and the Origins of Environmentalism, 1600–1800*. Cambridge:
    Cambridge University Press.
————. 1997. *Ecology, Climate and Empire: Colonialism and Global
    Environmental History, 1400–1940*. Cambridge: White Horse.
Grove, Richard, Vinita Damodaran and Satpal Sangwan (eds). 1998. *Nature
    and the Orient: Environmental History of South and Southeast Asia*. Delhi:
    Oxford University Press.

Guha, Amalendu. 1977. *Planter Raj to Swaraj: Freedom Movement and Electoral Politics in Assam, 1826–1947*. Delhi: Manohar Publishers

Guha, Ramachandra. 1989. *The Unquiet Woods: Ecological Change and Peasant Resistance in the Himalaya*. Delhi: Oxford University Press.

Gujarat Ecology Commission. 1994. *Current Ecological Status of Kachchh*. Vadodara: GEC.

Gupta, K.N. 1931. 'On Some Castes and Caste-Origins in Sylhet', *Indian Historical Quarterly*, 7(4): 715–26.

Gupta, Kamalakanta. 1967. *Copper-plates of Sylhet*. Sylhet: Lipika Enterprises.

Gyawali, Dipak. 2001. *Water in Nepal*. Kathmandu: Himal.

HRW (Human Rights Watch). 1999. *The Price of Oil*. Washington DC: Human Rights Watch.

———. 2002. *The Niger Delta: No Democratic Dividend*. Washington DC: Human Rights Watch.

———. 2003. *Testing Democracy*. Washington DC: Human Rights Watch.

Habermas, Jurgen. 1984. *The Theory of Communicative Action 1: Reason and the Rationalization of Society*. Boston: Beacon Press.

Habib, Irfan. 1982. *Atlas of Mughal India: Political and Economic Maps with Notes, Bibliography and Index*. Delhi: Oxford University Press.

Hale, Charles. 1994. *Resistance and Contradiction: Miskitu Indians and the Nicaraguan State, 1894–1987*. Stanford, CA: Stanford University Press.

Hall, Stuart. 1990. 'Cultural Identity and Diaspora', in J. Rutherford (ed.), *Identity: Community, Culture, Difference*. London: Lawrence and Wishart.

Hammer, J., 1996. 'Nigerian Crude', *Harper's Magazine*, June 1996: 58–68.

Hardin, Garrett. 1969. 'The Tragedy of the Commons', *Ekistics*, 160: 168–70.

Harding, Susan and Daniel Rosenberg. 2005. *Histories of the Future*. Duke University Press.

Headrick, Daniel R. 1988. *The Tentacles of Progress: Technology Transfer in the Age of Imperialism, 1850–1940*. New York: Oxford University Press.

Hecht, Susanna and Alexander Cockburn. 1989. *The Fate of the Forest: Developers, Destroyers and Defenders of the Amazon*. New York and London: Verso.

Heineman, R., W. Bluhm, S. Peterson, and E. Kearny. 1990. *The World of the Policy Analyst: Rationality, Values, and Politics*. Chatham, NJ: Chatham House Publishers.

Hendriks, F. 1994. 'Cars and Culture in Munich and Birmingham: The Case for Cultural Pluralism', in D.J. Coyle and R.J. Ellis (eds), *Politics, Policy and Culture*. Boulder, Colorado: Westview.

Hendriks, F. and S. Zourides. 1999. 'Cultural Biases and New Media for the Public Domain: Cui Bono?', in M. Thompson, G. Grendstad and P. Selle, P (eds), *Cultural Theory as Political Science*. London: Routledge.

Herman, E. S. and Noam Chomsky. 1988. *Manufacturing Consent: The Political Economy of the Mass Media*. New York: Pantheon Books

Herzfeld, Michael. 1997. *Cultural Intimacy: Social Poetics in the Nation-State*. London: Routledge.

Hill, Hal. 1996. *The Indonesian Economy Since 1966: Southeast Asia's Emerging Giant*. Cambridge: Cambridge University Press.

Hochschild, Adam. 1998. *King Leopold's Ghost: A Story of Greed, Terror, and Heroism in Colonial Africa*. Boston: Houghton Mifflin.

Hogendorn, Jan and Marion Johnson. 1986. *The Shell Money of the Slave Trade*. New York: Cambridge University Press.

Homer-Dixon, Thomas. 1991. 'On the Threshold: Environmental Changes as Causes of Acute Conflict', *International Security*, 16 (1): 76–116.

———. 1994. 'Environmental Scarcities and Violent Conflict: Evidence from Cases', *International Security*, 19 (1): 5–40.

———. 1999. *Environment, Scarcity and Violence*. Princeton: Princeton University Press.

Homer-Dixon T. and J. Blitt (eds). 1998. *Ecoviolence: Links among Environment, Population, and Security*. Lanham, MD.: Rowman and Littlefield.

Homer-Dixon, Thomas, J.H. Boutwell, and G.W. Rathjens. 1993. 'Environmental Change and Violent Conflict', *Scientific American*, 268 (2): 38–45.

Hood, C. 1998. *The Art of the State: Culture, Rhetoric and Public Management*. Oxford: Clarendon Press.

Hossain, Hameeda (ed.). 2001. *Human Rights in Bangladesh, 2000*. Dhaka: Ain o Shalish Kendra.

Huq, Nasser Ejazul. 1999. 'Mineral Resources of Sylhet', in Sharif Uddin Ahmed (ed.), *Sylhet: History and Heritage*. Dhaka: Bangladesh Itihas Samiti.

Hussain, Syed Ejaz. 2003. *The Bengal Sultanate: Politics, Economy, and Coins (AD 1205–1576)*. Delhi: Manohar Publishers.

Ibeanu, O. 2003. '(Sp)oils of Politics'. Paper delivered to a Conference on Oil and Human Rights, University of California, Berkeley, 24–26 January 2003.

Ikein, I. 1990. *The Impact of Oil on a Developing Country*. New York: Praeger.

Imam, Abu. 1999. 'Ancient Sylhet: History and Tradition', in Sharif Uddin Ahmed (ed.), *Sylhet: History and Heritage*. Dhaka: Bangladesh Itihas Samiti.

Irwin, A. 1995. *Citizen Science*. London: Routledge.

Islam, K. Z. 2002. 'The Bengal Award was a Perverse Award', *Weekly Holiday*. 2 February, 2002, http://www.weeklyholiday.net/080202/inret.html

Islam, Mohammad Amirul, Sabu S. Padmadas and Peter W. F. Smith. 2004. 'Men's Approval of Family Planning in Bangladesh', *Journal of Biosocial Science* (published online) 00: 1–13.

Islam, M. Ataharul. 1997. 'Population and Environment', in Sirajul Islam (ed.) *History of Bangladesh, 1704–1971*, 2nd edition. Dhaka: Asiatic Society of Bangladesh.

Islam, Sirajul. 1985. *Villages in the Haor Basin of Bangladesh*. Studies in Socio-Cultural Change in Rural Villages in Bangladesh, No. 4. Tokyo: Institute for the Study of Languages and Cultures of Asia and Africa.

———. 1989. *Rent and Raiyat: Society and Economy of Eastern Bengal, 1859–1928*. Dhaka: Asiatic Society of Bangladesh.

———. 1997. 'Economic History in Perspective', in Sirajul Islam (ed.), *History of Bangladesh, 1704–1971*, 2nd edition. Dhaka: Asiatic Society of Bangladesh.

——— (ed.). 2000. *Comilla District Records*. Dhaka: The Institute of Liberation Bangabandhu and Bangladesh Studies.

Jaeger, C., O. Renn, E. Rosa, and T. Webler. 1998. 'Decision Analysis and Rational Action', in S. Rayner and E. Malone (eds), *Human Choice and Climate Change: Volume 3, Tools for Policy Analysis*. Columbus, OH: Battelle Press.

Jasanoff, Shiela. 1990. *The Fifth Branch: Science Advisors as Policymakers*. Cambridge, MA: Harvard University Press.

Jeffery, Roger and Nandini Sundar (eds). 1999. *A New Moral Economy for India's Forests?: Discourses of Community and Participation*. New Delhi: Sage Publications.

Jensen, L. 1999. 'Images of Democracy in Danish Social Housing', in M. Thompson, G. Grendstad and P. Selle (eds), *Cultural Theory as Political Science*. London: Routledge.

Jung, Dietrich. 2003. *Shadow Globalization, Ethnic Conflicts and New Wars: A Political Economy of Intra-State War*. London: Routledge.

Kahl, Colin. 2006. *States, Scarcity, and Civil Strife in the Developing World*. Princeton, NJ: Princeton University Press.

Kakoty, Sanjeeb. 2005. 'Meghalaya-Sylhet: A Border Without History or Logic', *Himal South Asian*, November. Online: http://www.himalmag.com/2005/november/cover_story_8.html

Kaldor, Mary. 2007. *New and Old Wars: Organized Violence in a Global Era*, 2nd edition, Stanford, CA: Stanford University Press.

Kamal, A.H. Ahmed. 1988. 'The Decline of the Muslim League and the Ascendancy of the Bureaucracy in East Pakistan', Unpublished Ph.D. dissertation, Australian National University.

Kaplan, Robert D. 1994. 'The Coming Anarchy', *Atlantic Monthly*, 273(2): 44–76.

———. 2000. *The Coming Anarchy: Shattering the Dreams of the Post Cold War*. New York: Random House.

Kapucinski, Ryszard. 1982. *Shah of Shahs*. New York: Harcourt.

Kar, Bodhisattva. 2004. *What's in a Name: Politics of Spatial Imagination in Colonial Assam*. Guwahati: Centre of Northeast India and South and Southeast Asian Studies.

Karim, Abdul. 1985. *Social History of the Muslims of Bengal*. Chittagong: Baitush Sharif Islamic Research Institute.

———. 1992. *Corpus of the Arabic and Persian Inscriptions of Bengal*. Dhaka: Asiatic Society of Bengal.

———. 1997. 'Suba Bangla: Government and Politics', in Sirajul Islam (ed.), *History of Bangladesh, 1704–1971*, 2nd edition. Dhaka: Asiatic Society of Bangladesh.

———. 1999. 'Advent of Islam in Sylhet and Hazrat Shah Jalal (R)', in Sharif Uddin Ahmed (ed.), *Sylhet: History and Heritage*. Dhaka: Bangladesh Itihas Samiti.

Kemedi, Von. 2002. 'Oil on Troubled Waters', Berkeley: Environmental Politics Working Papers.

Klare, Michael. 2001. *Resource Wars*. New York: Metropolitan.

———. 2004. *Blood and Oil: The Dangers and Consequences of America's Growing Dependency on Imported Petroleum*. New York: Metropolitan Books.

Kolff, Dirk H.A. 1989. 'The End of an Ancien Regime: Colonial War in India, 1798–1818', in J.A. de Moor and H.L. Wesseling (eds), *Imperialism and War: Essays on Colonial Wars in Asia and Africa*. Leiden: E.J. Brill.

Kumar, Arun. 1995. 'Colonial Requirements and Engineering Education: The Public Works Department', in Roy MacLeod and Deepak Kumar (eds), *Technology and the Raj: Western Technology and Technical Transfers to India, 1700–1947*. New Delhi: Sage Publications.

Kutch Development Forum. 1993. *A Demand for Review of Water Allocation to Kutch: Recommendations, Observations, Extracts from Report of Review Group on Narmada*. KDF: Bombay.

Laban, B. 2002. 'Prospek Negatif Penebangan Liar di Taman Nasional Lore Lindu': *Indonesia Nature Conservation Newsletter* (INCL) 5 (10–11).

Latour, Bruno. 1987. *Science in Action: How to Follow Scientists and Engineers through Society*. Cambridge: Harvard University Press.

Le Billon, Philippe. 2001a. 'The Political Ecology of War: Natural Resources and Armed Conflicts', *Political Geography*, 20 (5): 561–84.

———. 2001b. 'Angola's Political Economy of War', *African Affairs*, 100 (399): 55–80.

———. 2005. *Fuelling War: Natural Resources and Armed Conflict*. Oxford: Routledge.

———. 2007. 'Fatal Transactions: Conflict Diamonds and the (Anti) Terrorist Consumer', in Derek Gregory and Allan Pred (eds), *Violent Geographies: Fear, Terror, and Political Violence*. New York: Routledge.

Leach, Melissa and Ian Scoones. 2002. 'Science and Citizenship in a Global Context'. Paper presented at Conference on Science and Citizenship in a Global Context. Institute for Development Studies, Brighton 12–13 December.

Lee, K. 1993. *Compass and Gyroscope*. Washington DC: Island Press.

Levidow, L. 2001. 'Genetically Modified Crops: What Transboundary Harmonization in Europe?', in J. Linnerooth-Bayer, R. Löfstedt, and G. Sjösted (eds), *Transboundary Risk Management*. London: Earthscan.

Leite, C. and J. Weidmann, 1999. *Does Mother Nature Corrupt?* IMF Working Paper. Washington DC: International Monetary Fund.

Leonard, D. and S. Strauss. 2003. *Africa's Stalled Development*. Boulder: Westview.

Leslie, Jacques. 2000. 'Running Dry: What Happens When the World no Longer has Enough Freshwater?' *Harper's Magazine*, 301 (1802) July: 37–52.

Levy, Marc. 1995. 'Is the Environment a National Security Issue?', *International Security*, 20 (2): 35–62.

Li, Tania M. 1996. 'Images of Community: Discourse and Strategy in Property Relations', *Development and Change*, 27 (2): 501–27.

———. 1999a. 'Marginality, Power and Production: Analysing Upland Transformations', in Tania M. Li (ed.), *Transforming the Indonesian Uplands*. London: Harwood Academic Publishers.

———. 1999b. 'Compromising Power: Development, Culture and Rule in Indonesia', *Cultural Anthropology*, 14 (3): 295–322.

———. 2000. 'Articulating Indigenous Identity in Indonesia: Resource Politics and the Tribal Slot', *Comparative Studies in Society and History*, 42 (1): 149–79.

———. 2001. 'Masyarakat Adat, Difference, and the Limits of Recognition in Indonesia's Forest Zone', *Modern Asian Studies*, 35 (3): 645–76.

———. 2002a. 'Ethnic Cleansing, Recursive Knowledge, and the Dilemmas of Sedentarism', *International Journal of Social Science*, 173: 361–71.

———. 2002b. 'Local Histories, Global Markets: Cocoa and Class in Upland Sulawesi', *Development and Change*, 33 (3): 415–37.

————. 2007. *The Will to Improve: Governmentality, Development and the Practice of Politics*. Durham, NC: Duke University Press.

Limerick, Patricia. 1987. *The Legacy of Conquest: The Unbroken Past of the American West*. New York: Norton.

Lindblom, C.E. 1977. *Politics and Markets: The World's Political-Economic Systems*. New York: Basic Books.

Lindsay, Alexander (ed.). 1858. *Lives of the Lindsays: or, A Memoir of the Houses of Crawford and Balcarres*. 2nd edition. London: John Murray.

Lindsay, Robert. 1858. 'Anecdotes of an Indian Life', in A. Lindsay (ed.), *Lives of the Lindsays: or, A Memoir of the Houses of Crawford and Balcarres*. 2nd edition. London: John Murray.

Lipschutz, Ronnie. 1997. 'Environmental Conflict and Environmental Determinism: The Relative Importance of Social and Natural Factors', in Nils Petter Gleditsch (ed.), *Conflict and the Environment*. Dordrecht: Kluwer.

Lonergan, Steve. 2001. 'Water and Conflict: Rhetoric and Reality', in Diehl and Gleditsch (eds), *Environmental Conflict*. Boulder: Westview.

Ludden, David. 1985. *Peasant History in South India*. Princeton: Princeton University Press. Second paperback edition published as *Early Capitalism and Local History in South India* with new Preface and additional Bibliography. Delhi: Oxford University Press, 2005. Available as ACLS History E-Book: http://ets.umdl.umich.edu/cgi/t/text/text-idx?c=acls; ;idno=heb02438

————. 1992. 'India's Development Regime', in N.B. Dirks (ed.), *Colonialism and Culture*. Ann Arbor, MI: University of Michigan Press.

————. 1999. *An Agrarian History of South Asia*. Cambridge: Cambridge University Press.

————. 2002. 'Spectres of Agrarian Territory in South India', *Indian Economic and Social History Review*, 39 (2–3): 233–58.

————. 2003a. 'Maps in the Mind and the Mobility of Asia', *Journal of Asian Studies*, 62 (3): 1057–78.

————. 2003b. *Where is Assam? Using Geographical History to Locate Current Social Realities*. Guwahati: Centre of Northeast India and South and Southeast Asian Studies. (Online version at http://www.himalmag.com/2005/november/cover_story_3.html)

————. 2003c. 'The First Boundary of Bangladesh on Sylhet's Northern Frontiers', *Journal of the Asiatic Society of Bangladesh*, 48 (1): 1–54.

————. 2006a. 'A Useable Past for a Post-national Present: Governance and Development in South Asia', *Journal of the Asiatic Society of Bangladesh*, 50 (1–2): 259–92.

————. 2006b. 'Development Regimes in South Asia: History and the Development Conundrum', *Economic and Political Weekly*, 40 (37): 4042–51.

————. 2006c. 'History and the Inequality Predicament in South Asia', Wertheim Lecture. University of Amsterdam, http://www.iias.nl/asia/wertheim/lectures/WL_Ludden.pdf

Mackenzie, Capt. Hector. 1861. *Report of the Revised Settlement of the Goojerat District*. Lahore: Hope Press.

Mackenzie, Fiona. 1998. *Land, Ecology and Resistance in Kenya 1880–1952*. New York: Heinemann.

Mahmood, A.B.M. 1970. *The Revenue Administration of Northern Bengal, 1765–1793*. Dacca: Pakistan National Institute of Public Administration.

Malkki, Liisa. 1992. 'National Geographic: The Rooting of Peoples and the Territorialisation of National Identity among Scholars and Refugees', *Cultural Anthropology*, 7 (1): 24–44.

Maloney, Clarence. 1980. *People of the Maldive Islands*. Bombay: Orient Longman.

Mamdani, Mahmood. 1996. *Citizen and Subject*. Princeton: Princeton University Press.

————. 1998. 'When Does a Settler become a Native?', Inaugural Lecture, University of Cape Town, manuscript.

————. 2000. *When Victims become Killers*. Princeton: Princeton University Press.

Mandal, Paresh Chandra. 1999. 'Sanskrit Language and Literature in Sylhet', in Sharif Uddin Ahmed (ed.), *Sylhet: History and Heritage*. Dhaka: Bangladesh Itihas Samiti.

Martin, Montgomery. 1838 [1976]. *The History, Antiquities, Topography, and Statistics of Eastern India (comprising the Districts of Behar, Shahabad, Bhagulpoor, Goruckpoor, Dinajepoor, Puraniya, Ronggopoor, and Assam)*. London: W.H. Allen. (Reprint Delhi: Cosmo Publications).

Mathews, Jessica T. 1989. 'Redefining Security', *Foreign Affairs*, 68 (2): 162–77.

Matthew, Richard, Mark Halle and Jason Switzer (eds). 2002. *Conserving the Peace: Resources, Livelihoods and Security*. Winnipeg: International Institute for Sustainable Development.

Mbembe, Achille. 2001. *On the Postcolony*. Berkeley: University of California Press.

McCarthy, J. 2000. '*Wild Logging': The Rise and Fall of Logging Networks and Biodiversity Conservation Projects on Sumatra's Rainforest Frontier*. Center for International Forestry Research Occasional Paper No. 31.

McKay, Bonnie and James Acheson. 1987. *The Question of the Commons: The Culture and Ecology of Communal Resources*. Tucson: University of Arizona Press.

McNeill, John Robert. 2001. *Something New under the Sun: An Environmental History of the Twentieth-Century World*. New York: W.W. Norton and Company.

Meadows, D.H., D.L. Meadows, J. Randers and W.W. Behrens III. 1974. *The Limits to Growth*. London: Pan.

Mehta, Lyla. 2001. 'The Manufacture of Popular Perceptions of Scarcity in Gujarat, India: Dams and Water-Related Narratives in Gujarat, India', *World Development*, 29 (12): 2025–41.

———. 2003. 'Struggles around "Publicness" and Access Rights: Perspectives from the Water Domain', in Inge Kaul, Pedro Conceiçao, Katell Le Goulven, and Ronald U. Mendoza (eds), *Providing Global Public Goods: Managing Globalisation*. New York: Oxford University Press.

———. 2005. *The Politics and Poetics of Water: Naturalising Scarcity in Western India*. New Delhi: Orient Longman.

——— (ed.). Forthcoming. *The Limits to Scarcity*. London: Earthscan.

Mehta, Uday Singh. 1999. *Liberalism and Empire: A Study in Nineteenth Century British Liberal Thought*. Chicago: University of Chicago Press.

Merchant, Carolyn. 1989. *Ecological Revolutions: Nature, Gender, and Science in New England*. Chapel Hill, NC: University of North Carolina Press.

Merrey, Douglas. 1983. 'Irrigation, Poverty and Social Change in a Village of Pakistani Punjab: An Historical and Cultural Ecological Analysis', Unpublished Ph.D. Dissertation, University of Pennsylvania.

Michel, Aloys A. 1967. *The Indus Rivers: A Study of the Effects of Partition*. New Haven, CT: Yale University Press.

Misra, Udayon. 2000. *The Periphery Strikes Back: Challenges to the Nation-State in Assam and Nagaland*. Shimla: Institute of Advanced Study.

Mital, K.V. 1986. *History of the Thomason College of Engineering, 1847–1949*. Roorkee: University of Roorkee.

Mitchell, Timothy. 2002. *Rule of Experts: Egypt, Techno-politics and Modernity*. Berkeley: University of California Press.

Mitra, Debendra Bijoy. 1991. *Monetary System in the Bengal Presidency, 1735–1835*. Calcutta: K.P. Bagchi.

Mohsin, K. M. 1997. 'Mughal Banking System', in Sirajul Islam (ed.), *History of Bangladesh, 1704–1971*, 2nd edition. Dhaka: Asiatic Society of Bangladesh.

Moore, Donald S. 1998. 'Subaltern Struggles and the Politics of Place: Remapping Resistance in Zimbabwe's Eastern Highlands', *Cultural Anthropology*, 13 (3): 344–81.

———. 1999. 'The Crucible of Cultural Politics: Reworking 'Development' in Zimbabwe's Eastern Highlands', *American Ethnologist*, 26 (3): 654–89.

Moore, Donald S., Anand Pandian and Jake Kosek. 2003. 'The Cultural Politics of Race and Nature: Terrains of Power and Practice', in D. S. Moore, J. Kosek and A. Pandian (eds), *Race, Nature and the Politics of Difference*. Durham, NC: Duke University Press.

Morse, Bradford, Thomas Berger, Donald Gamble and Hugh Brody. 1992. *Sardar Sarovar: Report of the Independent Review.* Ottawa: Resource Futures International Inc.

Morshed, Abul Kalam Manzur. 1999. 'Sylhet Dialect', in Sharif Uddin Ahmed (ed.), *Sylhet: History and Heritage.* Dhaka: Bangladesh Itihas Samiti.

Mosse, David. 2003. *The Rule of Water: Statecraft, Ecology, and Collective Action in South India.* Delhi: Oxford University Press.

Murishwar, Joy and Walter Fernandes. 1988. 'Marginalisation, Coping Mechanisms and Long-Term Solutions to Drought', *Social Action,* 38:162–78.

Myers, Norman. 1989. 'Environment and Security', *Foreign Policy,* 47: 23–41.

Naanen, B. 1995. 'Oil Producing Minorities and the Restructuring of Nigerian Federalism', *Journal of Commonwealth and Comparative Politics,* 33 (1): 46–58.

Nathan, Mir. 1936. *Bararistan-i-Ghaybi (A History of the Mughal Wars in Assam, Cooch Behar, Bengal, Bihar and Orissa during the reigns of Jahangir and Shah Jahan).* Translated by M. I. Borah. Guwahati: Government of Assam.

NDWC (Niger Delta Wetlands Commission). 2000. *Mediation and Conflict Resolution of the Crisis in Nembe.* Port Harcourt: Niger Delta Wetlands Commission.

Nelson, Diane. 1999. *A Finger in the Wound: Body Politics in Quincentennial Guatemala.* Berkeley: University of California Press.

Neumann, Roderick P. 2001. 'Disciplining Peasants in Tanzania: From State Violence to Self-Surveillance in Wildlife Conservation', in Peluso and Watts (eds), *Violent Environments.*

Ney, S. 1997. 'Why is Pension Reform so Difficult? The Institutional Limits to Reforming Social Security'. Paper presented at a joint LOS/IIASA (Norwegian Research Centre in Organisation and Management/ International Institute for Applied Systems Analysis) meeting on Security: Environmental and Social, Laxenburg, Austria, November.

Ney, S. and M. Thompson. 2000. 'Cultural Discourses in the Global Climate Change Debate', in E. Jochem, J. Sathaye and D. Bouille (eds), *Society, Behaviour and Climate Change Mitigation.* Dordrecht: Kluwer.

NFG (Nigerian Federal Government). 1996. *Ogoni Crisis.* Lagos: Ministry of Information, Nigerian Federal Government.

Niyogi, Puspa. 1967. *Brahman Settlements in Different Subdivisions of Ancient Bengal.* Calcutta: R.K. Maitra.

Ó Tuathail, Gearóid. 1997. 'At the End of Geopolitics? Reflections on a Plural Problematic at Century's End', *Alternatives,* 22 (1): 35–55.

Ó Tuathail, Gearóid and T. W. Luke. 1994. 'Present at the (Dis)integration: Deterritorialization and Reterritorialization in the New Wor(l)d Order', *Annals of the Association of American Geographers*, 84 (3): 381–98.

Obi, C. 2001. *The Changing Forms of Identity Politics in Nigeria*. Uppsala: Africa Institute.

Okilo, M. 1980. *Derivation: A Criterion of Revenue Allocation*. Port Harcourt: Rivers State Newspaper Corporation.

Okonta, Ike. 2002. *The Struggle of the Ogoni for Self-Determination*. D.Phil. thesis, Oxford University.

———. 2003. *When Citizens Revolt*. Unpublished manuscript. Berkeley: University of California.

Okonta, Ike and O. Douglas. 2001. *Where Vultures Feast*. San Francisco: Sierra Club.

Okpu, U. 1977. *Ethnic Minority Problems in Nigerian Politics*. Stockholm Wiksell.

O'Neill, C. 2001. 'Understanding the Impact of Participation in a Deliberative Process: A Social Learning Approach to Citizen Juries'. Paper presented at Conference on Developments in Public Participation and Innovations in Community Governance, Universitat Autonoma de Barcelona, Barcelona, 7–9 June.

Ong, Aihwa. 2006. *Neoliberalism as Exception: Mutations in Citizenship and Sovereignty*. Durham: Duke University Press.

O' Riordan, T. and S. Rayner. 1991. 'Risk Management for Global Environmental Change', *Global Environmental Change*, 1 (2): 91–108.

Osaghae, E. 1995. 'The Ogoni Uprising: Oil Politics, Minority Agitation and the Future of the Nigerian State', *African Affairs*, 94 (376): 325–44.

Painter, D. 1986. *Oil and the American Century*. Baltimore: Johns Hopkins University Press.

Pakem, B. 1987. 'State Formation in Pre-colonial Jaintia', in Surajit Sinha (ed.), *Tribal Polities and State Systems in Pre-Colonial Eastern and Northeastern India*. Calcutta: K. P. Bagchi.

Parry, G., G. Moyser, and N. Day. 1992. *Political Participation and Democracy in Britain*. Cambridge: Cambridge University Press.

Paschen, H., K. Gresser, G. Friedrichs, and F. Conrad. 1975. 'Some Problems of Evaluation in Technology Assessment Studies', *Methodological Guidelines for Social Assessment of Technologies*. Paris: OECD.

Pateman, C. 1970. *Participation and Democratic Theory*. Cambridge: Cambridge University Press.

Paterson, Matthew. 2007. *Automobile Politics: Ecology and Cultural Political Economy*. Cambridge: Cambridge University Press.

236

Paterson, Matthew and Simon Dalby. 2006. 'Empire's Ecological Tyreprints', *Environmental Politics*, 15 (1): 1–22.

Peet, Richard and Michael Watts. 1996. *Liberation Ecologies*. New York: Routledge.

Peluso, Nancy Lee. 1992. *Rich Forests, Poor People: Resource Control and Resistance in Java*. Berkeley: University of California Press.

———. 1996. 'Fruit Trees and Family Trees in an Anthropogenic Rainforest: Property Rights, Ethics of Access, and Environmental Change in Indonesia', *Comparative Studies in Society and History*, 38 (3): 510–48.

Peluso, Nancy and Emily Harwell. 2001. 'Territory, Custom, and the Cultural Politics of Ethnic War in West Kalimantan, Indonesia', in Nancy Peluso and Michael Watts (eds), *Violent Environments*. Ithaca: Cornell University Press.

Peluso, Nancy and Michael Watts (eds). 2001. *Violent Environments*. Ithaca, NY: Cornell University Press.

Perkin, H. 1989. *The Rise of Professional Society: England since 1880*. London: Routledge and Kegan Paul.

Perlin, Frank. 1993. *Monetary, Administrative, and Popular Infrastructures in Asia and Europe, 1500–1900*. Brookfield, VT: Ashgate.

Philip, Kavita. 2004. *Civilizing Natures: Race, Resources and Modernity in Colonial South India*. New Brunswick, NJ: Rutgers University Press.

Phillips, Alfred E. 1908. 'Irrigation Engineering', in Frederick E. Turneaure (ed.), *Cyclopedia of Civil Engineering*, v. 8. Chicago: American School of Correspondence.

Pirages, Dennis Clark and Theresa Manley DeGeest. 2004. *Ecological Security: An Evolutionary Perspective on Globalization*. Lanham, MD: Rowman and Littlefield.

Polanyi, Karl. 1957. *The Great Transformation: The Political and Economic Origins of Our Time*. Boston: Beacon.

Porter, T. 1995. *Trust in Numbers*. Princeton, NJ: Princeton University Press.

Postel, Sandra. 1994. *Dividing the Waters: Food Security, Ecosystem Health, and the New Politics of Scarcity*. Worldwatch Paper 132. Washington: The Worldwatch Institute.

Poulantzas, Nicos. 1978. *State, Power, Socialism*. London: New Left Books.

Punjab Public Works Department, Irrigation Branch. 1943. *A Manual of Irrigation Practice*, 1st edition. Lahore: Government Printing.

Putnam, Robert. 2000. *Bowling Alone*. New York: Harpers.

Rabinow, Paul. 1989. *French Modern: Norms and Forms of the Social Environment*. Cambridge: MIT Press.

Raffles, Hugh. 2002. *In Amazonia: A Natural History*. Princeton, NJ: Princeton University Press.

Raghavaiah, V. 1979. 'Tribal Revolts in Chronological Order: 1778 to 1991', in A.R. Desai (ed.), *Peasant Struggles in India*. Delhi: Oxford University Press.

Rahman, Hossain Zillur and S. Aminul Islam. 2002. *Local Governance and Community Capacities: Search for New Frontiers*. Dhaka: University Press Limited.

Rahman, M. M. 1999. 'Population of Sylhet', in Sharif Uddin Ahmed (ed.), *Sylhet: History and Heritage*. Dhaka: Bangladesh Itihas Samiti.

Rahman, Sayeed-ur. 1999. 'River Surma', in Sharif Uddin Ahmed (ed.), *Sylhet: History and Heritage*. Dhaka: Bangladesh Itihas Samiti.

Rainforest Action Network. 1997. *Human Rights and Environmental Operations Information on the Royal Dutch/Shell Group of Companies*. London: Rainforest Action Network.

Raj, P.A. 1991. *Facts. Sardar Sarovar Projects*. Gandhinagar: Narmada Nigam Limited.

Raju, K.C.B. 1995. 'Strategies to Combat Drought in Kutch'. Paper presented at a workshop on 'Strengthening of Community Participation in Disaster Reduction and Role of NGOs'. Mandvi: Vivekanand Research and Training Institute.

Rapoport, A. 1985. 'Uses of Experimental Games', in M. Grauer, M. Thompson and A. P. Wierzbicki (eds), *Plural Rationality and Interactive Decision Processes*. Berlin: Springer-Verlag.

Rashid, Harouner. 1991. *Geography of Bangladesh*. Dhaka: The University Press Limited.

Ray, Ratna. 1979. *Change in Bengal Agrarian Society, 1760–1850*. New Delhi: Oxford University Press.

Rayner, Steve. 1984. 'Disagreeing about Risk', in S. Hadden (ed.), *Risk Analysis, Institutions, and Public Policy*. Port Washington, NY: Associated Faculty Press.

———. 1987. 'Learning from the Blind Men and the Elephant', in V. Covello, Lester B. Lane, Alan Moghissi, and V.R.R. Uppuluri (eds), *Uncertainty in Risk Assessment, Risk Management and Decision Making*. New York: Plenum Press.

——— (ed.). 1993. 'The International Influence of NEPA', in S.G. Hilderbrand and J.B. Cannon (eds), *Environmental Analysis: The NEPA Experience*. Boca Raton: Lewis.

Rayner, Steve and R. Cantor. 1987. 'How Fair is Safe Enough', *Risk Analysis: An International Journal*, 7(1): 3–9.

Rayner, Steve and E. Malone. 1998. 'The Challenge of Climate Change to the Social Sciences', in S. Rayner and E. Malone (eds), *Human Choice and Climate Change: Volume 4, What have we Learned?* Columbus, OH: Battelle Press.

Renn, O., T. Webler, and P. Wiedemann, (eds). 1995. *Fairness and Competence in Citizen Participation*. Boston: Kluwer.

Renner, Michael. 2002. *The Anatomy of Resource Wars*. Worldwatch Paper No.162. Washington DC: Worldwatch Institute.

Riaz, Ali. 2005. 'Traditional Institutions as Tools of Political Islam in Bangladesh', *Journal of Asian and African Studies*', 40 (3): 171–96.

Richards, Paul. 1989. 'Agriculture as a Performance', in Robert Chambers, Arnold Pacey and Lori Ann Thrupp (eds), *Farmer First: Farmer Innovation and Agricultural Research*. London: Intermediate Technology Publications.

Robbins, Paul. 2004. *Political Ecology: A Critical Introduction*. Malden, MA: Blackwell.

Robinson, J. 1998. 'The Human Face of Socio-Ecological Modelling', in B. Wiman, I. Wiman, and S. Akker (eds), *The Art of Natural Resource Management: Poetics, Policy, Practice*. Lund: Lund University Press.

Rose, Nikolas. 1999. *Powers of Freedom: Reframing Political Thought*. Cambridge: Cambridge University Press.

Ross, Eric B. 1998. *The Malthus Factor: Poverty, Politics, and Population in Capitalist Development*. London: Zed.

Ross, Michael. 2001b. 'Does Oil Hinder Democracy?' *World Politics*, 53 (3): 325–61.

——— 2001a. *Extractive Sectors and the Poor*. New York: Oxfam America.

Rushbrook Williams, L.F. 1958. *The Black Hills: Kutch in History and Legend, A Study in Indian Local Loyalties*. London: Weidenfeld and Nicholson.

Rustomji, Kaikhosru J. 1929. *A Treatise on Customary Law in the Punjab*. Lahore: University Book Agency.

Sabatier, P. A. and H. C. Jenkins-Smith (eds). 1993. *Policy Change and Learning: An Advocacy Coalition Approach*. Boulder, CO: Westview Press.

Saberwal, V. and M. Rangarajan (eds). 2003. *Battles over Nature: Science and the Politics of Conservation*. Delhi: Permanent Black.

Sachs, Jeffrey and A. Warner. 1995. 'Natural Resource Abundance and Economic Growth', NBER Working Paper 5398. Cambridge, MA: National Bureau of Economic Research.

Sagoff, M. 1990. *The Economy of the Earth*. Cambridge: Cambridge University Press.

Said, Edward W. 1993. *Culture and Imperialism*. Knopf: New York.

Sangaji, A. 2001. *Menuju Pengelolaan TNLL Berbasis Masyarakat*. Yayasan Tanah Merdeka.

Sarmiento, Domingo. 1998 [1845]. *Facundo, or, Civilization and Barbarism*. Translated by Mary Mann. New York: Penguin.

Saro-Wiwa, Ken. 1990. *Similia: Essays on Anomic Nigeria*. Port Harcourt: Saros International Publishers.

————. 1992. *Genocide in Nigeria*. Port Harcourt: Saros International Publishers.

Saunders, Leslie S. 1873. *Report on the Revised Land Revenue Settlement of the Lahore District in the Lahore Division*. Lahore: Central Jail Press.

Schapiro, M. 1988. 'Judicial Selection and the Design of Clumsy Institutions', *Southern California Law Review*, 61 (3): 1555–69.

Schmink, Marianne and Charles Wood. 1992. *Contested Frontiers in Amazonia*. New York: Columbia University Press.

Schrauwers, A. 2001. 'The "Benevolent" Colonies of Johannes van den Bosch: Continuities in the Administration of Poverty in the Netherlands and Indonesia', *Comparative Studies in Society and History*, 43: 298–328.

Schwartzberg, Joseph E. (ed.). 1992. *Historical Atlas of South Asia*. New York: Oxford University Press.

Schweithelm, J., N. Wirawan, J. Elliott, and A. Khan. 1992. *Sulawesi Parks Program Land Use Survey and Socio-Economic Survey*. Lore Lindu National Park and Morawali Nature Reserve: Directorate General of Forest Protection and Nature Conservation, Ministry of Forestry, Government of Indonesia and the Nature Conservancy.

Scott, James C. 1995. 'State Simplifications: Nature, Space and People', *The Journal of Political Philosophy*, 3 (3): 191–233.

————. 1998. *Seeing Like a State: How Certain Schemes to Improve the Human Condition Have Failed*. New Haven, CT: Yale University Press.

Scott, James C., John Tehranian, and Jeremy Mathias. 2002. 'The Production of Legal Identities Proper to States: The Case of the Permanent Family Surname', *Comparative Studies in Society and History*. 44 (1): 4–44.

Scott-Moncrieff, Colin C. 1868. *Irrigation in Southern Europe: Being the Report of a Tour of Inspection of the Irrigation Works of France, Spain, and Italy, undertaken in 1867-68 for the Government of India*. London: E. & F. N. Spon.

Self, P. 1975. *Econocrats and the Policy Process: The Politics and Philosophy of Cost-benefit Analysis*. London: Macmillan.

Sen, Amartya. 1995. 'Rationality and Social Choice', *American Economic Review*, 49 (2): 711–25.

Serajud-din, A. M. 1964. 'The Revenue Administration of Chittagong, from 1761 to 1785', Unpublished Ph.D. dissertation, University of London.

Sethu Pillai, R.P. 1950. *Place-name suffixes in Tamil*. Madras: Published by Author.

Shah, Tushaar. 1993. *Groundwater Markets and Irrigation Development: Political Economy and Practical Policy*. Bombay: Oxford University Press.

Shaw, Rosalind. 1992. '"Nature", "Culture" and Disasters', in E. Croll and D. Parkin (eds), *Bush Base, Forest Farm: Culture, Environment and Development*. New York: Routledge.

Shiby, Atful Hye. 1999. 'Moulvi Abdul Karim and His Contributions to Muslim Education in Bengal', in Sharif Uddin Ahmed (ed.), *Sylhet: History and Heritage*. Dhaka: Bangladesh Itihas Samiti.

Siddiqi, Dina.M. 1998. 'Taslima Nasreen and Others: The Contest over Gender in Bangladesh', in Herbert L. Bodman and Nayereh Tohibi (eds), *Women in Muslim Societies: Diversity within Unity*. London: Lynne Reiner.

————. 2002. 'Of Consent and Contradiction: A Report on the Law and Practice of Forced Marriages in Bangladesh'. Unpublished paper. Dhaka: Ain o Shalish Kendra.

Siddiqui, Kamal. 1997. 'Land Reforms Since 1950', in Sirajul Islam (ed.), *History of Bangladesh, 1704–1971*, 2nd edition. Dhaka: Asiatic Society of Bangladesh.

Sinclair, Annette. 1998. 'A Statistical Analysis of Rainfall Data in Kutch', Mimeo. Brighton: Institute of Development Studies, University of Sussex.

Sirianni, C. and L. Friedland. 2000. *Civic Innovation in America: Community Empowerment, Public Policy, and the Movement for Civic Renewal*. Berkeley: University of California Press.

Sivaramakrishnan, K. 1999. *Modern Forests: Statemaking and Environmental Change in Colonial Eastern India*. Stanford, CA: Stanford University Press.

————. 2003. 'Conservation Crossroads: Indian Wildlife at the Intersection of Global Imperatives, Nationalist Anxieties, and Local Assertions', in V. Saberwal and M. Rangarajan (eds), *Battles over Nature: Science and the Politics of Conservation*. Delhi: Permanent Black.

Slotkin, Richard. 1992. *Gunfighter Nation: The Myth of the Frontier in Twentieth Century America*. New York: Atheneum.

Smith, Crosbie and M. Norton Wise. 1989. *Energy and Empire: A Biographical Study of Lord Kelvin*. Cambridge: Cambridge University Press.

Smith, Neil. 1984. *Uneven Development: Nature, Capital, and the Production of Space*. Oxford: Basil Blackwell.

————. 1992. 'Geography, Difference and the Politics of Scale', in J. Doherty, E. Graham and M. Malek (eds), *Postmodernism and the Social Sciences*. London: Macmillan.

Smith, Richard Saumarez. 1996. *Rule by Records: Land Registration and Village Custom in Early British Panjab*. Delhi: Oxford University Press.

Srivastava, Sanjay. 1998. *Constructing Post-Colonial India: National Character and the Doon School*. London and New York: Routledge.

Stone, Ian. 1984. *Canal Irrigation in British India: Perspectives in Technological Change in a Peasant Economy*. Cambridge: Cambridge University Press.

Stonich, Susan and Peter Vandergeest. 2001. 'Violence, Environment and Industrial Shrimp Farming', in Peluso and Watts (eds), *Violent Environments*. Ithaca, NY: Cornell University Press.

Stott, Philip and Sian Sullivan (eds). 2000. *Political Ecology: Science, Myth and Power*. London: Arnold.

Strickland, Claude Francis. 1940. *Deltaic Formation, with Special Reference to the Hydraulic Processes of the Ganges and the Brahmaputra*. Calcutta: Orient Longmans.

Suberu, R. 2001. *Federalism and Ethnic Conflict in Nigeria*. Washington DC: USIP.

Swain, Ashok. 2002. 'Environmental Cooperation in South Asia', in Ken Conca and Geoff Dabelko (eds), *Environmental Peacemaking*. Washington DC: Woodrow Wilson Center Press.

Tandon, Prakash. 1968. *Punjabi Century, 1857–1947*. Berkeley: University of California Press.

Taniguchi, Shinkichi. 1996, 'The Peasantry of Northern Bengal in the Late Eighteenth Century', in Peter Robb, Kaoru Sugihara, and Haruka Yanagisawa (eds), *Local Agrarian Society in Colonial India: Japanese Perspectives*. Delhi: Manohar Publishers.

Temple, Sir Richard. 1986a [1883]. 'Cooper's Hill College of Engineering', in Sir Richard Temple (ed.), *Oriental Experience*. Delhi: Gian Publishing House.

———. 1986b [1883]. 'Social Science in the British Empire Abroad', in Sir Richard Temple (ed.), *Oriental Experience*. Delhi: Gian Publishing House.

Thompson, M. 2000. 'Global Networks and Local Cultures: What are the Mismatches and What can be Done about Them?' in C. Engel and K.H. Keller (eds), *Understanding the Impact of Global Networks on Local Social, Political and Cultural Values*. Baden-Baden: Nomos.

Thompson, M., R.J. Ellis, and A. Wildavsky. 1990. *Cultural Theory*. Boulder, CO: Westview.

Thompson, M., G. Grendstad, and P. Selle (eds). 1999. *Cultural Theory as Political Science*. London: Routledge.

Thompson, M., S. Rayner, and S. Ney. 1998. 'Risk and Governance Part 2: Policy in a Complex and Plurally Perceived World', *Government and Opposition*, 33 (3):139–66.

Thompson, M., M. Warburton, and T. Hatley. 1986. *Uncertainty On a Himalayan Scale*. London: Milton Ash.

Tranvik, T., M. Thompson, and P. Selle. 2000. 'Doing Technology (and Democracy) the Pack-donkey's Way: The Technomorphic Approach to ICT Policy', in C. Engel and K. H. Keller (eds), *Governance of Global Networks in the Light of Differing Local Values*. Baden-Baden: Nomos.

Tsing, Anna Lowenhaupt. 1993. *In the Realm of the Diamond Queen*. Princeton: Princeton University Press.

———. 2000. 'Inside the Economy of Appearances', *Public Culture*, 12 (1): 115–44.

———. 2005. *Friction: An Ethnography of Global Connection*. Durham, NC: Duke University Press.

Tupper, C.L. 1881. *Punjab Customary Law*, 3 vols. Calcutta: Government Printing.

Turner, Frederick Jackson. 1994. 'The Significance of the Frontier in American History', in John Mack Faragher (ed.), *Rereading Frederick Jackson Turner*. New York: Henry Holt and Company.

UNDP (United Nations Development Programme). 2006. *Beyond Scarcity. Power, Poverty and the Global Water Crisis: Human Development Report 2006*. Palgrave: Basingstoke.

Van Asselt, M. 2000. *Perspectives on Risk and Uncertainty*. Dordrecht: Kluwer.

van Schendel, Willem. (ed.). 1992. *Francis Hamilton Buchanan in Southeast Bengal (1798)*. Dhaka: University Press Limited.

———. 2002. 'Geographies of Knowing, Geographies of Ignorance: Jumping Scale in Southeast Asia', *Environment & Planning D: Society & Space*, 20 (6): 647–69.

———. 2005. *The Bengal Borderland: Beyond State and Nation in South Asia*. London: Anthem.

Verba, S., K. Schlozman, and H. Brady. 1995. *Voice and Equality*. Cambridge, MA: Harvard University Press.

Verweij, M. 1999. 'Whose Behaviour is Affected by International Anarchy?' in M. Thompson, G. Grendstad and P. Selle (eds). *Cultural Theory as Political Science*. London: Routledge.

———. 2000. *Transboundary Environmental Problems and Cultural Theory: The Protection of the Rhine and the Great Lakes*. London: Palgrave.

———. 2001. 'Forget The Hague: Curb Global Warming Instead'. Seminar paper presented at IIASA (International Institute for Applied Systems Analysis), 18 January, Laxenburg, Austria.

VIKSAT. n.d. *Debating the Options: Groundwater Management in the Face of Scarcity, Gujarat, India*. Ahmedabad: VIKSAT.

Vitalis, Robert. 2002. 'Black Gold, White Crude', *Diplomatic History*, 26 (2):185–213.

Wade, Robert. 1988. *Village Republics: Economic Conditions for Collective Action in South India*. Cambridge: Cambridge University Press.

WALHI (Wahana Lingkungan Hidup Indonesia). 2001a. *Kontroversi Dongi Dongi*. Jakarta: WALHI.

———. 2001b. *Lembaran Fakta: Taman Nasional Lore Lindu*. Jakarta: WALHI.

———. 2001c. *Pendudukan Dongi Dongi Oleh Forum Petani Merdeka* (FPM): Jakarta: WALHI.

———. 2002. *Laporan Tim Investigasi Wilayah Tongoa-Kamarora dan Dongi-Dongi* (*Kawasan* Tnll), 18–20 July, Palu: WALHI.

Watts, Michael. 1998. 'Islamic Modernities?' in J. Holston (ed.), *Cities and Citizenship*. Durham: Duke University Press.

———. 2000. *Struggles over Geography*. Hettner Lectures. Heidelberg: University of Heidelberg.

———. 2001. 'Petro-Violence: Community, Extraction, and Political Ecology of a Mythic Commodity', in N. Peluso and M. Watts (eds), *Violent Environments*. Ithaca, NY: Cornell University Press.

———. 2004. 'Antimonies of Community: Some Thoughts on Geography, Resources and Empire', *Transactions of the Institute of British Geographers*, NS 29: 195–216.

WCED (World Commission on Environment and Development). 1987. *Our Common Future*. Oxford: Oxford University Press.

Wescoat, James. 2002. 'Water Rights in South Asia and the United States: Comparative Perspectives, 1873–1996', in John Richards (ed.), *Land, Property and the Environment*. Oakland: Institute for Contemporary Studies Press.

Whitehead, Alfred North. 1948. *Science and the Modern World*. New York: Mentor.

Wicks, Robert S. 1992. *Money, Markets and Trade in Early Southeast Asia*. Ithaca: Cornell University Press.

Willcocks, Sir William. 1935. *Sixty Years in the East*. Edinburgh: William Blackwood.

Williams, Raymond. 1976. *Keywords: A Vocabulary of Culture and Society*. New York: Oxford University Press.

———. 1980. *Problems in Materialism and Culture*. London: Verso.

Williamson, O. 1975. *Markets and Hierarchies, Analysis and Anti-Trust Implications*. New York: Free Press.

Wilson, Herbert M. . 1893. *Manual of Irrigation Engineering*, 1st edition. New York: John Wiley & Sons.

———. 1909. *Irrigation Engineering*, 6th edition. New York: John Wiley & Sons.

Winpenny, James. 1994. *Managing Water as an Economic Resource*. London and New York: Routledge.

Wise, M. Norton and Crosbie Smith. 1989–90. 'Work and Waste: Political Economy and Natural Philosophy in Nineteenth Century Britain', *History of Science*, 27: 263–301; 27: 391–449; 28: 221–61.

Worster, Donald. 1985. *Rivers of Empire: Water, Aridity and the Growth of the American West*. New York: Pantheon Books.

———. 1992. *Under Western Skies: Nature and History in the American West*. New York: Oxford University Press.

Wynne, B. 1982. *Rationality and Ritual: The Windscale Inquiry and Nuclear Decision in Britain*. Chalfont St. Giles: British Society for the History of Science.

———. 2002. 'Science and Citizenship in a Global Context: Challenges from New Technologies'. Paper presented at Conference on Science and Citizenship in a Global Context. Institute for Development Studies, Brighton, 12-13 December.

Xenos, Nicholas. 1989. *Scarcity and Modernity*. London: Routledge.

Yappa, Lakshman. 1993. 'What are Improved Seeds? An Epistemology of the Green Revolution', *Economic Geography*, 69 (3): 254–73.

Yergin, Daniel. 1991. *The Prize*. New York: Random House.

Zerner, Charles E. 2003. *Culture and the Question of Rights: Forests, Coasts, and Seas in Southeast Asia*. Durham, NC: Duke University Press.

Contributors

AMITA BAVISKAR is Associate Professor, Institute of Economic Growth, Delhi.

SIMON DALBY is Professor, Department of Geography and Environmental Studies, Carleton University, Ottawa.

DAVID GILMARTIN teaches in the Department of History, North Carolina State University.

TANIA MURRAY LI is Professor, Department of Anthropology, University of Toronto.

DAVID LUDDEN is Professor, History Department, New York University.

LYLA MEHTA is Research Fellow, Institute of Development Studies, University of Sussex.

STEVE RAYNER is James Martin Professor of Science and Civilization and Director of the James Martin Institute, University of Oxford.

MICHAEL THOMPSON is Fellow, James Martin Institute for Science and Civilization, University of Oxford.

ANNA TSING is Professor of Anthropology, University of California, Santa Cruz.

MICHAEL WATTS is Class of 63 Professor of Geography and Director of African Studies, University of California, Berkeley.

Index